Speaking Out for Animals

Speaking Out for Animals

*True Stories about Real People
who Rescue Animals*

Kim W. Stallwood

Lantern Books • New York
A Division of Booklight Inc.

To all animal advocates, and to the animals we have yet to liberate.

2001
Lantern Books
One Union Square West, Suite 201
New York, NY 10003

The photograph on the cover, of eleven-year-old Danielle Williams holding Mia, he beloved six-year-old cat, was taken by her father, John Elliott

All royalties from the sale of this book will be donated to the Animal Rights Network Inc., and its programs, including *The Animals' Agenda.*

Printed in the United States of America

Library of Congress Cataloging-in-Publication Data

Stallwood, Kim W.
  Speaking out for animals : true stories about real people who rescue animals / [edited by] by Kim W. Stallwood.
    p. cm.
  ISBN 1-930051-34-4 (alk. paper)
 1. Animal rights activists—Case studies. 2. Animal welfare. 3. Animal rights. 4. Animal rescue. 5. Stallwood, Kim W.

HV4715 .S64 2001
179'.3—dc21

2001029462

Table of Contents ～

Foreword viii

Acknowledgments xiii

Introduction—Kim W. Stallwood 1

Section One: Voices for Animals

Introduction—Kim W. Stallwood 7

The Extraordinary Activist: an interview with Paul McCartney
—Kim W. Stallwood and Jill Howard Church 8

The Art of Friendship: an interview with Brian Clarke
—Kim W. Stallwood and Jill Howard Church 26

A Muse with A Mission: an interview with Carla Lane
—Kim W. Stallwood and Jill Howard Church 31

A Conversation with Peter Singer—Kim W. Stallwood 34

To Serve and Protect: Sgt. Sherry Schlueter—Jill Howard Church .49

Rod Coronado—Laura A. Moretti 61

The Body Shop: an interview with Anita Roddick
—Kim W. Stallwood 73

Wayne Pacelle, unplugged—*The Animals' Agenda* 77

A Conversation with Tatyana Pavlova—Martin Rowe 88

Animal Passions: an interview with Jeffrey Masson
—Kim Sturla 93

Ahimsa with Attitude: an interview with Maneka Gandhi
—Mia MacDonald 98

Pacheco after PETA—Jill Howard Church 103

Something to Believe In: an interview with Rikki Rockett
—Kirsten Rosenberg 107

A New Order in the Court: an interview with Steve Wise
—*The Animals' Agenda* 113

Section Two: Happy Endings
Introduction—Kim W. Stallwood 119
The Ties That Bind—Laura A. Moretti .120
Keiko Goes Home—Mark Berman 122
Hope, the Pig and Ivan the Gorilla—The Animals' Agenda 124
Annabelle, The Baby Broiler Hen—Karen Davis 126
A Dog Named Bear and the Calico Cat—Jane Erdhart 127
Arthur and Annie—Cathy C. Gaynor .129
New Life for Elephants—Kirsten Rosenberg 131
Abandoned Pigs Find the Good Life—Kirsten Rosenberg 132
Putting a Face on Meat—Kirsten Rosenberg 133
In Emily's Hoofprints—Kit Paraventi .135
Popcorn Ponies—Kirsten Rosenberg .137
Birdman of Puerto Rico—Pat Valls-Trelles 138
An Angel with a Wagging Tail—Dawn Willis Solero 139
The Buckshire Twelve—Laura Moretti 140
The Heart of Harbinger—Kit Paraventi 142
Rusti's Angel—Peter Hnath and Sherryl Volpone 145
Butch and Sundance: The Last Stand—Kit Paraventi 147
Death Row Pardon—Kit Paraventi 149
Lilly—Matt Kelly 152
Homeward Bound—Kirsten Rosenberg 154
Saving Sasha—Pat Derby 156
No Little Piggies Went to Market—Lorri Bauston 158
Belka's Longshot—Kirsten Rosenberg 160
Saving Trudy—Carol McKenna 162
Miracles and Joy—Carol Buckley 164
Cassie and Michelle's Comeback—Kirsten Rosenberg 167
 Purrfect Outcome for Hillgrove Cats—Carol McKenna 169
A Lesson in Life—Rachelle Detweiler .171
Bray-ving a Battered Past—Rachelle Detweiler 173
What the Cat Dragged Home—Rachelle Detweiler 175
Running like a Wolf—Rachelle Detweiler 177

Section Three: Unsung Heroes
Introduction—Kim W. Stallwood 181

Tony & Vicki Moore—Kim W. Stallwood 183
Ladies of the Night—Kirsten Rosenberg 185
Bill Dyer—Laura A. Moretti 187
Linda Hatfield—Kit Paraventi 189
Sue McCrosky—Jill Howard Church 192
Rick Bogle—Kit Paraventi 194
Hillary Morris—Kit Paraventi 197
Steve Hindi—Jill Howard Church 199
Coby and Hans Siegenthaller—Kit Paraventi 202
Ed Blotzer—Rebecca Taksel 204
Sherry DeBoer—Kit Paraventi 207
Buffalo Nations—Kit Paraventi 210
Sean Day—Kit Paraventi 212
Amanda Walker-Serrano—Lynn Manheim 215
Gerda Deterer—Erin Geoghegan 217
Sally Mackler—Valerie Schneider and Kirsten Rosenberg 220
Matt & Mary Kelly—Kit Paraventi 222
Phyllis Lahti—Kirsten Rosenberg 224
Evelyn Wood—Patricia A. Wismer 227
Eric Mills—Kirsten Rosenberg 229
Janet Halliburton—Rachelle Detweiler 231

Contributors 234
Organizations 236
About *The Animals' Agenda* 241

Foreword ❦ JANE GOODALL

C HANCES ARE, IF YOU ARE READING THIS BOOK, THAT you already care about animals, and are shocked, as I am, about the inhumane treatment inflicted on so many animal species by that most destructive of all animals: us. In the face of so much animal suffering around the world—caused by intensive farming, trapping for fur, hunting for "sport," testing for medical research and the pharmaceutical industry, use in the circus, advertising and other forms of "entertainment," the pet industry, and many other practices—feelings of frustration, anger, and helplessness sometimes get the better of us. How can we, as individuals, possibly make a difference?

And how did the world get to be this way? The indigenous people of the world hunted for food, but they respected the animals they killed and offered up a prayer of thanks. The animals lived wild and free until their death. It is very different today. Animals, so often, are considered mere "things"—mindless and lacking in feelings. And this attitude, only too often, is fostered in our own children. I was lucky, for my early fascination with animals, common to most children, was nurtured and guided by a very perceptive mother. When I was eighteen months old she found me in bed with a handful of earthworms. Instead of scolding me she just said quietly, "Jane, if you keep them here they'll die. They need the earth." I gathered up the worms and toddled with them into the garden. Thus her gentle wisdom guided my early exploration of the animal world.

Children quickly learn from those around them, especially from those they love, and those they admire. Animals attract children who can very easily learn to be kind. But children can equally learn to treat them with indifference, even cruelty. They soon realize that the animals chosen to share their homes are to be loved, but that mice and rats and insects should be killed along with other "pests." They discover that it's OK to kill animals for food or for their skins. Many learn that it is manly to shoot them for sport. Above all, children are often told that animals don't have feelings like ours, don't feel pain in the same way. This is how teachers persuade sensitive students to kill and dissect an animal in class. And so our children typically come to accept the status quo. Even if they want to protest the system, how, in the face of so much opposition, can they really effect change?

Even so, there are few adults who honestly believe that animals have no feelings. But huge numbers of people are brainwashed into accepting cruel practices because that is the way things are. They become numbed, "all pity choked by custom of fell deed." Others try to hide away because they cannot bear the suffering but they lack the will to try to do anything about it, or, even if they would like to help, they feel that it wouldn't do any good. Or they are inhibited by social pressure, do not want to be classified along with "crazy" animal activists.

That is why this collection of inspiring tales is so important. They are true tales about individuals who have dared to take positive action against cruelty to animals and won, individuals who have made a difference. They are stories selected from *The Animals' Agenda* magazine, which has, for more than two decades, discussed all aspects of animal rights, brought together from many sources. Thus the magazine has helped to raise awareness. And, even more importantly, it has reported the efforts made by individuals, or groups of individuals, to effect change, and celebrated their victories—the small victories at a local level as well as the larger victories that have, in some cases, led to new anti-cruelty legislation. In the struggle against the powerful forces that make the exploitation of animals their business, nothing is more encouraging than reading about success.

Let me share one story. It began when I watched a group of boys in Kigoma, Tanzania, teasing a sick puppy. They were not deliberately cruel, just irritating and giggling. I went out to remonstrate. "You can't do anything about their attitude," said one of my European companions. "It's all over Africa. Tanzanian kids are almost always cruel to dogs." For one thing, that is not true, although the Muslims mostly believe that dogs are unclean and must not be touched (which is untrue—the Koran teaches only that one should avoid their saliva). For another, these boys were actually stroking the mother, and the pup's two litter mates. And finally, this particular incident was not "all over Africa"—it was happening outside our window. So out I went. "You like your dogs, don't you?" I asked. Yes, they did. I pointed out that their teasing was as if a giant of another species tormented one of them. Would they like that? "No." Do you think the puppy likes it? "No." So why are you doing it? A shrug of the shoulders. I asked if they would like to help me with our Roots & Shoots program (that involves young people in fifty countries in hands-on projects to make the world a better place for animals, the environment, and their human community). We discussed how they could share their understanding of dogs with the other children in their village, and the boys, talking excitedly, went off, carrying the puppy.

Two years later an American teacher from a school in Bombay came up to me at a conference. She told me how, when she was first posted to India, she felt she could not work there because of the sheer number of starving, mangy, and clearly suffering stray dogs on the streets. She couldn't sleep at night for worrying. Then, back in the United States for her leave, she talked to an old friend of hers, a veterinarian. What could she do? She was desperate. By some extraordinary chance, he had attended one of my lectures that year, and I had told the story about the little boys and the puppy. "Why don't you go back and take it one dog at a time?" With great pride she told how she had taken in and treated and neutered one stray, then found it a home.

Then she did the same with another, and another, and another. One, then two, then more of her friends were inspired to help her. They raised money and built a shelter. Gradually, the number of strays was decreasing. More importantly, a number of caring people could see that they were making a difference—one dog at a time.

We can never hope, in the unforeseeable future, to eradicate all cruelty to animals. We humans have an unfortunate cruel streak in our makeup; think how cruel we can be to each other. But we can strive, realistically, to bring to an end the mass cruelty that is, implicitly or explicitly, currently condoned by society as a whole. This will happen as more and more people begin to understand the immorality of these practices—and the fact that they can actually do something about it. We live in a consumer-driven society, and we can help to bring about change by making ethical choices in what we buy (and even more importantly, what we do not buy). There are more and more cruelty-free products on the market; we must seek them out and share our knowledge with our friends. We can eliminate the cruel use of animals in circuses and other forms of entertainment by refusing to go to performances of this sort and by turning off our TV sets. We can refuse to buy dogs or cats from puppy mills or pet shops, and instead adopt unwanted animals from shelters. More and more alternatives to the use of live animals in pharmaceutical and product testing are being found; we must insist on legislation that enforces their use, once they have proven safe and effective. The list of simple ways that we can, collectively, ensure change is a long one.

Kim W. Stallwood, in gathering together stories of determination and courage, stories emphasizing the power of individual action, has produced a book that will have an important impact on those who read it. The voices of the animal advocates speak from every page: some quietly, some with resonant shouts, together encouraging all who care about animal suffering to work even harder to effect change. Let the volume of these joined voices penetrate the minds and hearts of those who hide from the pain and suffering of the animal world because they feel powerless to help, inspiring them to take action. The sense of accomplishment and joy that comes from helping even one animal is the reward that encourages further action.

As we move into this new millennium I truly hope that we shall gradually become a more caring and compassionate society. That more and more people will join the ranks of those Speaking Out for Animals. And that we shall reach the point when our children's children look back on this era, on the way we treat animals today, with the same horror as the German nation in the 21st century looks back on the unspeakable actions of Nazi Germany in the Third Reich.

Jane Goodall

Acknowledgments ∼

SINCE 1979 *THE ANIMALS' AGENDA* AND THE ANIMAL Rights Network Inc. (ARN), its not-for-profit publisher, have been nurtured and sustained by thousands of readers, supporters, and volunteers. ARN's board of directors, honorary board, and advisory board consist of the great and the good of international animal advocacy. Like-minded organizations and foundations have also played a significant role in helping us help animals. I would like to thank them all for their dedication and inspiration.

I would also like to recognize ARN's and *Agenda's* staff members, who labor tirelessly for the animals. In particular, special thanks are due for this anthology to Suzanne McMillan for research, and to Jill Howard Church and Kirsten Rosenberg for editorial counsel. Further, *Agenda's* writers, including those in this volume, donate their time and expertise. Quite simply, we would not exist without them. Thank you.

Since I became a vegetarian in 1974, I have had the privilege of meeting animal advocates from throughout the world. Each one influenced my thinking about the moral status of animals and a new society free from animal cruelty and exploitation, and our role in its creation. It would take a book to recognize everyone. Please know, however, that you have been an inspiration, for which I am grateful.

Finally, there are the sentient beings—human and nonhuman—whom I have had (or still have) the pleasure of living with that I would like to simply say thank you to: Annabelle ("Piggy"), Bambino ("Beano"), Boobaa, Caesar, Effy, Emmy, Gary, Henry, Honey, Markie, Queenie, Spot, Tiddles, and Veda.

Kim W. Stallwood

Introduction KIM W. STALLWOOD

W HAT MOTIVATES SOMEONE TO ACT ON BEHALF OF animals? I believe the answer lies in the personal stories of the people who are featured in *Speaking Out for Animals*, and the animals they have saved.

For **Paul and Linda McCartney**, it was making the connection between the lamb they were eating and the sheep they saw playing outside on their Scottish farm. They became vegetarians.

For hunter **Steve Hindi**, it was attending the infamous pigeon shoot in Hegins, Pennsylvania—where captive birds were shot at close range—that made him realize all hunting is wrong. He went on to form the Chicago Animal Rights Coalition (now called Showing Animals Respect and Kindness).

For **Coby and Hans Siegenthaller**, it was being raised in Holland during World War II in families with vegetarian parents who opened up their homes to Jewish fugitives. After they met in a group for young vegetarians, they married, emigrated to the United States, and became stalwarts of the animal rights movement in Southern California.

For young **Amanda Walker-Serrano**, it was learning that her third-grade class was planning a trip to the circus. Upset about the plight of performing animals, she organized a petition, educated her schoolmates, and attracted considerable media attention.

For **Gerda Deterer**, it was a child who brought her a baby robin to care for. From then on, for more than twenty years, Gerda has opened her home to many rescued birds whom she nurses back to health.

These caring people—and the other compassionate people featured in this book—are in many respects ordinary people doing extraordinary things for animals. Whether they are internationally celebrated musicians like the McCartneys or a Maryland homemaker like Gerda, they have incorporated into their lives everyday acts of kindness toward animals.

For me it was spending one summer working in a chicken-processing plant.

In 1971, I began a three-year course in French cuisine and hotel and restaurant management at a college in London. During my second summer vacation I was expected to work in the profession. I had dutifully done this the first year by working in a restaurant kitchen, but decided against doing it the second because I thought I'd be spending my career doing such work. Friends at other colleges and universities had taken summer jobs at a nearby processing plant; it paid well, and would last only ten weeks. And I wanted to buy my first car.

I recall never wanting to see the chickens being slaughtered. I worked on the post-slaughter part of the production line. The workers at the front end had to start work a half hour earlier than the rest of us because it took that amount of time to begin the process of hanging the live chicken on the conveyor belt, kill and eviscerate her, and run the body through the scalding tank to remove the feathers and supposedly sanitize the carcass.

I stood on the production line with dead chickens approaching me every minute. The birds' bodies were neatly folded in preparation for the freezing process. Someone up the line placed a weight label on each chicken's breast. My job, for eight hours a day, was to place the dead bird in a plastic bag, while keeping the weight label in position, and then squeeze out the air, twist the bag, and seal it by running it through a sticky tape machine. Thus the chickens were taken to the freezer.

I could never bring myself to watch the chickens being slaughtered, but I knew then that I hated it taking place. The smell of thousands of live birds, fresh from the factory farm, and their death hung like a pall over the plant and its surrounding area.

When I returned to college for my final year, I could not wait to meet up with a fellow student one year younger whom I had a crush on. Amanda was the only vegetarian I knew at this time, and I could not wait to play the macho role of trying to make her upset over what I had done during the summer. Instead, we argued, from September to December, until I realized what I had been responsible for was wrong.

I became a vegetarian on January 1, 1974. I had another six months to go on my course. How was I to cook meat and taste it if I was a vegetarian? "Fake it," said Amanda. "Pretend you tasted it." Notwithstanding some diligent experimentation with alcohol and drugs, I did not have to worry about faking it because my teachers knew I was one of the more able students and did not worry about me.

Two years later, I shunned all animal products and became a vegan. I abandoned the pretense that was called my career, and fate led me to Compassion In World Farming, where I became the organization's first campaigns manager. For more than twenty-five years I have worked full-time for animal rights in the United Kingdom and United States, and have had the pleasure of meeting animal advocates from around the world. I consider it to be a privilege to be the executive director of the Animal Rights Network Inc., the not-for-profit publisher of *The Animals' Agenda*, the world's premier animal rights magazine.

Animal advocates come in all shapes and sizes, but the media's portrayal of us does not reflect what I believe the vast majority of us are like: caring, compassionate, and thoughtful people who want passionately to make a difference for animals, people, and the environment. In contrast, animal activists are portrayed in popular culture as being either an emotional group of harmless eccentrics or dangerous fanatics who care more about animals than people.

Ken Shapiro, executive director of Psychologists for the Ethical Treatment of Animals, once characterized animal advocates as "caring sleuths": a hybrid, if you will, of Sherlock Holmes and Mother Teresa. Caring sleuths are "always on the job of caring, seeing, and actively investigating suffering." We make it our business to witness animal suffering, and in doing so seek to expose it with the intention of preventing its recurrence.[1]

Animals have always been the focus of human attention. From the prehistoric cave paintings in Lascaux, France, to the latest Disney movie, animals feature prominently in our interpretation of the world around us. Our way of looking at animals ranges from the benevolent to the malevolent. We put them on altars for worship and for sacrifice.[2]

The 1975 publication of **Peter Singer's** landmark book, *Animal Liberation*, is generally recognized as the beginning of today's animal rights movement.[3] Singer said in my interview with him that his goal in writing the book was to "bring about a situation where we give the same consideration to the interests of nonhuman animals as we give to our own." He envisioned a society that "ceases to exploit animals, ceases to discount their interests, and ceases to sacrifice their major interests for the much more minor interests of our own." (See "A Conversation with Peter Singer," page 33.)

Animal rights philosophies like Singer's help to make sense of the world we live in because they help organize our thoughts and explain why things are the way they are. Animal advocates are clearly a group of people who reject the view of animals as property, but we must live in a society that is largely dependent upon the consumption of dead animals.

Speaking Out for Animals shows how animal advocates dedicate themselves to creating a peaceful world for all beings that increasing numbers of people—including philosophers, artists, elected representatives, teachers, parents, and children—envision. This book testifies that the activities of animal advocates are as diverse as the individuals themselves.

Since 1979, *The Animals' Agenda* has recorded and reported on the animal rights movement. This anthology comprises a selection of the interviews and profiles published since I became the Editor in Chief in 1993. The one common theme that is present in all of the pieces is compassion. I believe compassion for animals is one of the most important and vital human emotions that we can ever experience. It opens the door to a heightened sensitivity to all beings, irrespective of their species, because as we question how animals are so mistreated, we also inevitably ask how humans can be so unkind. Individual acts of animal cruelty and institutionalized exploitation, such as that found on factory farms and in research laboratories, are a human—not an animal—problem.

This is why the inspiring stories of people like Amanda Walker-Serrano and the Siegenthallers are so important. They inspire us to always speak out for animals.

---

1. Ken Shapiro, "The Caring Sleuth" (Baltimore: *The Animals' Agenda*; January/February 1994, 44–45).
2. See Francis Klingender, *Animals in Art and Thought* (Cambridge: The MIT Press, 1971); Jacques Boudet, *Man & Beast* (New York: Golden Press, 1964); and Keith Thomas, *Man and the Natural World* (New York: Pantheon Books, 1983).
3. Peter Singer, *Animal Liberation* (New York: New York Review, 1975; second edition, 1990).

1: Voices for Animals ∼

Introduction ∼ KIM W. STALLWOOD

PEOPLE FROM DIFFERENT WALKS OF LIFE CAN OFTEN find themselves treading the same path to animal liberation. Regardless of where we begin, it's where we end up that counts. For some people helping animals is only part of their life's work; for others, it is their life's work. What follows, from *The Animals' Agenda*, are profiles and conversations with some very special individuals who show how regardless of privilege or politics, fame or fortitude, people who put their individual talents to work for animals can lead by example.

For some people—usually men, in my experience, who most often perpetrate or benefit from animal cruelty—a passion for helping animals is viewed as a weakness in human character. They believe, for example, that hunting animals, eating meat, and other forms of animal use are healthy signs of masculinity and superiority over the natural world—which they believe is here for our control and domination. They see animal advocates as namby-pamby bleeding hearts suffering from "Bambi syndrome."

It would not be hard for anyone to believe, after reading these interviews, that each one of these courageous people demonstrates the greatest tenacity to help anyone and the most compassion to feel empathy for any being that the human condition is capable of experiencing. The common characteristic among them all is the ability to feel compassion—deep compassion for all—which I believe is the true hallmark of what makes us human.

7

The Extraordinary Activist
An Interview with Paul McCartney

KIM W. STALLWOOD
AND
JILL HOWARD CHURCH

A S ANIMAL ACTIVISTS, PAUL AND LINDA MCCARTNEY were quite famous and quite average at the same time. Despite their success and wealth, they dealt with animal issues on a daily basis: What to eat, what to wear, what to say to the unenlightened. They read *The Animals' Agenda* to learn about current events in the animal movement, and wrote protest letters to companies involved in animal abuse. They incorporated their beliefs into their "day jobs," Paul writing songs inspired by or concerning animals and Linda writing cookbooks and creating a vegetarian food business.

Soon after Linda's death from breast cancer in April 1998, Paul contacted *The Animals' Agenda* and explained that he wanted to break his silence and reiterate his commitment to animal rights campaigns, using primarily animal-related publications instead of the mainstream press. He began speaking to vegetarian groups and related activists, promoting the release of Linda's *Wide Prairie* album, and honoring her memory by continuing the work they both believed in so passionately.

In November 1998, the former Beatle met with *Agenda* Editor in Chief Kim Stallwood and Senior Editor Jill Howard Church to discuss his life with Linda, vegetarianism, hunting, fishing, vivisection, and other issues, not as a celebrity spouting off but as a genuinely concerned and committed activist seeking to strengthen and advance the humane movement. *Agenda* also spoke with British television writer **Carla Lane** and renowned artist **Brian Clarke**, close friends of the McCartneys.

When it comes to animal rights, Paul McCartney doesn't just talk the talk, he walks the walk—in vinyl Doc Martens boots.

8

You've been doing a lot of interviews lately. Has this been a way of promoting Linda's album and animal issues at the same time?

Yeah, the original thing was that because Linda was so visible and really our family spokesperson, I had the luxury of just backing up all her ideas, going to events with her, but always pushing her to the fore. That was my luxury. And we'd make all the decisions together, like about her foods and stuff and whether we'd donate to a certain cause, so really it was the two of us doing it all through the last twenty years. But because she was most visible, I had the feeling that when she was no longer there that a lot of people around the world might get very disappointed and think, "Oh God"—which is true, we've lost a great advocate. But rather than have them think we've lost a great advocate and there's no one to take her place, I just wanted to remind people—and myself in some ways—that I was sort of there on all the decisions.

And in actual fact, once she had the graciousness to say to me that it was actually me that suggested we went veggie, which I can't remember. So I just wanted to reassure people that it wouldn't suddenly mean a big hole where the McCartney family wasn't weighing in where it had been for twenty years, in vegetarianism, and food, and animal welfare, and in all the kind of connected things.

So that's where rather than coming to the press and saying what they wanted, which was, you know, "How are you coping with the grief?", rather than intrude into that period of my life I felt happier just doing what Linda would have done, which was just to talk. She might have been doing this interview.

Did you make plans with her to carry on certain things when you knew she wouldn't be here?

Well, we never knew, fortunately, but we would say, "If anything ever happens...." She said to us she'd like her food thing to continue. When someone dies people assume, "Oh well now who's going to do it?" But the great thing was when Linda got into the food thing I was very much part of it. I just thought with food, it's far better for a woman to do it. I'm not being sexist; the way I am, it just felt better. She was just the best cook in the house, too. It was kind of practical.

Who taught her to cook?
Nobody. She picked it all up. Her mom wasn't around [Linda's mother died in a plane crash when Linda was a teenager], and her mom was a good cook. But Lin used to like to hang out in the kitchen a lot. I used to joke with her that she was from a rich family, and she said, "We weren't that rich." She used to like to hang out with whoever was doing the cooking, which would sometimes be a cook. So I said, "Well that's rich, I don't care what you say." So we had a bit of fun over that. But she learned to cook because she loved food.

When she was a kid she would raid the cocktail cabinet for the silver-skinned onions—not the martini. And we ended up once writing to Heinz about putting preservatives in these blessed silver-skins, 'cause I got to love them so much. But they wrote back the standard letter, "It's to improve shelf life." Which doesn't matter! You shouldn't be doing it, they were great!

But I think Linda learned to cook out of necessity, out of loving food, and then just over the years she learned to be a very good cook. I think she took one or two little courses, too, but it was really instinctive.

And when she came to do her cookbooks, people would say, "How many tomatoes are you using?" and she'd say, "I don't know, a few." She'd just pick 'em, she'd go, "That looks enough." And so they'd have to say, "Stop the process! Measure them." You know, they'd weigh them, however many grams, or "four whole tomatoes."

So we always had the benefit of that, it was really good cooking. Real big sort of Italian-style meals with the kitchen smelling proper. And I still boast, because our kids are great cooks, I still boast that it's the finest restaurant in Britain.

How did her vegetarian food compare to vegetarian food that you'd been exposed to before?
Generally speaking, when we first started on it, it lacked imagination. Both of us were highly into the principle of not eating our friends, which is basically how we saw it; it was a compassionate thing rather

than a health thing. Then we started and we found this sort of missing ingredient, because most meals are the meat and "the other stuff," so we were just doing "the other stuff," and it was a bit bland. But very soon she started, "Well, we'll put pasta in there," or these sort of baked beans or mashed potatoes or some macaroni cheese. And out of that her repertoire grew. We used to work together on the "macaroni turkey," we used to call it, because it used to be a development of macaroni cheese that we'd slice. We'd leave it [in the refrigerator] for a few days and it firms up a bit. It was like a rice pudding. We could actually slice it so we could get our sort of token slices for the Christmas meal. We didn't have to [eat] what we used to call "rabbit food." That was always the joke with veggies.

Over the years it got to the state where it is now, which is really very lusty. So I think Linda took the fear out of cooking. And all the kids loved it. And she'd start them off, and me.

I know I'm a great chopper, which you need in a lot of food. "Anyone want to volunteer for chopping the garlic?" [Points to himself] Me. And I'm good at that, I enjoy the art of it, you know, I kind of like art. "What do you want, finely chopped?" You know, I respond well to direction. So it was Linda's thing, she communicated this passion. And she also saw it as an art, cooking. And it is. We talk about it being the greatest concept art. You prepare this fantastic stuff and within half an hour it's gone. What a concept! And then you start over. We always saw it as almost like a philosophical thing.

And it was 'round about that time that I'd go, like, to Nashville and someone would say, "You wanna go fishin'?" You know, good old boys time. And I'd say, "Sure." This was before we went veggie. And I'd find myself fishing in a pond and if I'd get lucky after a few hours I'd pick out this fish. And I'd see him flailing around and I remember thinking, "Oh God, I really am ending your life." This is it. I'm the "final man," as Carla [Lane] says in one of her lyrics on Linda's album. And I mean it, "This is your judgment day." And I didn't want to be that! So I put him back in. And after that I just started to question whether I wanted to do that kind of thing. Invariably, the answer was "No, you don't." But I'd been tricked by convention, by tradition, by good old boys.

One of my problems is hunting in the States. I feel very sorry. Because in American culture it's the beautiful thing for the boy and his father. But I feel sad for the sort of dad who's been brought up traditional—"Now come on, son, we'll go crack a few beers, we'll get in the tent"—I mean, I can see that. But my problem is you've got to take something's life, someone's life, and you're just reinforcing this brutal effect on your son. And it's this idea of, "We're in this kind of society, lad, you know, we must do this."

So whilst I do see the traditional aspect, that is why Linda and I tried to keep the food looking sort of traditional. I mean, we barbecue for instance. Married to an American, we barbecue. And it looks exactly the same, in fact it's better than what my memory was of traditional sort of "yuck." We gradually just got to be able to eat very well, which was like the first problem—not seeming too untraditional when people came 'round. "Are you going to have a burger?" "What? Aren't you veggie?" "Oh, have a glass of wine and a burger." "You drink?" They think you're something strange. And as Linda used to say, "You're only cutting one item out of your diet. Big deal."

Do you remember who the other first vegetarians you met were? Were there other vegetarians who influenced you?
No, it was completely our own decision, in Scotland [after] seeing the lambs gamboling. I only knew of a couple of vegetarians. There was a guy, Yehudi Menuhin, a famous fiddler, that I knew was. There actually weren't that many then, strangely enough, because even Carla Lane wasn't. When we met Carla, and she was going on about [animals], and Linda said, "Carla, are you veggie?" She said—people used to say to us—"Getting there." We used to say, "There's no such thing as half a virgin." We had to temper our view in the end. We said, "OK, getting there is good. It's a step." You mellow a bit on all that stuff. Carla said, "I'm getting there, I don't eat any red meat." "Oh, you eat the white stuff?" And as Linda said, "It's still got red blood. It

doesn't bleed green blood, love. It's still just the same. It's got a face, and its mommy loves it," as Linda would put it. So it was basically out of this compassion and this waking up to this idea, this nice modern idea, that maybe we can question what we do. That we don't just have to automatically do everything our parents told us to. Not out of rebellion so much as out of, "We've got to make our own way in life." *Editor's note: Carla Lane later clarified she had been a vegetarian prior to meeting the McCartneys.*

Your son, James, is vegan. Has veganism played a role in the family diet?
James is now twenty-one, so all our kids are sort of moving away from home, they've moved, really. But he will come home for a few days and then we eat vegan. And I don't bother trying to not be vegan. It's as easy for me to eat vegan as not.

Among vegetarians there's always the "How vegan are you?"
Well, James is completely vegan, and I'm "getting there"[*laughs*]. I enjoy soy milk a lot, which I didn't think I would, but then again I didn't think I'd like skimmed milk after having had full-fat all my life. Now I couldn't go near full-fat milk, but I will [use] skimmed milk if someone's having an ordinary cup of tea. But over here it isn't too clever because we've got a BSE [mad cow disease] risk in the milk.

A lot of vegetarians were obviously upset in general because of Linda's death, but the fact that she developed cancer on such a healthy lifestyle seemed especially ironic. Was she upset by that fact?
Yeah, obviously it was a major upset just at the fact itself, but yeah, it was a sort of secondary thing. It's like, "Oh, shit." We'd been saying that we believed it reduces the risk, which I still do think is true. And I think probably the way she was able to be so brave during her treatment and sort of not complain—we almost had a good time during the two and a half years of her treatment; almost, well you can't say you really had a good time—but I think that [her diet] had a lot to

do with the resistance she built up. But I still don't know what caused [the cancer]. She used to think it could have been dietary, she said, "You know, for an awful lot of my life I had meat," and used to like the steak quite rare. That's the old traditionalist kind of thing. So we never knew, really. There was quite a possibility it could have been a genetic thing. I have to tell you, they don't know.

[In an interview with the BBC on October 22, 1998, Paul McCartney said, "I'm finding out now that there is quite a lot of animal experimentation—some of it, I suppose, absolutely necessary when you come down to the final tests before people." In a letter to the editor that was published in USA Today on October 28, 1998, Jacquie Calnan, president of Americans for Medical Progress, wrote, "In McCartney's case, it took the death of his wife, Linda, from breast cancer to convince him to go beyond the glib words of animal rights activists and take a closer look at the vital role of animal research in medicine."]

Americans for Medical Progress, which is a biomedical group in the United States, published a letter in *USA Today* after your BBC interview about the "absolutely necessary" comment on animal testing. Would you like another chance to clarify that?
Yes. What happened during our treatment was this very sort of difficult moment where people would put it differently, they'd say, "If your child was dying, and the only way you could save your child was some form of animal experimentation, what would you do?" It's a real dilemma, it's very, very difficult. And we'd always say, "Well, you'd have to see the circumstances." It had always been our worst nightmare scenario. And so what I said in that interview was that in America, before any drug whatsoever can go on the market, there's this statutory requirement for it to be tested on animals before humans. So I was talking about that. Obviously I would prefer that it wasn't so, but I suspect that unless you can get the government to change its mind, there is some sort of requirement at that point, and at that point only.

As far as I'm concerned, I'm totally opposed to all animal experimentation whatsoever. Even this type. But at this fine end of this talking point, there is this very, very difficult period, full stop, to get stuff onto the market for AIDS, cancer, for all these things. It would be so great to see a cure. But I wouldn't want scientists to now think, "Aha! He's given in on that point," because I haven't at all.

It's very telling that they actually did this, they actually took the situation and manipulated it around.
They take it out of context and they completely switched the meaning around.

They labeled it "An Ex-Beatle's Courage"—he had the "courage" to say his animal rights convictions were complete crap once it came down to him being faced with his wife's illness.
Yes, I saw that, and they completely misinterpreted, but then again, what else is new? And I've had letters over the years from people saying "You've come out against animal experimentation, do you realize what you're doing? We at Maryland University, or whatever it was, are involved [in] all sorts of da-da-da." In fact, I'm engaged in letters at the moment just about exactly this, where it's a very difficult thing for me to give to cancer charities when I know there's animal experimentation. Because I know what Linda thought about that.

Tell us about the video.
Linda did a song on her new album called "The White Coated Man," which was Carla's words that Linda and I set to music. That's a very poignant lyric, so the video is filmed from the point of view of a rabbit. We get a small inkling of what they go through as the viewer.

We wanted to make something hard-hitting that I know Linda would have liked, but at the same time something that would actually get shown. Because that's the trouble, if you're so hard-hitting they just say, "Well, we're not going to use it. Our licensing laws will not allow it." It's like [when] the Norwegians got mad at us because we showed a film before our tour that showed them whaling. And they wrote to us and said, "Children under fifteen should not be allowed to see this." We said, "We are merely projecting images on a wall. If you don't want them to see it, you stop it. We're just reporting what you do."

And actually Linda and I did have to be quite courageous in that because the band that were working with us were a bit unsure of that film because they weren't all veggies and it was a fairly uncompromising film that Kevin Gardner made for us. It was showing anal electrocution and stuff like that, and people don't want to know about that. That's very shocking. But then we did the "Paul's Furs" thing with PETA [People for the Ethical Treatment of Animals]. It said, "Get your free fur video, save thousands," and it was great. *The New Yorker* [where the advertisement ran] got a little bit peeved with me because I'd sort of tricked them.

But the thing is that every little bit helps, all these campaigns. Because even though I know all your readers sort of support this thing, it's a bit of a difficult life, standing up. And as Linda and I always used to say, "For what? These 'dumb' animals? Nobody's getting paid around here." It's not all the usual enticements of society, like pay, holidays. It's exactly the opposite. It's a bloody difficult life. One friend of ours, an animal activist, picked up something in the jungle that he won't get rid of his whole life. And that's the price he's got to pay, what for some "dumb" pigs? Exactly that, for some "dumb" pigs. But that's why we do it, but it isn't easy. You can certainly think of an easier life to carve out for yourself. It's just a passion that we're blessed to have.

And I think a lot of your readers will understand that it's not easy for them being the odd man out in the crowd.
Stella just went to Japan, she said, "They couldn't believe I didn't eat fish." It was Linda, I think, getting massaged on our tour in Japan, and the woman couldn't believe her complexion—Linda had very lovely skin—and she said, "Oh, you eat lots of beef, huh?" And Linda said, "Ooo, no! Just the opposite."

Do people ever ask you if you eat chicken?
[*Chuckles*] Oh that's a vegetable, isn't it? Chicken and fish are officially vegetables now. I think you have to be strong, you've got to stick to all your principles. I used to call Linda "Mrs. Pankhurst" [a leading British suffragist], my "little Mrs. Pankhurst." Because you know, all you guys who are doing this, all us guys who are doing this, it's not an easy life. You get made fun of a lot, but you've got to stick with it. And I think the gratifying thing is we see things happening. We see the California horses got some kind of reprieve, we see that Gillette isn't testing, possibly because of that campaign I did through PETA. And this is the gratification. [*See editor's note on page 25.*]

Like the [British] cosmetics testing ban announced two days ago.
And we could only dream about all of this [before], and now it is actually coming online, and that is really gratifying. Linda and I actually had been surprised at the speed at which it's come around, because when we started twenty years ago, we said, "Oh, maybe in about a hundred years' time you'll see it happening." We were prepared for it to be a slow, inevitable grind toward sense. Every so often you get a little spurt. You go, "Wow! So many more veggies."

What about the future, as far as animal rights stuff you plan to do?
I'm not a great planner, so it's when somebody comes along, if you ask me to do an interview, I'll say, "Yeah, OK," and that's my role. We keep on plugging vegetarianism, because I think that is one of the single greatest things someone can do. And so many animal activists still aren't. What we want to try and do is to try and educate young people. For instance, we've got an animated film that will come out at some point and that's really aimed at young kids. It's a very lovely little animation thing, and it's sweet, and it's a song, and it's a celebration. But the idea is, we see a shot of a deer for instance, like Bambi, and one of the characters says, "Do you believe someone wanted to shoot and eat that lovely animal?" So you have to, I think, infiltrate kids. Let's face it, the other side infiltrates. We pay for all the meat adverts; we

give them a very large amount of money out of our taxes, even us veggies pay for the meat adverts over here. So I have no sort of worry about infiltrating on the other side, I think that's exactly what we ought to do.

I like the idea that little kids, when they watch [the movie] *Babe*, will say, "Is that a pig? What is that, Mommy? Is that a sheep? Oh, no thanks." I think that's a good thing for the future.

As Linda and I used to say to people, "Look, you want to do something to save the planet, go veggie." In one move. People are so frightened of it, though. And as someone said recently, "People don't like to be inconvenienced." And I can relate to that.

Was it difficult raising your children vegetarian?
We've brought them all up [vegetarian], except Heather, who's the eldest, who was part of our conversion. Then all the others almost from birth, I think. The only time it came into question really was when we were in a hotel and they'd say, "What's a barbecue?" We'd say, "Well, it's chickens, it's a cow, or it's this," and we'd explain what it is. And they'd say, "Can we try it?" And we'd say, "Yeah, OK." We're not that strict. "Yeah, try it, this has got to be your decision." So they'd try it and luckily for us they'd say, "Ooo, we don't like it. It is chicken, I'd rather have the [live] chicken." We had chickens at home. You struggle with all those things, trying to find your way. I think one of the good things is that we who perhaps are little bit more advanced just from doing it a bit longer can sympathize with people who are still struggling with all this shit they're having to put up with.

Did your kids do any other forms of activism?
[Fashion designer] Stella's done [an anti-]fur thing recently. They're just coming into it. You see, we all had the luxury of Linda; we could just say, "Yeah, way to go, Lin!" "Yeah, I'm coming to this one!", "I'll raise that donation." She was not only the spokesperson, [she was] the office it all went through. So the kids dealt with being veggies and are

now very proud of it. James, being vegan, just did a sort of [anti-]milk thing, wrote a letter, and that was put about in a few places.

My most surprising thing about milk is this new ["Got milk?"] campaign in America with the white over the top lip. I always used to be very supportive of milk because we've all been brought up [that way]. My mother was a nurse, so I had all the old traditional medical values. She died when I was a teenager, but I know she would have said when she heard I went veggie, "Where are you going to get your protein?" So I, like she, was a great advocate of milk. We've begun to reassess that. Someone pointed out that we're the only animals who feeds its young milk after the first year. And I actually think the people, the ones with the [white] upper lip, all think like I used to think.

Did the milk industry ever approach you?
I don't think so. But I sympathize with those people. I used to remind Linda that the Beatles were nonvegetarians, and I said, "And we were OK people." We still wanted the world to be a better place, we just didn't know. So that made us have more sympathy and compassion for people who didn't know yet. I quite like that. I'm sort of glad I wasn't a veggie all my life because it gives me a perspective that I can relate to people who are having trouble. I can say, "Oh, I know exactly that problem. You know what you do? You do *this*. Here's Linda's book." There's always an answer.

Tell us about some of the animals you've had over the years.
Oh, I'd love to tell you about the animals. I personally never had a pet growing up, because my mom and dad both worked. And even the day we saw free puppies going and my brother and I thought, "Definite, we'll get one," we couldn't have one. So my first pet was when I was living alone as one of the Beatles and I got an Old English sheepdog called Martha, and I loved her dearly; she was beautiful, she was really good for me; we were good for each other. I remember John Lennon coming 'round and saying, "God, I've never seen you with an animal

before." I was being so affectionate it took him aback, he'd not seen that side of my character. Because you don't do that with humans—not as obviously anyway.

And then I had two cats called Pyramus and Thisbe, which showed my literary bent, and then I had three—they all had to be cool names, of course—that were called Jesus, Mary, and Joseph. And then as a family, Linda and I, after Martha died, we then got another Old English sheepdog and we eventually had a litter by the one after her. We kept two of the puppies, so that meant we've got three now. I have four dogs at home, three English sheepdogs and Stella's dog, the mutt. She'd hate me to say that!

Everyone will want to know, are the dogs "fixed"?
Yes, they are.

That was the correct answer.
Oh good.

Any cats?
We have Picasso, we have Motley, and Seal, a very beautiful Russian Blue. We have two terrapins...Linda was fantastic with animals. She didn't have many pets. She had a dog called Missy, [who] wasn't allowed on the bed, but she had her trained so that if her parents ever came [the dog] jumped down on the floor; the rest of the time she was on the bed. Plus horses, she was horse mad. She never owned her own horse, although she'd ridden at Madison Square Garden, so she was a fantastic rider. But her parents didn't understand how to buy her a horse, even though they had the money. And she used to look out of her window every Christmas morning half expecting to see a horse on the lawn. She used to tell me that, a very poignant story. The good payoff, then, was that I was able to be the one that bought her her first horse, called Cinnamon, a big chestnut mare of Irish extraction. She was being bred as a polo horse, so it was good she came to us because I think she wouldn't have had as good a time. Well, none of the

animals would have had as good a time because we really spoil them and let them live out their lives.

Linda bought a stallion from America when we were on tour, this lovely stallion called Lucky Spot, and he was an Appaloosa Foundation stallion. We brought him back to England and bred off him with this other American Foundation mare who'd come across the Mojave Desert while she was in foal to come to England. We used racehorse facilities, so it was as if she was a million-dollar stud, she got good treatment. And there came a crisis at one point about five or six years ago when she was lying in the field with something obviously wrong with her stomach. They said it might be colic, and the vet said, "There is an operation that requires six vets." It's a huge procedure, costs a lot. I said, "I'm not worried about the cost." I walked the horse around and I said, "Look, you're going to go with them and let them do what they're going to do because you need this, and this is something you should do." And the vet said she might not even survive the anesthetic. We rang that evening: "How did it go?" He said, "She's had the operation, it was totally successful, she's standing up and she's eating." We said, "Yo, that's our baby!" So she was fantastic. She was called Malaspina Maid, and she lived three more years after that. She was over thirty, which is pretty old for a horse.

Were there specific animals that helped Linda while she was going through her tough times?
The dogs were very good, and her horse. Her Appaloosa stallion, son of Lucky Spot, is called Blankit. And he's beautiful. He's tough. But she talked to him like he was a big puppy dog. He's a couple of tons of horse, and a full stallion, so she's not messing around here. He's not gelded, which quiets them down, [jokingly] as it would you or I.

On Flaming Pie you wrote the song "Little Willow" for the family of Maureen Starkey [Ringo Starr's former wife], after her death. Have those words come back to help you?

I wrote "Little Willow" before we knew anything about Linda's diagnosis, and there was a terrible moment when we were listening to it. It always used to make us cry anyway, but once Linda was diagnosed it was terrible, because we looked at each other and she said, "Oh God, it's about me now." And it was horrible, it was a very sad moment.

But you know, none of us get out of this alive, and you have got to look at it philosophically. As I said at the New York memorial service, we shouldn't judge a life by its length. You could have people who live forever and be complete idiots. You can have people who live just a few special years and it's quite often the case that people get what they have to say said, and then they find that they don't live that long. And I certainly think in many ways that was Linda's thing. Except you know, it's horrible for me 'cause she was my best friend. And for the kids, because they were her best friends, too. So it's tragic from that point of view.

But you've got to go on, we've all got to go on. We're all involved in a struggle, we're all involved in trying to change the world. The last thing she would want is that any of us would be not encouraged by her death. She would want us to go the other way, and I think it's had that effect. That was why I made the point when I made a statement about how I felt, to say, "And if you want to pay tribute to Linda, do the one she would have liked best [go vegetarian]." Which got me in a lot of trouble; a lot of people said, "Oh, typical grandstanding, showboating, even when his wife's died." Well, I knew that she would have wanted that. It came to me, I knew she would nudge me—"Use it, use it for all it's worth." And I told Carla [Lane] and people like that, "This is so difficult, but we've gotta play this out. We've got to use all this media attention for what it's worth, for everything we can get out of it, because even in the most horrible of circumstances she would want us, and I would want us, to use the moment."

Did you and she believe in heaven?

That's such a big question. I wouldn't say we had a conception of heaven. It's like, "Do you believe in God?" Linda and I pretty much shared the kind of view where I would say, "God is the word 'good' with an 'o' taken out." And I have a feeling, sort of historically, that it was personified by the priests and other people who wrote the literature. Because it's easier for people to understand if you say it's a big guy with a white beard. But when you ask people, "OK, how do you see God?", even the most committed of Christians have a little trouble with that. You say, "Well, I'm not sure it is a guy with a white beard." For instance, somebody a few years back said that God might be a woman. Well I must say, since Linda's died, I've thought, "Have I got a contender!" [*laughs*] That would be my most devout wish, I could handle that. She's a real good candidate; she'd be very merciful, yet tough as nails.

We were very spiritual, and still are, believing goodness, believing all of that. But as to whether there actually is a place called heaven and a man in a white beard called God, I just don't know. I don't know whether [her spirit] is lodged in a place called heaven, but I think it's in a good place because of who she is.

Linda and I were amazed for years to hear Stephen Hawking, the scientist, say that they've discovered now that we are made of the same things that stars are made of, sort of a molecular base. And Linda and I loved that, we said, "OK, we're stardust."

❦

> One of my hopes for the future is that the various animal groups, that can sometimes find themselves disagreeing over tactics, will realize, "We've got to get together and help each other."
> —Paul McCartney to *The Animals' Agenda*

Cow

Placid creature
Standing in your June field
With one more day of grazing
Before the slatted truck

Trusting creature
Going to meet the final man
With nothing on your face

Except for that familiar beauty

And he will eat you
Because he didn't look

From the song "Cow" by Carla Lane, Linda McCartney, and Paul McCartney, from the album, *Wide Prairie*.

Little Willow

Sleep, little willow
Peace gonna follow
Time will heal your wounds

Grow to the heavens
Now and forever
Always came too soon

From the song "Little Willow" by Paul McCartney, from the album, *Flaming Pie*.

A Personal Postscript by Kim W. Stallwood

Nothing can prepare you for a meeting with Paul McCartney. It was one of the most nerve-racking experiences of my life. He is, of course, nothing but charming and friendly. There's no escaping, however, that you're meeting a living legend. During the interview, one half of me concentrated on Paul's responses to our questions while the other half was thinking, "F—k me, I'm sitting on a sofa with Paul McCartney!"

During the interview Paul talked about how some people try to catch activists off-guard by asking if they wear leather shoes. "You'll notice my very leather-looking shoes," Paul said, putting one foot on the coffee table, "but they're not leather." What followed is one of those classic moments when animal activists start comparing plastic shoes. Except that this was me with Sir Paul McCartney!

Typically, I have to complain about my pair of crippling, nonleather shoes that had begun to self-destruct after just a few days of walking around London. Vegan they were; comfortable they were not.

Paul took off one boot, sniffed it, and said, "I used these for two world tours."

He then promised to buy Jill and me a pair of shoes each from Vegetarian Shoes in Brighton, England, which is where he buys his.

Thanking him but thinking nothing more about it, we completed the interview.

Paul's office was one step ahead, however, because when I returned to the *Agenda* office they had already sent a fax asking for our U.K. shoes sizes.

Two weeks later, a box arrived containing two pairs of shoes. I forwarded Jill's on to her, which she proudly wears and will someday add to her collection of Beatles memorabilia.

I donated my pair to *Agenda*'s library and archive.

I will show them to you for a small donation.

☙

Editor's note: 1998 California voters approved a measure with 59.4 percent to ban the commercial sale of horse for human consumption. In November 1996, Gillette announced a moratorium on animal testing.

The Art of Friendship
An Interview with
Brian Clarke
KIM W. STALLWOOD
AND
JILL HOWARD CHURCH

B RIAN CLARKE HAS EARNED GREAT ACCLAIM AS A
talented and award-winning artist. His exquisite paintings and
stained-glass creations grace museums and buildings the world
over, and he designed fabulous sets for Paul McCartney's world
concert tours.

Brian was one of Linda McCartney's closest friends for many years;
the two occasionally collaborated, and he dedicated his stained-glass
piece "The Glass Wall" to her in 1998. His November 1998 interview
in London with *The Animals' Agenda* marked the first time since
Linda's death that he spoke at length publicly—and very poignantly—
about her life and work.

How did you first meet Linda?
My art dealer was Robert Frasier back in the late '70s, and he was a
seminal figure in the '60s pop art movement. He'd been a friend of
Paul's since the very early days of the Beatles, and in fact he and Paul
had developed a great kind of sympathy with each other regarding
their mutual interest in art. And Robert one day said, "I'd like you to
meet this photographer I know, I think you'd get on very well," and he
took me around to meet Linda. She was pregnant with James at the
time, and we hit it off instantly. And then as the years went on we
worked together on lots of things, Paul and I and Linda and I, and
became great friends.

When did the animal consciousness bit start?
Like, after about fifteen minutes, I think.

How come?
Because at the time I had the kind of open honesty that you can only have when you're really young and you don't know that it's disadvantageous [*laughing*]. You tell everybody everything. And I'd just got a new boyfriend, and I said to Linda—I'd only known her half an hour or something—and I happened to make some remark about this to Linda. And she said to me, "Does he eat meat?" And I said, "Yeah, I think so." She said, "Oh, I don't know how you can kiss somebody who eats meat!" [*laughs*] And it seemed such an odd thing to say, it made me laugh.

Linda had very hands-on contact with animals, particularly at home. It's the nearest I've ever seen to a Disney cartoon [*laughs*]. All manner of dogs and rabbits and birds and God knows what. And Paul talks to them all, of course. They stop the car when they're driving and they chat to the animals and call out. And it's very nice, it's not kind of nuts. It seems like you've entered another kind of experience.

We shoot pheasants in England a lot, as you know, or shoot anything really, and on their land in Sussex they allow the pheasants to roam free. And they do all kinds of things to attract the pheasants onto their land so that once on, they're safe. And they've kind of spread the word among each other, these pheasants and rabbits and hares and things, because the place is absolutely teeming with them. There's obviously something about that area that attracts all these animals, because I've never seen so many.

She's the best friend I've ever had, really....I've never heard Linda say anything to anybody with the intention of even remotely impressing them. It really wasn't in her nature to try and make people feel less important than she was or herself feel or be viewed as important. She didn't see herself as important, and it embarrassed her that people thought she was. You could be at a party or a dinner, and Linda would somehow find some cleaning lady, some waiter, who had a sheepdog, and she would be going at it all night about, "No, no, no, you don't have to give it meat..." and she'd create big friends. And the next day she'd be sending photographs and cookbooks to the waiter, the driver, the cleaner, whoever it was, and she would hardly notice that Robert DeNiro or Dustin Hoffman was there. She had no interest in rank or station or position or wealth or authority. I've never met any people who are more dignified in that position than [Paul and Linda] are. Linda actively and demonstrably believed that everybody was equal. And she made it absolutely clear in her treatment of people that it was no effort to her; that's really in her soul what she felt.

I always think of Linda as a vegetarian person rather than an animal rights person, but of course she was both. She used to say, "I want the truck driver to understand that he can eat vegetarian food, that it doesn't make him a [wimp]." We were in Australia, and there were all these huge kind of butch riggers on the tour, and somebody was complaining about the fact that they only had vegetarian food on the tour, and they thought it wasn't manly, eating all this stuff. And Paul said, [in Liverpool accent], "Gorillas are vegetarians, you know." [laughs].

She would never be fazed by who it was she was trying to convince of the rightness of this. And she would spend an equal amount of time trying to persuade my housekeeper as she would trying to persuade a prime minister or a president. And she had regular access to both kinds of people. We were staying at the Okura Hotel in Tokyo a few years ago, and they'd kind of put aside the pool for Paul and Linda to use, but at a certain time of day the prime minister of Japan was going to use it. And when Linda heard this, she needed to know which one of these men was the prime minister because she had to tell him about the whales. And it was very important, she was, like, [looks around frantically] fighting to find the right guy. She believed that it was her job.

And she got a lot of stick for it. If you look at the things she is supposed to have done wrong in her life, the things that she was so relentlessly hounded for in the press: [counting on his fingers] She married the guy she fell in love with; she was American; she didn't shave her legs; and she didn't like to kill or eat animals. Oh, and she can't sing. Give me a break! And she carried it. She never complained. Even when she was sick, she never complained.

How did she cope with the illness?
[*Pause*] She didn't moan. She got upset, of course, and every now and again it would express itself. She really loved her family, and the idea that she was leaving them was very, very painful to her. I think that there's a lot said about Paul and Linda's love affair and how remarkable it was in show business terms, and what an unusual thing for two people living in that extraordinary bubble. But I think that the love affair that existed between Paul and Linda was very, very rare. It brought a beauty out in both of them. It was a unique thing, in my experience, their relationship, and it was founded entirely on affection. And when Linda became ill, he showed strengths of an extraordinary nature that I didn't know he had.

What would you say about her photography?
In telling you about her photography I can tell you something very much about her character. When I first became excited about photography in the 1970s, I was a punk rocker. I'm forty-five now—I've been a very young kind of '60s guy, and I've been a Beatles fan, but I was a bit too young to be really in that frame, and I was a little bit too old to be a punk, but I got into punk because it fought the kind of conventional constrictions that everything was being held in—the commercial, and the banality of it all. And photography I approached in the same way. It was really where the action was at in the '70s, the photographers were the people who were pushing the barriers out, who were addressing the really hard issues. Painting had become decorative in the hands of the kind of late pop painters like [David] Hockney and Peter Blake...it had just become weak and charming. The photographers were the ones addressing the really serious issues.

Linda, as a photographer, struck me as very odd because she was capable of embracing those kind of really tough issues and yet at the same time, she lent to the way she looked at the world through her lens a femininity, a tenderness. And that wasn't altogether in the kind of swing of things then. But it was a genuine tenderness, and she was never ashamed of it. Look at the things she would continually photograph: animals, her family, landscape—the delicate things. I was involved with a lot of really great photographers at that time. David Bailey was and is one of my closest friends; [Richard] Avedon, Ralph Gibson, Harry Callahan, Aaron Siskind—the real heavyweights of the day—Helmut Newton, they're all my friends, I know them all. And Linda was different. There was a tenderness, and she managed to approach those issues but with a...I don't want to say it, because by using the word "motherly" it seems to rob Linda of something else she had, which was sexuality. Linda was a very sexy woman, very sexy. And when Paul and Linda were together they were a sexy couple. They looked like they had sex. There was always a kind of grin on both of their faces, and they were continually pecking at each other. All the time, couldn't keep their hands off each other, right to the end, right to the end.

And Linda's photography expressed that. It expressed the way human beings make contact with each other, the way humans make contact with animals. And she saw no hierarchy, I'll tell ya. As far as she was concerned, someone who'd kick a dog would kick a person. Somebody who would be insensitive to an animal's needs would be insensitive to a human's needs. And she was not one of those animal rights people—and I've met them, believe me—who doesn't actually like people very much. That was not Linda McCartney. She saw the animal kingdom as encompassing everything that moved, and she used to say, "I won't eat anything with a face." It was that that got me, it was that that turned me veggie.

She wanted people to be vegetarian so they'd be happy, so that they'd feel more like they were part of nature. And when she was in her element, down on the farm, she was so happy. And it was a happiness that she really wasn't content to keep to herself.

The Animals' Agenda *extends special thanks to Nancy Dolinger for helping to make this interview possible.*

≋

A Muse with a Mission
An Interview with Carla Lane

KIM W. STALLWOOD
AND
JILL HOWARD CHURCH

LIVERPOOL NATIVE CARLA LANE FIRST MADE A NAME for herself by becoming one of Britain's most successful television comedy writers. But she has also become well known for her more serious side, one wholly devoted to rescuing animals and fighting cruelty. Her sanctuary, Animaline, provides shelter and rehabilitation for dozens of wild and domestic animals in rural England, while her investigative organization, Animal Information Network Ltd., exposes abuse, such as Europe's live animal export trade. A vegetarian for the past thirty-five years, she tirelessly uses her fame and talents to bring attention to the plight of abused creatures.

In November 1998, Carla spoke with *The Animals' Agenda* about her close friendship with Linda McCartney, with whom she co-wrote the songs "The White Coated Man" and "Cow" on Linda's *Wide Prairie* album.

Tell us about the two songs.
Linda just happened to say to me, "Do you write poetry?" I said yes. So she said, "Would you send me some?" And I did. And then about two or three weeks later she rang me up and she said, "Would you like to come on over and watch Paul doing some recording?" I said yes, that would be great. It was a lovely sunny day, I always remember. I heard this beautiful music coming from the mill. And then I heard someone singing, which turned out to be Linda, and suddenly I thought, "I know those words!" It was "White Coated Man." Paul

31

said, "Come on, now, Carla, you've got to rap." So I did it. But it was all done for fun, there was no commercial feeling, it was eight years ago. We did both songs and I came out feeling really elated, because it was a change from writing for television.

When did you know she was ill?
Somebody just rang me and said, "Did you know that Linda had cancer?" And I didn't know, because Linda and I never talked about that sort of thing. That was how it was. We used to talk about how we were going to change the world, and how animals were going to benefit by our dual things we were doing. She used to say to me, "You do the talking, I'll do the cooking."

And then just before she went away [to America], she rang me and we just talked normally. She said to me, "Are you going to bring me some chickens over?" I'd rescued 500 chickens from a farm, [and] I said, "Are you going to take some of these from me?" She said, "OK, I'll have some." Now in my mind, that spelled "I'm all right." I said, "When are you coming back?" She said, "On the eighth." I said, "I'll be there on the ninth with quite a lot." So that was it. And then at the end of the conversation she said, "Things are not going well for me, Carla." And I said, lightheartedly, "Oh, you're going to be OK." Because I thought, [since] she hadn't had a mastectomy, that perhaps was the next move. So I said, "You'll be all right. I've had a word with Buddha along in the hall." And her words were, "Yeah, well, when you talk to him next, ask him to get this shit out of my body." I'll always remember that. And I thought, "This is not good." And then we had a few more words, and she always used to end by saying, "Bye! Love you lots!" you know, in that merry way. And she said, "Carla, I love you, Carla." And my heart turned over—it was like goodbye.

When did you start your sanctuary?
Nearly seven years ago. But I started rescuing animals in London about fifteen years ago. In those days I was rich—I'm afraid those days are long gone—so I used to go around saving animals. I used to buy

horses that were going for slaughter, and I found myself with about sixteen of them, and I was paying someone else to look after them. And then one day I went to the studio and I was about three hours getting there and two hours getting back, and I thought, "Oh, I don't want all this, I'm going to live in the country." I thought, "Well, I'll make the effort, and then I can say to myself, 'Well, you tried to leave.' " And lo and behold, two titled people came along and bought my house in two weeks. So we started looking around. And when I first saw this place, I thought, "It's much too big, there's forty-four rooms here, and I just don't need that." But I did need the twelve stables. So we moved in, and the neighbors—well, there aren't any immediate neighbors, but those far away must've seen this terrible procession!

What message would you convey to *Agenda* readers?
Just keep fighting—never give up, never stop talking, writing, shouting, singing. Be a voice for them and never grow tired of it. Don't let people put you off by calling you names; just acknowledge that we are the cranks and loonies of the world, and we feel that what we know merits what we're doing.

A Conversation
with Peter Singer

KIM W. STALLWOOD

I N 1975, A TWENTY-NINE-YEAR-OLD AUSTRALIAN PHILO-
sopher named Peter Singer published *Animal Liberation*, the book
that is often credited with launching the modern animal rights
movement. Since *Animal Liberation* was published, Singer has written
or co-written fifteen other books, including *Animal Factories* (with
Jim Mason), *Practical Ethics*, and *How Are We to Live?* Singer also has
edited or co-edited nine additional books, including *In Defense of
Animals*, *Animal Rights and Human Obligations*, and *The Great Ape
Project* (with Paola Cavalieri).

Born in Melbourne, Australia, Singer was educated at the
University of Melbourne and the University of Oxford. Formerly a
professor of philosophy and co-director of the Institute of Ethics and
Public Affairs, and deputy director of the Center for Human Bioethics
at Monash University in Melbourne, Singer is now the DeCamp
Professor of Bioethics at Princeton University. He has also taught at
five other universities around the world, including the University of
Oxford and New York University.

Singer is married to Renata Diamond; they have three daughters.
When he is not writing, teaching, lecturing, or traveling, Singer enjoys
bushwalking, swimming, and growing fruits and vegetables.

In 1994, Singer was in the United States to promote The Great Ape
Project. *The Animals' Agenda* visited with him in the offices of St.
Martin's Press, publisher of *The Great Ape Project*, in New York.

Why did you become a philosopher?
I was always interested in doing things that would contribute to public debates about ethical and political issues. Philosophy offered the potential for doing that. I was quite unsure about becoming a philosopher for some time during my university career. I didn't make the decision until after I had graduated. That was a time when philosophy was going through some interesting changes. After spending a lot of time rather fruitlessly analyzing the meanings of words, it was just starting to get involved in debates about the Vietnam conflict, civil disobedience, racial rights, and so on.

You recently co-edited *The Great Ape Project* with Paola Cavalieri. What do you hope this book will accomplish?
I hope it will help to build a bridge between us and other species. We're asking that the community of equals, as we call it, the community of beings for whom we accept the same ultimate, basic rights, should cease to be the species *homo sapiens* and should become the great apes as a whole. If we were to accomplish that, and people were to accept that all species of great apes are not items of property, but are beings with rights, equals, if you like, persons in the full sense, both legally and morally, that would be a historic expansion of that community of equals. Once that community ceases to be identical with the species *homo sapiens*, a lot of other possibilities open up. We're making a case for one rather narrowly defined group at the moment, but we don't disguise the fact that cases may be made for other species as well.

Why do you think the public is going to be more receptive to the idea of bringing great apes into the human sphere of ethics first as opposed to any other species?
For a number of reasons. One is that because of the work that's been done by Jane Goodall—and the apes' ability to communicate through signing—we now know so much more about the apes and about their emotional and social lives in which we recognize ourselves very

directly. People who see the great apes on film or hear reports of their signing can recognize themselves and recognize the interests and desires of the apes as rather like theirs. Because of that close likeness, we identify more immediately with the apes.

Secondly, we are not embedded in a culture that ruthlessly exploits the great apes in a large-scale way—as we are embedded in a culture that exploits pigs and chickens and so on. So the kind of psychological opposition people have to considering an idea that would force them to change their diet—and the much more tangible opposition of industries prepared to put millions of dollars into fighting us—isn't going to be there in the case of great apes.

What's the current status of the declaration that people can sign in support of including the great apes in the community of equals?
Quite a number of people have written to us from England, where the book has been out for more than eight months. In Australia about 1,200 people have signed up as supporters. We were also pleased to have endorsements from a well-known author like Douglas Adams and a distinguished biological scientist like Richard Dawkins, who did not previously have a track record of support for animal liberation causes. And I just had a letter from a woman who works with Carl Sagan. He's indicated that he's supportive of it. [*Editor's Note: Carl Sagan died in 1996. For more on the Great Ape Project, see www.greatapeproject.org.*]

What's the next stage for The Great Ape Project?
We've already had letters of support from people in thirty countries. We want to build up national groups in each of those countries. Then we want to think about helping particular great apes whose conditions of imprisonment are blatantly ones of deprivation and torture. We would try to get them into a sanctuary or reservation where we can provide for their needs. At the same time we would keep in the forefront the idea that The Great Ape Project is not simply rescuing animals from inhumane conditions, it's really trying to extend the community of equals. We might go to people in politics, trying to get

resolutions of principle on this matter. We might go through the courts. I'm having some discussions with lawyers in America about those possibilities. And eventually we might go to the United Nations, trying to get them to pass a declaration on the great apes akin to the declarations on the rights of children or women or the disabled.

Next year [1995] will mark the 20th anniversary of the publication of *Animal Liberation*. What were your original goals when you wrote the book and have they been accomplished?
My goals were to bring about a situation where we give the same consideration to the interests of nonhuman animals as we give to our own. That would mean a society that ceases to exploit animals, ceases to discount their interests, and ceases to sacrifice their major interests for the much more minor interests of our own. Obviously that goal has not been accomplished at all. What has been accomplished is this: First, a movement now exists that didn't really exist in 1975, so there is an organizational base from which to work for the accomplishment of those goals. Second, there have been some changes in the severity of our exploitation of animals in a wide variety of fields. In this country there has been a move away from testing cosmetics on animals, and apparently there's been quite a significant drop in the number of animals used in laboratory experiments, according to the report from the Tufts University Center for Animals and Public Policy. There's also been a significant impact on the fur trade.

Are you surprised at the growth of the movement and the growth of all these issues during the last twenty years?
That's hard to say, because I didn't know what to expect. You've got to remember that the book was written in the early 1970s when a lot of things seemed possible that perhaps people have become more cynical about now. My expectations ranged all the way from having mass support for goals such as getting rid of factory farming, which seems to me to be absolutely indefensible. But that hasn't come, so in that sense the book hasn't reached my expectations. Yet in more pessimistic

moments I thought, "Ah, well, this is too utopian. It's going to cause a flap, then be forgotten." But that hasn't happened, either. So I guess the book's success has been somewhere between my more optimistic and more pessimistic expectations.

What do you think is the most difficult challenge facing the animal rights movement now?
To maintain the momentum that was built up during the 1980s. We took our opponents, to some extent, by surprise. At first they laughed at us. They didn't take us seriously. That allowed us a sympathetic hearing with the media and made it relatively easy to get a lot of attention. It's now become harder. Our opponents have cleverly exploited this idea that the movement is full of terrorists or fanatical extremists. There's a real danger to the movement in getting painted into that corner.

How do we avoid that?
First, by making it clear that we do not support any violence toward human beings. Second, by showing that we are prepared to talk to our opponents and to work with them to devise concrete ways that will allow them to do the things they want to do without exploiting animals. We have to show that we are not anti-science, but we want to see ways in which scientific research can be achieved without the exploitation of animals. We are not anti-farmer, but we want to see ways in which farmers can make a living and produce food without exploiting animals.

Where do you think the message of animal rights has not gotten through, and what can we do about it?
In the United States the message about food and farm animals has not got through effectively. The United States is well behind Europe, not that Europe has reached the state we want to see, but there's a lot more awareness in Europe of the fact that food animals live in miserable

conditions that do not satisfy their needs and that it's not impossible to change this.

More ultimately, the ethical argument, the anti-speciesism argument, has not got through enough with most people. It hasn't been taken seriously enough perhaps, or it hasn't been understood. We have to keep hammering away at the fundamental philosophical point that animals have interests and the fact that animals are not of our species is not a reason for ignoring or discounting those interests.

How would you rate the movement's effectiveness in relating the issue of the interests of animals toward the interests of women and minorities?
From my experience there is a fairly solid and reasonably active group of feminists who are concerned about the animal movement, ranging from, I guess, ecofeminists who take a broader view of feminism and nature, to some of those who have written specifically about the animal movement, like Carol Adams [author of *The Sexual Politics of Meat*].

We've been less successful in involving minorities in the movement. Obviously we ought to try more. At the same time we have to understand that they may have their own priorities. Because a lot of their problems have not been met, they would naturally see them as more urgent.

How far should we compromise when we seek legislation for animals?
I'm prepared to support any legislation that reduces the suffering of animals or enables them to meet their needs more fully. I'm not prepared to bargain away the more far-reaching goals of the movement for the sake of those reforms. In other words, I'm prepared to support, say, the European move to get rid of the battery cage for hens, even though raising hens is obviously still compatible with a fair amount of exploitation. I'm not prepared to say, "If this happens, I will give up any sort of suggestions that we need to go further." [*See Editor's note.*]

If you could get hens out of cages and into free-range or deep-litter systems, you might switch to other priorities because hens would not be among the most severely exploited animals. But it's important to see these reforms as stepping stones on the path to further goals, not as the be-all and end-all of the campaign.

You're involved with ANZFAS: the Australian and New Zealand Federation of Animal Societies. Can you tell us how that movement has evolved? And do you see parallels between their evolution and what you're aware of that's happening in this country or in Europe? ANZFAS evolved as an attempt to get the various Australian animal rights, animal liberation, and animal welfare groups together because we have a federal system where we need to make representations to state government on specific issues, but we also need to have a voice at the federal level for a number of other issues. We felt that there were few groups representing the movement at a national level. When the national government would call for submissions on any particular issue, there would be forty different groups that might make submissions, but none of them had the expertise or the time to research the issues properly. So we invited the groups to join our federation, which would represent their concerns at a national level. They might still put in submissions if they wished, but we would have the expertise to look at this sort of thing properly. About forty-five different organizations joined. The ones that stayed out were either the SPCAs, who basically felt they had their own national organization and state branches, and a few of the most hard-line anti-vivisection groups. ANZFAS hasn't been able to keep the entire movement together, that would be unrealistic, but it's kept the solid middle body together. That includes animal liberation groups as well as some shelters and so on.

ANZFAS has put members on various government committees in the department of primary industries, committees that are developing codes of practice for the keeping of hens and cattle. I think it's done a very useful sort of work. I don't really know of anything similar in other countries. I don't think there is anything drawing the movement together in the United States.

There's nothing here in the United States. In fact, the animal rights movement is proposing that something like that should be formed here. I'm not aware of anything similar in Britain. Does ANZFAS have its own budget, its own staff? Where does it get its funding?
ANZFAS gets its funding partly from member society subscriptions, but they're pretty low because the idea is to keep in as many member societies as possible. It also has its own individual members who joined in order to give it direct support, and it has a couple of larger donors who have given it money from time to time. Our government now gives some money directly to bodies who represent movements at political levels. These are called administrative services grants. The government recognizes that the existence of ANZFAS means that if it [the government] wants to consult with the animal movement, it can do so with one request, one letter, rather than having to find forty-five different bodies and go around to them.

Does ANZFAS get active when there's a general election or in other statewide elections?
It has at times, but that took a major amount of funds. In the last couple of elections it hasn't been as active. It really is struggling with the workload it has. Essentially it has a full-time executive director, a secretary, and a part-time assistant.

Why do you think cooperation and unity among organizations and individuals within the animal rights movement is notoriously difficult to accomplish?
This is not a movement that is going to attract large numbers of people who conform to what others say. That might be one factor. Otherwise, I don't think it's a whole lot worse than other voluntary movements, where there are splits and friction, too. People fighting for a cause they passionately believe in get upset when things don't work or when

people do things in a way that they see as not being right. But we shouldn't think we are a whole lot worse than any other groups.

The opposition seems to be much more willing to band together to fight us. How come they are and we're not?
Don't forget that they're not passionately committed to an ethical cause. They're basically concerned to keep us off so they can continue to make their profit. In that sense, there's less of a sense of commitment and dedication, almost desperation, which, I think, gets people to be a little short-fused with each other.

Is there a similar counter initiative in Australia?
Yes. There's a group that calls itself, rather misleadingly, the Animal Welfare Federation of Australia, which consists of circuses, animal experimenters, factory farmers, and so on. They haven't made a very big impact, fortunately.

The scientists in Australia, the animal experimenters, do not present a united front of opposition. In fact, the leaders of the animal experimentation issue within our United Health and Medical Research Council—the equivalent of the U.S. National Institutes of Health—do not join the Animal Welfare Federation. They are very willing to talk to the animal rights movement, to recognize that there is a need for reforms and for getting fairly stringent codes in place and so on. In that sense we've had a less polarized debate. And you could say that the Animal Welfare Federation of Australia has actually split the relatively small number of extremists who think that animal research should be absolutely unfettered and don't want to talk to us from the majority of more moderate scientists who recognize the serious ethical issue there.

In the United States companion animals have received increased attention from people in the animal rights movement, particularly with regard to solving the overpopulation problem. Yet some animal rights people think that having a companion animal is exploitative, per se, while others disagree. **Do you think it's possible to live with an animal and not be part of an exploitative situation?**

It's certainly possible. At present, of course, there are many companion animals who have no future except to be killed or to live fairly miserable lives as strays. I don't see any sense in criticizing people who take in those animals and give them the best possible lives they can and treat them as much as they can as equals, as you would treat a human companion.

I certainly don't think people should go out and buy companion animals. Ultimately, we may have a society in which we phase out those companion animals whom we have to kill other animals in order to feed. It's not an ideal situation to have companion animals who are carnivorous by nature. But we don't live in a society that's vegetarian, so that's a long-term solution. At the present stage I think it is possible to have a companion animal in an ethical way.

Would your goal, ultimately, be a society in which people, after having somehow solved the present surplus-animal problem, would ideally live without companion animals?

No, I wouldn't say that. I think there may be species who can benefit from living with us and with whom we can live in a symbiotic relationship. If we solve the problem of having to exploit other animals in order to feed companion animals, then I don't see a problem about the possibility of those interspecies relationships.

Do you have interspecies relationships at home?

We have a cat who was given to us by a friend who had taken the cat in as a stray. We've also had some rats that have come to us in other ways, and they've been companions as well. There's still one of them around.

Do you ever become overwhelmed with so much animal suffering and misery in the world?

I wouldn't say overwhelmed. There are always opportunities for feeling that you're making some impact. One can, I guess, get a certain feeling of desperation about how hard it is to keep making that impact, and there are times when I get depressed about the difficulty of making progress. For me the greatest way out of that is to go back to being with people who are trying to make a difference. That is part of a long tradition, and I'm not just thinking about the animal tradition. I'm thinking about a broader, civilizing tradition, an attempt to produce a more humane, just society. That tradition has included the slave trade reformers and the prison reformers and people all the way back to Roman and Greek times. That tradition clearly is never going to die out, and I feel consolation in knowing that the tradition is here and is a strong one.

In the second edition of *Practical Ethics* you talk about your experiences in Germany and Austria. You spoke about how opponents to the views you expressed in *Practical Ethics* campaigned to close the conferences at which you were going to speak. And at one point you were actually physically assaulted.
I had my glasses smashed, that's right.

What kind of impact did that have on your thinking about the legitimate forms of tactics that animal advocates should use?
This was a fairly distressing experience. And quite an ironic one given my family background. My parents were Jewish refugees who came to Australia from Vienna in 1938 after the Nazis took over Austria. Given that three of my four grandparents died in Nazi camps, I saw it as deeply ironic that because I mentioned the word euthanasia, which is a word that the Nazis used for something quite different, I was denounced as in some way supporting a fascist or Nazi platform. There was an amazing depth of ignorance in these people. Many of them did not know that I had written anything on animals. In fact, they would ask the opposite questions. "Why have you committed

your life to promoting euthanasia?" Which obviously is not something I've done.

This incident strengthened my commitment toward free speech. It strengthened my belief that rational debate and exchange of ideas are really the way forward because you can see that there's just so much ignorance to be overcome. To some extent what happened to me in Germany has made me a bit uncomfortable on some occasions in the [animal] movement because I think there are elements in all movements which are, perhaps, not sufficiently open to the possibility that some of the things they're saying are a bit simplistic and not well-founded. And we can only change that by encouraging a freer debate and not trying to impose a group mentality on the movement as a whole.

What are you most proud of accomplishing?
Oh, I think writing *Animal Liberation*. I've changed a few things in the second edition, but basically it's a book that's stood the test of time. The other thing I'm pleased with is that people keep coming up to me and saying, "Your book changed our lives. We've abandoned exploiting animals and are involved in the movement." I am pleased both personally and as a professional philosopher to have shown that philosophy and rational argument can make a difference.

What do you think has been added to the animal rights movement by the feminist critique of animal oppression?
The feminist critique has, perhaps, made some of us who are inclined to look at things in a rational way realize that we have not given enough attention to emotional connections to animals and to caring attitudes towards them. We should try to extend people's emotional attachment and commitment to animals, and we ought to try to get people to empathize more with the less charismatic, less attractive animals. That's something I've gotten from the feminist critique.

What is your opinion of ecofeminism, which argues that both utilitarian calculations and natural rights theories are an integral part of the dominant patriarchal culture that exploits animals?
I'm not sure that all those who consider themselves ecofeminists would adopt that position. I've spoken to some who would accept the idea of equal consideration of all animals, although they may not think it goes far enough. Still, they wouldn't reject equal consideration as part of patriarchal domination. I think ecofeminists would recognize that an equal-consideration viewpoint provides a moral stance from which you get away from domination.

There are several strains of ecofeminism. I couldn't speak for all of them, but my position is compatible with much of what ecofeminists are talking about. If they're saying, for example, the male attitude has been disastrous for the planet and for other species, I certainly agree. And I'm inclined to accept that, in general, women have more of a long-term sense of responsibility for the planet as they often do for human relationships. You could speculate on the reasons for that, whether men have been socialized into this dominant attitude or if women are, in some way, naturally more long-term in their perspective.

Do you think animal liberation can be accomplished under patriarchy?
The goals of care and commitment for animals—like the goals for oppressed minorities, indigenous peoples, and the ecological systems of the planet—are subversive of patriarchy. Therefore, if we accomplish animal liberation, we are simultaneously undermining a patriarchal society, so that it wouldn't exist by the time we got to our goal; but that's not to say we have to eliminate patriarchy before working towards animal liberation.

Can animal liberation be accomplished under capitalism?
I don't think animal liberation can be accomplished under a system that promotes greed and personal self-interest as the natural goals for

every individual. To some extent, then, animal liberation would have to be accomplished under a dramatically modified capitalism, but it still would be a system that allows free markets to perform certain functions. I don't see any reason for assuming that government control of the economy in itself brings about animal liberation. My inclination is towards smaller-scale, regional community development, which allows a place for markets and for exchange but would not be the global-scale capitalist system we know today.

Do you think we will accomplish animal liberation in our lifetime?
Animal liberation will not be accomplished until we persuade people that we don't have the right to dominate and exploit animals. We cannot accomplish that while the prevailing diet is based on the assumption that animals are here to produce food for us rather than to lead lives of their own. That's the underlying buttress of speciesism, and it may be the last one we get rid of. When we do, if other forms of speciesism still exist, they will collapse. If society ceased to regard animals as food, they would cease to be regarded as fur coats or laboratory tools or anything else. I don't expect to see that in my lifetime. We've seen steps towards it, but eliminating an animal-based diet is a bigger and more historical change than the abolition of slavery, which was not so central in the lives and economy of the people in the New World at the time that the reformists began to abolish it. Yet it took them from the late 18th century until the middle of the 19th century to abolish slavery.

If you were not a philosopher, but, say, a public information officer for the animal rights movement, what message would you articulate to combat the strategy of the anti-animal rights forces?
I would try to revive grassroots initiatives, to get people in their own communities prepared to stand up and say, "I want to make a difference in the way animals are treated." I'm going to tell other people why I'm not eating animals. I'm going to make it easier for others to do this by pointing out that there are vegetarian alternatives

available. I'm going to look out for cases of animal abuse. If I'm a student or a parent, I'm going to see that there are alternatives to using animals in classes. We need to promote that level of local activity. It's too easy for people to feel that because they write a check once a year to some organization, that's the extent of their responsibility for the movement. I'd like people to realize that living an ethical life is worthwhile in itself. It's not just as a side issue to the goal of pursuing a career.

Are you concerned about the image of the animal rights movement and the backlash against the movement?
The backlash is effective at combating specific initiatives from large animal rights groups, but it's less effective at the grassroots level because it can't be everywhere at once. The backlash is fueled by a few well-heeled professional organizations who employ other professionals to fight us full time. Reviving a grassroots movement is one way of combating those professionals. People in local communities are going to be more influenced by those they know, respect, and work with than they are by outsiders. We also must keep hitting the fact that opponents of the animal rights movement are defending their financial self-interest. When we get people to see that, I think they will automatically discount the kinds of things professionals say against us.

≈

Editor's note: Farm Ministers from the European Union agreed in 1999 to ban the use of battery cages for laying hens starting January 1, 2012. During the phase-out period that runs from 2003 to 2012, European farmers will have to give each hen eighty-five square inches of space, rather than the current seventy square inches. This means removing one hen from a cage that normally contains five.

To Serve
and Protect
Sergeant Sherry Schlueter

JILL HOWARD CHURCH

T HESE DAYS, IN THE COURSE OF CONTENTIOUS SOCIAL change, it's not uncommon to find animal rights activists in the back seat of a police car. But in Broward County, Florida, there's one activist who not only rides in the front seat, she's steering an entire police detective unit that brings animal abusers to justice.

Since 1995, Sergeant Sherry Schlueter has led the Abuse and Neglect Unit of the Broward County sheriff's office Investigative Services Division. This unique unit—the first and only one of its kind in the country—consists of Schlueter and six full-time detectives charged with investigating the abuse of animals, children, elderly persons, and disabled adults. It is demanding work involving hundreds of individual cases that bring the officers face to face (or face to muzzle) with some of the most vulnerable victims of human violence. Hollywood might call it *SPCA Blue*.

Woof, Whine, and Wail

Schlueter's unit covers most of the unincorporated sections of Broward County, plus a few cities that contract with the county. In 1997, the unit investigated nearly 200 incidents of animal abuse and neglect in addition to more than 1,000 human-related cases. The crimes themselves—ranging from dog fights and horse beatings to the abandonment and "collecting" of animals—are no different from horrific acts committed against animals nationwide, but the way they are dealt with is. The critical difference has been Schlueter's determination to create a law enforcement entity that takes such cases seriously, both for the sake of the victims and for the well-being of the community as a whole.

"I'm extremely sensitive to the suffering of others," Schlueter says. "I have no tolerance whatsoever for the oppression or exploitation or abuse of other beings, human or nonhuman." She strongly argues that violence is violence, regardless of the victim's age, gender, species, or physical condition.

Schlueter has put those principles into action in a way that makes herself and her unit increasingly conspicuous. They are either praised by humane advocates as examples of how the police should treat crimes against animals, or are criticized and ridiculed by others in law enforcement who treat the unit's focus as something of a joke.

Detective Mike Vadnal handles animal cases almost exclusively, and Detective John Murray also has extensive animal experience.

The Collector

Sergeant Sherry Schlueter's reputation as an expert on animals and the law has brought her to the small community of Parkland, Florida, where police lieutenant John Grimes has asked her to help determine whether a local animal "collector" is violating cruelty statutes.

On a patch of undeveloped property at the end of a dirt road, an old white-and-peach trailer sits next to a small pond. A row of caged chickens sits to one side; a pen with two potbellied pigs is on the other. A dusty white goose struts like a sentry, honking an alert. Several dogs and guinea fowl run about, and cats lounge and linger inside and out. A mixed rottweiler barks at the end of a chain near a doghouse.

Schlueter, Grimes, and officer David Keeler approach the seventy-two-year-old resident, a woman who seems friendly but a bit confused. Schlueter explains that there have been concerns about the animals and asks if the officers might have a look around, which they are granted. Inside, open bags of cat food let the approximately

Detectives Bob Parr, Chris McCoy, Ken Kaminsky, and Craig DeGuiceis devote most of their time to child, elder, and disabled adult cases.

Murray, who joined the unit at his own request six years ago, explains that most crimes against animals stem from basic neglect of cats and dogs. "Three quarters of our cases are just ignorance on people's part," he observes. "They don't understand the legal obligations of animal ownership." The more severe cases of beatings and intentional deaths are more serious, however. The source of that kind of behavior, he says, "has just been an absolute indifference to animals."

. "When I first started in this unit I didn't realize how serious the [animal abuse] situation really was," he says. "There's a whole lot more of it than you really thought."

Murray's most horrific case was that of Pepsi, a female black Labrador mix found drowned in a canal in 1994. An electrical cord

twenty-five feline residents snack as they please. Despite the catty smell and the worn furnishings, the place is relatively clean, but the potential for greater problems is evident.

Schlueter gently asks the woman how many animals there are, where they came from, and whether they have been neutered and vaccinated. She explains that several of the dogs need immediate grooming and/or medical attention, and that vaccination for rabies is a must for the cats and dogs. She acknowledges the woman's kindness and generosity for taking in so many homeless animals, but suggests that the woman needs help caring for them and that some could be placed for adoption.

After phoning the woman's landlord, who agrees to arrange for assistance, Schlueter calls the local humane society and arranges for two of the young, healthy dogs to be taken to the shelter. The local officers will follow up on the rest. The woman will receive practical aid for herself and the animals, and the situation will be monitored so that both legal troubles and animal abuse can be avoided. ❧

had been tied around her neck, attached to a thirty-five-pound concrete block. She had been killed by her "owner's" brother for eating food meant for the brother's puppy. The reason for her increased appetite became clear after necropsy: Pepsi was pregnant. The file photos show Pepsi's face frozen in a contorted mask of agony, eyes bulging and tongue protruding. Murray says the image haunts him still. The perpetrator was convicted of not one but two counts of felony cruelty, one for Pepsi and one for the puppy who died inside her—an example of how thoroughly and seriously this group of officers takes its work.

But Murray acknowledges that even within police circles the unit and its work are not always taken seriously. "We take a lot of ribbing,"

The Pits

The business card taped to the dashboard of his weathered gold sedan reads "Ace Ventura: Pet Detective," but Broward County detective Mike Vadnal has the street smarts and cool exterior that Ace could only envy. Vadnal's wraparound shades and I-know-what's-going-down attitude seem borrowed from primetime drama—a bit of Starsky minus Hutch. He has been investigating animal abuse cases for six years, with special emphasis on dog fighting. Only a few blocks from the sheriff's office in Fort Lauderdale, he cruises a run-down neighborhood where pit bull breeders and fighters are common. He pulls over in one driveway next door to "a big-time dope dealer" to check out a brindle-colored pit bull dragging a thirty-pound weight to keep him from jumping the fence. The barking dog shows no scars from recent fights, so Vadnal moves on.

"It's a game," he explains. He knows the fighters and they know him, but both sides know that police must witness actual fights or have more solid evidence to make an arrest. A man passing by recognizes Vadnal and stops near the car. "You the dog man!" he says. There seems to be an odd rapport between the residents and the police. "You get to know some of the people on the street," Vadnal he admits, from those who think the unit is a waste of resources compared to crimes like murder and robbery. Schlueter's extensive experience has been more harsh. "I have endured the most brutal ridicule you can imagine from law enforcement," she says. Other officers have made animal noises over the police radio, and have referred to the unit as "The Geese Police," "Hoof and Woof," "Paws and Claws," and—to encompass all the groups it represents—"Woof, Whine, and Wail."

Still, Murray says, the unit gets good administrative support, and he praises Schlueter's guidance. "She definitely has compassion for victims of all species," he says.

says. "Some of them talk to you, some of them don't." In this area, dog fighting often goes hand in hand with drugs and weapons, and anyone caught talking to detectives could be labeled a snitch.

As he patrols another neighborhood farther north where a mangled cat may have been used as pit bull bait, residents eye Vadnal warily. He searches in vain for several teenage boys—he calls all of them "goofballs," no malice intended—who might know something about the case. He ends up at the home of an older teen whose three dogs were confiscated after being found deprived of proper shelter and water. The boy obviously knows where dog fights take place, but hesitates to name names. Vadnal tries to tempt him with information about cash rewards. Maybe next time.

Vadnal says dog fighting is increasing in south Florida, both among organized groups with big money at stake as well as in ordinary neighborhoods where teenagers fight dogs as a macho ritual.

"It's easy to get fed up with the human race," he admits, but he seems to believe in the ability of law enforcement to make things better one case at a time. "I think more police are sensitive to the needs of victims, and animals and children and the elderly are three types of victims that will definitely need your help." ✒

The Compassionate Cop

After meeting Sherry Schlueter, it is easy to conclude that her job in law enforcement is as much a calling as a career. Protecting animals is her life's work, and her work has largely become her life. Her distinctive attitude is unavoidably augmented by her distinctive looks. But don't anyone dare call her a "babe with a badge" or any other obnoxious label; Schlueter is no Charlie's Angel of Mercy. She is smart, disciplined, and as tough as she needs to be; but she is also fair, kind, and deeply committed to nonviolence both personally and professionally. She has turned her natural affinity for animals and her desire to help them into a career that has spanned more than twenty-six years with no end in sight.

"Nobody was surprised at who I became," she says. Her history makes a good case for predestination. Her success makes a good argument for cloning.

As a child she kicked other kids out of her yard for stomping ants. Schoolmates remember her rescuing spiders in the classroom. Watching *The Wizard of Oz* made her fear for Toto, not Dorothy. She worked in a veterinarian's office during high school and was a volunteer investigator for the Humane Society of Broward County (HSBC) before being hired by the HSBC in 1972. As a court-appointed investigative agent she had limited powers of confiscation and arrest but didn't have the clout she needed to be more effective.

So in 1979 she approached Sheriff Bob Butterworth (now Florida's attorney general) and convinced him of the need to devote more resources to animal crimes. Schlueter credits Butterworth with being "progressive enough and wise enough" to see the merit of the project, and his wisdom also prompted him to hire Schlueter for the job. This required her to enroll in the police academy, from which she graduated in 1980 after 640 hours of study and training. Not an easy task for anyone, but for Schlueter it was what she had to do to be in a better position to help animals.

Since starting animal investigations in her teens, she explains, "I had to teach myself everything I knew. I found it astonishing that the law enforcement officers didn't know anything about the cruelty statutes."

She spent two years assigned to road patrol in order to learn standard police procedures but continued to do animal investigations on personal time, with Butterworth's permission. In 1982 she became a one-person Animal Cruelty Investigation Unit. Schlueter was promoted to sergeant in 1986, and the following year was allotted two more detectives for her unit, which had been expanded to cover agricultural crimes. She was also put in charge of supervising several other investigative and specialty units.

The Abuse and Neglect Unit was formed in 1995, which took Schlueter off most field investigations but put her squarely in control of a pioneering program. After reviewing crime reports from patrol officers, Schlueter analyzes the cases and assigns them to the individual detectives, who then gather information that can be used for prosecutions. The detectives attend courses and seminars dealing with human and animal abuse, and they help cross-train each other by handling a variety of cases, although each tends to specialize in only one or two areas.

The outcomes of the investigations vary. Some go to trial, some end in plea bargains, and others are rectified with counseling or other forms of intervention. The officers follow up to make sure abuses aren't repeated. If animals are in immediate jeopardy, they are taken to shelters or veterinarians; those beyond help are euthanized. "Regardless of the criminality of the situation," Schlueter explains, "we will leave the victims better off after our intervention."

The unit's animal-related caseload remains busy all year. In addition to the never-ending incidents of dogs and cats left without adequate food and shelter are the more egregious cases involving baiting and fighting, ritual sacrifices, and torture, such as the case involving a Doberman doused with gasoline and set ablaze by several young teenagers for no apparent reason. The presence of the detective unit seems to indicate that such incidents are getting more attention from both the public and law enforcement.

"I believe more cases are reported because they [citizens] feel somebody will do something about it," Schlueter says. "It is in communities where no one investigates that no one reports."

Schlueter's own public profile rose considerably in 1995 as a result of an abuse case that made national headlines. Oakland Park resident Robert Homrighous was charged with putting nine newborn puppies into a paper bag and burying them alive in his back yard. The pups' mother, a rottweiler named Sheba, broke free from her chain and dug them up with help from a neighbor who saw her frantic struggle.

Three of the puppies died, but the rest were confiscated along with Sheba and another adult dog. Homrighous pleaded no contest to several cruelty charges and was fined $1,000 and permanently prohibited from owning any other dogs or cats. The outrageous incident drew massive media attention, and put Schlueter's name, face, and message on shows like *Leeza* and *Oprah*, plus the pages of *People* and countless other publications. The outpouring of sympathy for the

SSAAFFEE

One of Sherry Schlueter's biggest frustrations is the difficulty of finding and paying for the care of animals confiscated during abuse cases. For children and other needy people there are government-funded agencies and foster homes; for animals the only recourse is cooperative shelters, veterinarians, and willing individuals (including Schlueter herself) who seldom have all the resources they need. Although Schlueter tries to get financial restitution for animal care as part of court settlements or judgments, there is little official support for such measures.

To address this problem, she has established the Sherry L. Schlueter Foundation, Inc., an umbrella group for several private funds that she administers under the business name of the Sherry Schlueter Anti-Abuse Foundation for Ethical Endeavors (SSAAFFEE). The Fund for Abused Animals is used to compensate shelters or individuals who take in confiscated animals who are not dogs and unmitigated contempt for Homrighous gave Schlueter further proof that animal abuse cases do matter to the public.

Schlueter's work isn't without conflict or compromise, however. She opposes the idea of using dogs and horses in police work, but agreed to oversee the mounted police unit so that she could have some control over the horses' treatment. She has to limit her personal expressions of protest because of her standing in the community.

"The public cannot separate Sergeant Sherry Schlueter, law enforcement officer, from Sherry Schlueter, activist," she acknowledges. But she supports the concept of civil disobedience, calling it "an American right to challenge bad laws." She wears a nylon gun belt and badge holder while on plainclothes duty but wears the standard-issue leather ones when in formal uniform, choosing not to belabor the issue. "I've had to compromise very little," she says. Yet it is her refusal to compromise her ethics that has brought her so far.

As a teenager she became a vegetarian without knowing any others who forsook flesh. She now calls herself an "obnoxiously strict"

cared for by law enforcement agencies, such as the six horses currently in custody whose care tops $2,500 a month. The Domestic Violence Companion Animal Rescue Effort helps battered women seeking shelter find temporary care for their companion animals rather than leave them behind. Schlueter gives her pager number to such women so that she can be available at a moment's notice when the women are ready to flee. The third fund is the Crimestoppers Animal Abuse Reward Fund, which offers money to individuals who provide information regarding abuse cases.

Schlueter's fundraising efforts must be done separately from the official business of the Broward County sheriff's office, which cannot accept donations directly. Anyone interested in contributing to the foundation or learning more about her programs may contact her at 2601 W. Broward Blvd., Fort Lauderdale, FL 33312; phone (954) 321-4830. ✒

vegan, relying mostly on raw foods if and when she finds time to eat between her daytime police work, her evening off-duty jobs for extra income, and her weekend engagements as a singer at church and social events. An avid long-distance runner, Schlueter somehow finds time to run marathons and help organize the annual Special Olympics Law Enforcement Torch Run, which involves teams of officers in a relay from one end of Broward County to the other. Schlueter, however, has the stamina to run the entire distance.

The Cycle of Violence

One of Schlueter's major themes—a concept that goes to the core of her unit's presence—is that there exists in society a cycle of violence. It is generally well known that victims of child abuse often become abusers themselves later in life. It is similarly true that people who abuse animals often "graduate" to abusing people. For this reason, Schlueter believes, it is important to treat crimes against animals seriously not only for their own sake but also because of the implications they have for continued violence.

"You have to care about the crime of animal cruelty and treat it professionally because it is an indicator crime," she explains, not something that can or should be chalked up to childhood pranks or "boys being boys."

Schlueter teaches this concept at regular presentations to police academy cadets as well as to social service and civic groups related to domestic violence. She explains that the same man who beats his dog may very well beat his wife and children also. She often quotes anthropologist Margaret Mead, who said, "The most dangerous thing that can happen to a child is for a child to torture or kill an animal and get away with it." She reminds her audiences that such serial killers as Jeffrey Dahmer and David "Son of Sam" Berkowitz began as animal abusers. She also notes that the American Society for the Prevention of Cruelty to Animals was founded as an organization devoted to the welfare of both children and animals. She explains the difference between sympathy and empathy, the latter being more significant in changing human behavior. Addressing groups not directly related to animal welfare "gives me the forum to introduce this topic to people who otherwise wouldn't hear it," she says.

Schlueter takes a corresponding view when dealing with the perpetrators of violence, in that she also recognizes the value of a cycle of compassion. When the public was spitting epithets over the Sheba incident, Schlueter took extra care to treat Homrighous with respect and civility so that no part of her actions could be used in judgment against her or the rest of the police unit.

"I certainly enjoy the opportunity to take an evil person to jail," she admits. "But the reality is that that doesn't necessarily benefit the animal....The animal doesn't enjoy any sense of revenge or delight" if the defendant is treated harshly. Her interactions with Homrighous eventually prompted him to relinquish custody of all of his dogs—to her personally, not to any county agency—so that they could be placed in better homes.

Schlueter advocates such an unemotional approach to anyone interested in pursuing a career as a humane officer or police officer. "Always be objective no matter what your personal feelings are," she advises. "So many people who want to be humane officers can't control their emotions." Her job, she says, is to "investigate, present [evidence], and be fair," not punitive. That kind of conduct has helped her earn respect amid difficult circumstances, and some judges now ask for her input when deciding sentences.

The Long Haul

The future of the Broward County sheriff's office Abuse and Neglect Unit seems stable given its successes and steady workload. But Schlueter gets visibly irritated when discussing the reasons why similar units aren't in place all over the country.

"I think the biggest obstacle is to get law enforcement to embrace this concept [of taking animal issues seriously]," she says, and to assign resources that will not only deal with such crimes but help prevent them as well. She says those who mistreat animals are "generally violent, sadistic abusers" who endanger all of society. "Law enforcement should be ashamed to have not fulfilled their obligation to this [kind of] state victim."

Schlueter is a vocal advocate for upgrading state statutes so that cruelty to animals is considered a felony and not a misdemeanor. "One of the strongest reasons I wanted to create the [Florida] felony statute is because law enforcement officers take felonies more seriously." She says the Florida statute, which she wrote in 1988 and which was enacted in 1989, has had "a profound effect" on the way humane laws are enforced in the state. Eighteen states currently have some form of felony animal abuse laws, and legislation to create similar statutes is pending in another ten.

Ironically, the success of Schlueter's career may also be a stumbling block for her future advancement. She says that she could have achieved a higher rank by now but would likely have had to transfer to another department to do so, and she refuses to leave the unit she worked so hard to create. She would like to expand her unit further and incorporate sex crimes into its purview. Being an effective advocate for society's most voiceless victims, she says, "would make me extremely happy....I eat, sleep, and live my work." Still, she admits, "I don't know why after so many years of doing this I haven't burned out or gone crazy." And although she would consider the right offer to move elsewhere, her professional and personal investments in the Broward County system are substantial, and she must consider issues of seniority and retirement.

In the meantime, Schlueter will continue her personal journey and do her best to keep the Abuse and Neglect Unit running. Going the distance is something she knows a lot about.

❧

Editor's note: Sgt. Sherry Schlueter was recently promoted to the position of Lieutenant, and directs the Family and Victim Services Unit of the Broward County Sheriff's Office in Florida.

From Activist to Prison
and Back Again
Rod Coronado

LAURA A. MORETTI

THIRTY-TWO-YEAR-OLD ROD CORONADO HOLDS A NEW $20 bill to the window light and studies it, as if he's never been to America. In fact, he's a native: a mixed-blood Yaqui Indian. But for more than three and a half years and for the next six months, he's been, and will be, an inmate in the U.S. federal prison system for his illegal direct action activities. Rod is spending the last six months of his incarceration at a so-called halfway house in northwest Oregon until his release in September 1999.

I can tell he hasn't seen cash in awhile, and he's smiling, almost mesmerized by the currency. "Looks like Monopoly™ money," he finally says of the new design.

At his office desk at the *Earth First! Journal* in Eugene, Oregon, where he's allowed to work as an editorial assistant, Rod is dressed in black jeans and hiking boots, a forest green shirt and a string of beads. His long black hair is slightly graying and tied into a ponytail. He seems taller, larger, than I remember him. And calmer. It has been five years. Back then, things were, well, chaotic.

Rod was hunted down like a beast on the run for his role in fur farm animal liberations—among other things. He was charged after his capture in a seven-count indictment for arson and destruction of property, including one count of conspiracy and interstate racketeering.

The various charges were related to an Oregon State University (OSU) fur farm fire that burned an experimental feed building and destroyed research records; an $800,000 fire at a mink farm feed distributor that supplied OSU and dozens of other Northwest fur farms; the theft of six mink and the destruction of research at a Washington State University fur farm; a fire at an Oregon mink farm's pelt-processing building; twenty-four coyotes being rescued from a Utah State University research facility as well as destruction of its lab; and the removal of two mink and the burning of thirty-two years of mink farm research at a Michigan State University campus, all of which occurred between 1990 and 1992.

After spending time in prison, Rod opted for a nontestimony plea-bargain and return to the struggle. His action caused dissension, mudslinging, a sense of betrayal, and mutual disappointment within the animal rights community. For many in the animal liberation movement, Rod's case was the door through which we would all be taken to the promised land: his trial would be the perfect place to expose our concerns, voice our values, speak loudly to an attentive public. It would be the ultimate political statement. For Rod, however, it was quite possibly a terminal loss of freedom—and so he opted for a nontestimony plea-bargain and return to the struggle.

And the fallout was nasty. To begin with, he was accused of not living up to his convictions. Yet his lifelong service in direct action is formidable. In the early 1980s, Rod worked with Paul Watson aboard the Sea Shepherd. (Watson's ship is involved in direct action protecting whales and other animals from being hunted illegally.) In 1986, Coronado was arrested and beaten in the Faroe Islands for disrupting the annual pilot whale slaughter there. That same year he also disabled Iceland's illegal whaling station and helped to sink two of its four whaling ships. He participated in fox hunt protest actions with England's Hunt Saboteurs, helped stage anti-vivisection rallies, worked with Earth First! against trophy hunting, and co-founded the Hunt Saboteurs in America to protect bighorn sheep in the Mojave Desert.

With the help of Friends of Animals, Rod launched an undercover (and unprecedented) investigation of fur farm animal abuse across

America, grisly video of which found its way to commercial television, specifically *60 Minutes*. Never before had an unsuspecting public seen how mink were made into fur coats: the twisting of tiny heads, the broken necks, the writhing, the screaming.

"I am a warrior," Rod writes in one of his Strong Hearts publications he produced from prison. "I was unaccustomed to witnessing such cruelty without doing something about it." In an unprecedented action, Rod bought out the fur farm where he witnessed the mink killings, and then rehabilitated and released the remaining two bobcats, two lynx, and sixty mink in the Northwest wilderness.

Again, dissension arose among the ranks regarding how Rod chose to rehabilitate those animals, feeding the freed predators live prey to teach them to hunt in the wild. Some labeled Rod a hypocrite, and— in letters to the ALF-friendly magazine *No Compromise*—told him that, in the end, the animals would be "disappointed" in him. I have now found my next question.

How would you describe yourself?

I consider myself an indigenous traditionalist, meaning I believe in animal rights, human rights, land rights, water rights, air rights. I respect and revere all sentient creatures. So I don't consider myself an animal rights activist or a human rights activist, because to me if you believe in the rights of one living thing, you must believe in the rights of all living things, in all of creation.

Even if it means killing some to save others?

The definition of animal liberation, as it pertains to the fur farm industry, is to turn those animals back to the wilderness where they're not dependent on humans for their survival. That to me is real animal liberation. Our goal wasn't just to free those animals, but to prove to the industry and the rest of the movement that animal liberation for fur farm prisoners could actually mean returning them to the wild.

In 1991 there hadn't been any fur farm liberations in the United States. We knew if such raids were ever to come, one of the biggest arguments against them would be that the animals released from the cages would cruelly starve to death in nature. We needed to prove they could be successfully rehabilitated, and to increase their chances of survival, we had to do some short-term, temporary live-feeding.

We could then return them into the wilderness where they were on their own. If that meant surviving great; if that meant starving to death, that's nature, you know. A lot of animals starve in nature. Nature can be cruel. I don't believe animal liberation is defined by the elimination of cruelty because harmony sometimes necessitates sacrifice.

By returning these animals to the wild, we were putting the pieces together and allowing nature to take its course. We set the stage for people who now liberate fur farm animals by arguing that these animals *do* belong in the wilderness. They are native American animals.

Some have suggested it would have been more in keeping with animal rights to have humanely euthanized the mink.
I think such a solution shows a tendency to be single-issue oriented. Even as vegans, just because we don't personally ingest any animals into our bodies doesn't mean we're not contributing to animal exploitation or killing. Rather than split hairs and look at individual instances where some animals are being killed, we need to focus on our lifestyles. So many animal rights activists drive cars, and yet the oil industry is responsible for an incredible amount of habitat and animal destruction.

That's where my political beliefs merge with my Native American beliefs. We're not taught to absolve ourselves from any kind of inter-action with nature; we're taught to minimize our impact on nature so that ultimately we're walking as simply as possible on the earth, and causing the least amount of suffering—and not just for animals, but for plant life, for human life, for all life. That's my own personal goal.

Anything that attacks the individual behavior of one person, one activist, is a distraction from that larger objective that we are all, in a sense, fighting for.

So what is your diet today?
I'm a vegan and don't believe in supporting the animal food industry, but I also don't enjoy supporting the plant food industry, either, because of its dependency on chemicals, its support of biotechnology, its pollution runoff into waterways, [and] predator control. There are lots of reasons to be opposed to modern farming, not just factory farming.

But what about the rights of living "food" animals?
Food animals are the modern equivalent of human slaves at this period in time because their sole purpose in our reality is to fulfill human luxury. And it's very representative of our separation from nature that we allow an animal's existence to be based solely on how it can serve us. Ultimately, all food animals should be bred out of existence. They not only suffer immeasurably themselves, but the conditions they're forced to live in degrade the environment.

In the case of fur farm animals, we're talking about animals who've only been removed from the wild less than a hundred years. They are genetically identical to their wild cousins. It's one of the better causes the animal rights movement could argue for because there's no need to address the issues we face with food animals, such as what do we do with these animals once they've stopped being raised for food? On the fur farm, all we have to do is open the cages and let nature take its course.

We knew, at the time [of our direct action], the fur farm industry would come under greater attack. It would be necessary when that happened that we be able to prove there had been a project in which animals were successfully returned to the wild. As for the live-feeding, many animal sanctuaries are forced to perpetually sanction feeding meat byproducts to animals who are going to live long lives under human dependency. It was less of a compromise for us to feed the mink live animals for a short period than to cage them and feed them the dead animals of an exploitive and destructive industry for the rest of their lives.

We cannot fail to recognize that in nature there is a dependency among animals on the lives of each other, and we can't impress our morality on that.

Rod waits patiently for the next question after a ringing telephone breaks the conversation. Is he being polite? Or have years of prison disciplined him? He is confident, I see that now. He is unafraid of the questions, for he has already faced the enemy. And there is pride in that dark gaze— for he is a survivor. His people, his heritage, are survivors.

In 1995, at the time of his ALF-related convictions, Rod was also sentenced to fifty-seven months (served concurrently) for stealing a notebook from the Little Bighorn museum during a visit there. He held the journal hostage while issuing this statement: "We demand equal representation at the battlefield in the form of displays and exhibits approved by the American Indian Movement. The explanation of the justified actions of Crazy Horse and Sitting Bull to defend their home and people at the Little Bighorn is necessary before the notebook can be returned."

How do you feel about killing animals for use in indigenous ceremonies?

Personally, my traditional ceremonial regalia has always been acquired from road-kill animals or naturally killed animals I've found while hiking. I've encouraged people within my community not to support the fur industry because a lot of people who require certain artifacts only know to get them from powwows and places where commercial trappers sell their wares. And they agree with me that it's not right; these people [trappers] aren't showing respect for the animals.

I do support the U.S. Fish & Wildlife Service's policy in which it provides eagle feathers and parts from animals taken illegally or found dead. I don't think it's necessary to kill any of our animal relations to preserve the ceremonies that honor them. All cultures and people evolve, but that doesn't mean one has to lose one's cultural identity; it just means changing the context of it.

And so it isn't just the white people who are out of balance; it's also the black man and the brown man, because the worldview that sees nature, humans, and animals only as resources isn't unique to somebody's skin color. It's a way of thinking, not a way of ethnicity. Anyone can be influenced by the corruption of power and money.

How does Native America view the animal rights movement?
I don't think traditional indigenous people separate animal rights from human rights or natural rights. There's no concept that just recognizes animals. Everything is inclusive of natural creation. The impression native communities have of animal rights is unfortunately one in which they perceive a moral superiority because [animal rights activists] have a lack of understanding of other people's way of living, other people's way of harmony with nature.

As a result, that presents a conflict to Native American people when they view animal rights, because the people who exemplify animal rights are judging the Indian culture's perception of nature as opposed to trying to understand it.

We have to rethink how we present animal rights to native people. Instead of trying to force on them just another product of colonialization, which many Indians see animal rights as being, we have to recognize we probably have more to learn from the traditionals, by being able to learn that the attitudes we so far afford to animals need to be extended to the rest of the natural world. It doesn't just stop at animals.

How are we supposed to justify opposing indigenous gray whale hunting when we [protest] in ships and boats that are dependent on supporting the petrochemical industry which degrades people in other countries, as well as animals and the environment, too? That's a type of hypocrisy that I, as an indigenous person, see, and I don't believe it can be separated. You can't just be opposed to killing animals, in my opinion. You have to be opposed to the destruction of all natural creation.

How does your personality fit into this worldview?

[*Rod turns his head, looking across his desk out the window. He is quiet a long time before he speaks, and his voice takes on a peaceful tone, a warmth and confidence.*]

Resisting the forces that destroy nature is just natural to me. That isn't a political statement; for me, it's a spiritual statement, an ecological statement, it's something I do because it's necessary for life on earth. You look around you, anywhere, and you'll see nature resisting, fighting back everything man has and is doing to her. You'll see her breaking up the sidewalks, splitting roads; you'll see animals learning to overcome the threats humans have imposed on them, animals like the coyote, who has actually expanded her range and increased her litter size despite the genocidal war against her people.

We need to replicate nature in that way. Everything we need to learn to live in harmony with nature can be seen in the animals and earth. Anything we may have lost in the hundreds of years of colonization, in the time we've been separated from nature, can be regained simply by looking back at nature and seeing how she survives.

Did you learn anything in prison?

[*He looks at me again, seemingly snapped from a trance.*] I've learned a lot. I think it showed me more than anything that the power of nature, the power of the beliefs we fight for, is going to require sacrifices much greater than the one I was forced to make. When we hope to accomplish the goals and visions for the world we propose, we're not going to get it by holding back, by protecting our privileges in this society, which is most responsible for the destruction of the natural world. It's going to require that we separate from it; in essence, to become a traitor to the society that has bred us. We need to make sacrifices. As activists that means risking our own lives and our own freedom.

Every day I was in prison, I never had any regret for my actions because I knew why I was there. Through nature's presence in my life, even when I was locked up, whether it was feeding a hummingbird or watching a storm pass or looking at a full moon, I was able to open myself up to the love of my animal relations. It's not enough to say you love them. You have to show them in deeds.

Every time the moon rose or the stars shone or an animal flew by, that was Earth's way of saying I wasn't forgotten. Such a relationship can help us endure anything. And endure is what we must do because we have a lot more sacrifice to make before we even come close to achieving the goals we have set for ourselves.

Are you angry?
Of course I'm angry. I'm very angry. I don't have hatred, though. Hatred is a power they [the opposing forces] control, a power that reinforces everything they believe in. I'm motivated by the things that led me to take direct action, by my feelings of love. It wasn't because I was angry at vivisectors, it was because I loved my animal relations so much who were suffering in their labs that I was willing to do anything to rescue them. It's more important to be motivated by love than hate, because it's a power they cannot control, a power Earth teaches you through her own examples. Love is uncontrollable, in a sense. To be motivated by it is the most noble thing a human being can do. And that relationship, that love, will bring us back to the circle of life.

What's it like to be able to work again?
It's a big change, a good change. It's just weird because when I was in prison I could be one way; I was dealing with the same thing every day: the numbness, the zombies, the walking dead. I could just zone out and be in my own world. But coming here [to the *Earth First!* office] I'm able to be myself, completely. I can be alive again. Then, every night, I go back to the other reality: to rules and cops. And that's hard. It's harder than prison was. And county inmates are whiners, big-time whiners. They don't have the respect you learn in prison.

People wake up at 5 a.m. and talk to each other across the room. "Hey, Joe, what's up?" You don't do that in prison, you get your head smashed, you know?

Looking down that road ahead of you...
My role in the struggle now is to represent that sacred relationship with the natural world and try to convey it not just to those who are destroying her and her animal children, but even to my own allies, who might easily fall victim to hatred and to burnout and frustration. One thing I'd like to accomplish for animal rights, for animal liberation, for the environmental movement, is to remind people that through direct action comes power, the type of power that really does give us the strength to endure what we must in the future.

Having gained some access to that power, it's important to me to speak out in its defense, especially in a time when the ones who are fighting acts of violence in our society are being called terrorists. People such as myself should stand up and defend ALF and Earth First! as anti-terrorists. The real terrorists are those with six-figure salaries who are reaping their profits from the blood of our animal and earth relations.

How do you propose we do that?
We do that by being united, by not bickering among ourselves when it comes to the tactics some of us are unfamiliar with, tactics that allow or ascribe more rights to life than to property. You can't commit a violent act against property, in my opinion. If you're going to be a moral judge of anyone, then be a moral judge of those who have the most blood on their hands. You may not agree with what some activists are doing, but their very perseverance to adhere to nonviolent principles by not harming any living thing deserves—at least—our quiet support rather than public condemnation.

We mustn't show the public we're divided on this principle. We must show them we're a strong and united movement, we all believe we're a part of a legitimate struggle fighting toward the same end. In that sense, exploit any attention activists create through direct action, whether legal or illegal, and just use it, whether they are above- or underground activists. Get the truth out there.

Do you think your actions had an effect on the fur industry as a whole?

Absolutely. All you have to do is look at its bottom line. They're spending more money now on security and protection from animal rights activists than they ever have. Fur farmers have to factor in the threat of an Animal Liberation Front raid. They have to explain to their bankers how they're going to protect themselves against such threats, actions that could destabilize their income. Fur farmers today not only worry about whether they can get the fur quality from their mink, they worry whether the ALF is going to pay them a visit.

The posters, the bumperstickers, the demonstrations, the protests are keeping a relentless pressure on the industry, and are pushing it to the edge. What'll push them over is going to be sabotage. The industry has survived to this day because it's been able to endure the protests. That's where the ALF best serves our struggle, and it's our obligation to take full advantage of the window of opportunity they've created by continuing to put pressure on the industry, on the retail outlets, in the public eye. If we can't win the fur farm issue, we sure as hell can't win the factory farm wars.

And compromise is our struggle's enemy. We can't not say where we really come from. We can't not say we're not against all hunting. We have to be honest, and sure, we'll work on a ballot initiative to ban hound hunting in the state, but if people ask us, let's not lie, let's say we're opposed to all hunting.

It hurts our cause when people feel they're being deceived. We have to be real about that. Incremental change is fine, but when they ask us to condemn the people breaking the law, let's refuse to do so. When they ask us to accept twenty-five percent change rather than

100 percent, let's make it known to them from the start that's not what we're about.

We *are* abolitionists.

⸙

Editor's note: This interview took place at the offices of Earth First! *in Eugene, Oregon, in 1999. Rod continues to be active for animals and the earth, including writing for* No Compromise, *the militant, direct action newspaper of grassroots animal liberation and their supporters.*

Compassion, Commitment, and Commerce
Anita Roddick

KIM W. STALLWOOD

I N 1976 ANITA RODDICK OPENED A SMALL STORE IN Brighton, England, to sell naturally based, non-animal-tested skin and hair care products. Today, The Body Shop has more than 1,300 stores in forty-five countries. Worldwide retail sales exceeded $750 million in 1995. Throughout the company's twenty-year history, The Body Shop has balanced a commitment to progressive business practices with compassion for animals, people, and the environment.

From the beginning The Body Shop rejected the image and excesses of the conventional cosmetics industry. The company sells more than 500 products for women, men, and children, using minimal packaging and encouraging customers to recycle or refill containers in the stores. The Body Shop Foundation awarded grants to the British Union for the Abolition of Vivisection for alternatives to product testing on animals, and to the Environmental Investigation Agency for endangered species protection.

The Body Shop is a World Sponsor of World Animal Awareness Week, including the World Congress and the March for the Animals. *The Animals' Agenda* spoke with founder Anita Roddick in the Spring of 1996.

What is your policy on animal testing?
The Body Shop is against animal testing of cosmetics and toiletries, products, and ingredients. We have never tested or commissioned others to test our products or their ingredients on animals.

What originally inspired you to sell products that have not been tested on animals?

When I opened the first branch of The Body Shop twenty years ago, I was against animal testing. It seemed to me then and it still seems to me cruel and totally unacceptable to sacrifice animals for human vanity. We have used our influence and resources to press hard for a ban on such testing. We will continue to do so until we succeed.

How difficult has it been to implement this policy?

It's been easy and tough. Easy because from day one I believed it was plain wrong to test on animals, so we haven't done it. Tough because we've had twenty years of fighting the mainstream cosmetics industry and trying to effect change. For The Body Shop it's always a question of, can we do better? Can we put more pressure on suppliers to stop testing? Can we find a new way to press the politicians to ban the tests? We examine every ingredient from every supplier. We won't buy any ingredient that a supplier has tested on animals after December 31, 1990, for another cosmetics company. We employ a staff simply to ensure our suppliers comply.

How critical has this policy been to the success of The Body Shop?

"Against Animal Testing" is in the soul of The Body Shop. It sets us apart from others in the industry. We do not believe skin and hair care products are the body and blood of Jesus Christ. We absolutely believe that human and animal rights and respect for the environment are. We're proud of that, and of the great support we get from our staff and customers for taking this position.

Do you have plans to phase out all animal-derived ingredients from your products?

The Body Shop is not a vegan company. We do use honey, milk, and lanolin, although we do make great and serious efforts to make sure that the lanolin comes from sheep that receive the highest standards of care. We have never used musk from deer or spermaceti oil from whales. Our soaps are 100 percent vegetable-based, as is all our glycerin. But we do use gelatin in our bath beads. Whether we should is a serious debate in the company. We are actively looking for an alternative that can do the same job. Our Product Information Manual lists facts about each of our products, including a full ingredient listing. It also gives information on products not suitable for vegans to ensure that their beliefs are not compromised when buying a product.

Please explain the mission, goals, and accomplishments of The Body Shop Foundation.
The Body Shop makes great skin and hair care products. But our mission is to achieve social and environmental change. Our Trading Charter lays down how we do that by trading honorably with respect for people, animals, and the planet. We believe that business is absolutely part of life. Your values in work should be the same as those at home. That's why we just published our Animal Protection Statement as part of our Values Report.

Why did The Body Shop decide to become an international sponsor of World Animal Awareness Week?
Animal protection is a vital issue of The Body Shop. We believe in empowering our franchisees, staff, and customers on issues which matter to them. We have worked closely with the animal protection movement internationally to end cosmetics testing on animals and in the fight to protect endangered species. In 1994, we ran our largest-ever international campaign on the illegal trade in endangered species such as tigers and bears. We raised over three million signatures on a petition calling for enforcement of the Regulations of the Convention on the International Trade in Endangered Species of Wild Fauna and Flora (CITES). Supporting World Animal Awareness Week continues our tradition of getting behind key events and organizations seeking to improve the lot of animals, the environment, and the protection of human rights. The event also ties in perfectly with our plan to campaign around the world during this year on the [issue of]

cosmetics testing. Later we will press the European Union to enforce its proposed ban on cosmetic tests on animals from January 1, 1998.

How would you apply your marketing talent to the animal rights movement?

I already try by putting clear, factual, motivational, and empowering information and campaigns in our stores, be it [about] domestic violence, the destruction of the rain forest, or animal testing. The animal movement needs to be clear about what we want to achieve and make achieving it accessible to people. Be positive. Offer alternatives to consumers and to companies. Lead by example but don't preach. Be brave. Have big ideas and make them happen. Look up and out, not down and in. Never give up!

Which issues do you think the animal rights movement can succeed in accomplishing in the next twenty years?

The Body Shop is twenty years old, and in that time we've seen enormous changes. Just look at cosmetics testing. We've seen consumers become aware and active on the issue, leading to a substantial fall in the number of animals used in such tests. We've also seen many companies taking up the cause. This year there's a chance to ban the tests in Europe. In the next twenty we must see an end to such tests worldwide. There must be stricter enforcement of measures designed to protect the thousands of endangered species. Concern about animals and their treatment will spread and grow. Tighter laws on intensive farming, hunting, and many other areas must surely follow. With courage, passion, and imagination, everything is possible!

Editor's note: On April 3, 2001, the European Parliament voted to ban the sale of animal tested cosmetic products as well as animal testing of cosmetics within the European Union.

Wayne Pacelle, Unplugged

THE ANIMALS' AGENDA

B Y THE TIME HE GRADUATED FROM YALE IN 1987, Wayne Pacelle was "really consumed by animal issues. I wanted to devote my full energies to them, and *Agenda* [where he signed on as an assistant editor] provided me with an outlet to do that."

One promotion and a little more than a year later, Pacelle was anointed by [the late] Cleveland Amory as the director of The Fund for Animals. During his five years at The Fund, Pacelle established a reputation as someone with the courage to confront hunters in the field and the political savvy to help get initiatives passed in California (which outlawed mountain lion hunting) and Colorado (which outlawed spring, bait, and hound hunting of black bears). Then, just when most people in the movement had assumed that one day Pacelle would be president of The Fund, he quit his post to take a newly created vice presidency at The Humane Society of the United States. That decision, he says, "was one of the hardest ones I've ever had to make in my life." In an interview with *The Animals' Agenda*, Pacelle, twenty-nine, reveals his reasons for leaving The Fund and discusses the goals he hopes to meet at HSUS. [*See Editor's note on page 87.*]

How would you describe HSUS's philosophical position?
We describe ourselves as an animal protection organization. We're more pragmatic than dogmatic. We focus on tangible reform. I find the distinction between animal welfare and animal rights less useful than I once did. The difference between animal welfare and animal rights

on a range of issues, such as the use of animals in circuses, fur, rodeo, puppy mills, trapping, and hunting, is a distinction without a difference. Our mission is captured in our name. We want to create a humane society that takes into account the interests of animals and that eliminates the gratuitous harm by humans. If HSUS differs from other groups markedly, it may differ in tactics, but less in ideology.

What is the HSUS strategy for accomplishing its goals?
We attempt to work within the system—through the courts, the legislative process, mass education, and the media—to advance our ideas in the broadest court of public opinion.

That's the mission of the public relations department: to advance tangible reforms and to foster a vision of a humane society and deliver it to the broadest audience. Our decision to enter into electoral activity and major lobbying activity is an affirmation of our commitment to working within the system.

Does HSUS do much demonstrating? I don't know that I've ever seen a newspaper that said, "Representatives of The HSUS picketed such and such."
For the most part that is correct. Our regional office in New Jersey conducts an annual protest at the Great Swamp National Wildlife Refuge to protest hunting, and there have been some fur demonstrations from time to time, but it's fair to say that demonstrating is not a major tactic employed by HSUS.

What's the rationale behind the decision?
The rationale relates to our ability to work effectively in other arenas. I recognize the importance of demonstrations and direct action in our social movement, but it's not what HSUS does best; and HSUS's resources need to be deployed running initiatives, drafting legislation, speaking to college audiences, and so forth. Those are the areas where we use our talent pool to best advantage.

Has that part of your personal operating style been changed somewhat then?
It was changing when I was still at The Fund. I have been arrested many times, and I have led hunt protests in the field all across the country, but I decided that the best way for me to use my skills was in other arenas. I firmly believe there is a place for civil disobedience in our movement. I don't think HSUS needs to contribute substantially to civil disobedience. We need not undermine it, but we need not contribute to it.

Does your appointment indicate any change in HSUS's position?
I don't think so. The HSUS, like the movement, is a mosaic. There are people of different political backgrounds and different beliefs. My political views are known, and HSUS was aware of them. In some areas my views would go beyond what HSUS's views are, but that's healthy for an organization. By no means am I the first vegan to work for HSUS.

Please explain your responsibilities at HSUS.
I am in charge of two departments: government affairs and public relations. The government affairs department oversees our interactions with local, state, and federal legislative bodies as well as executive agencies. The PR department is our connection to the media.

What do the media people do in addition to turning out press releases?
We're organizing press conferences, and we're trying to get news coverage in the print and electronic media about animal issues. We write letters to the editor and op-ed pieces and try to get newspapers to do editorials endorsing our views. We manage the talents of HSUS in interacting with the media. We pitch a story and get attention then we put the media person covering that story in touch with one of our experts.

What do the government affairs people do?
They're dealing with USDA [U.S. Department of Agriculture] people, with U.S. Fish and Wildlife Service people; they're lobbying on Capitol Hill; they're drafting legislation.

They created a new vice president's position for you. Was that part of either the condition or the motivation for your moving to HSUS?
It was not specifically said that way, but these were two areas where HSUS wanted to enhance its profile, and it was logical that they would carve out a new position.

How many members do you have currently?
HSUS has 2.1 million members and constituents, and we want to have five million members in five years. Another of our goals is to develop the tools to advance the cause for animals most effectively. In short, we want power; we want credibility. We now have more than 100 active campaigns at HSUS. We want to see all those campaigns mature, and we want tangible results. [*See Editor's note on page 87.*]

What do you want to accomplish during the short term?
We will be introducing four pieces of original legislation in the next Congress: one to ban canned hunts, one to reduce the cruelties associated with horse transport in this country, one to establish a freedom of information act for lab animal experiments in the United States, and one relating to pet theft. That legislation would hopefully eliminate Class B dealers, which is a category of people who are collecting animals with the intent to sell them to research laboratories.

Institutionally, we're in the process of creating a (C)(4) organization. HSUS is a 501(C)(3) organization. Only a limited amount of its budget can be allocated to direct and grassroots lobbying, and it is excluded from engaging in any electioneering activities. We intend to form a (C)(4) which is, in effect, a lobbying arm, and some of us independently hope to be able to establish a related political action committee to really establish the movement's first solid political lobbying apparatus. That is one of the main reasons I came to HSUS. We intend to make candidates responsive to humane concerns. It would not be an overstatement to say that the animal movement is considered impotent by some political observers. Our numbers have simply not translated into political power. Until we graduate to electoral involvement and major political activity, we are not doing all we can to help animals. We need to have policy makers respond to our wishes and our concerns. We need to make animals part of the political agenda. [*See Editor's note on page 87.*]

Does the makeup of Congress affect your strategy for making animal protection issues part of the nation's political agenda?
Whether Democrats or Republicans are in charge is a secondary issue. The primary concerns are these: Are we organizing at the grassroots level? Are we making animal issues important to candidates on both sides of the aisle? We need to govern from the bottom up, but at present the animal rights movement has more lobbyists in Washington, D.C., than grassroots organizers across the country.

Not every success of the animal protection movement occurred when there was a Democratic majority in both houses of Congress and a Democratic president. In fact, the last two Congresses did not meet the expectations many people had for the Clinton administration. Only one piece of environmental legislation was passed. So in some ways the new Congress presents opportunities.

I do think, however, that we are going to be at a loss on wildlife issues. The people in charge of the wildlife committees in Congress are inveterate hunters and trappers. Don Young [R-AK], who is chairperson of the House Public Lands and Resources Committee, and Frank Murkowski [R-AK], who is chairperson of the Senate Energy and Natural Resources Committee, are absolutely abysmal on wildlife protection issues. [*See Editor's note on page 87.*]

We may see advances on other issues, such as research, where the government is paying scientists to do animal experiments. It depends on the issue, but we don't look at the next two years as being absolutely blacked out. There are real areas for advance, we simply need to adjust our campaigns to recognize that the leadership is different.

What sort of adjustments will that realization require?
Directing our campaigns toward cutting government expenditures that go to harming animals, the ADC [Animal Damage Control, now called Wildlife Services] or certain types of animal research, for example. We also could stress more law-enforcement issues that are bread-and-butter issues for the Republican party. On wildlife issues we'll have to take more of a defensive posture and seek to hold what we have rather than to pursue measurable gains.

In 1994, you were involved in two successful statewide ballot initiatives; in fact, you led the Oregon campaign to halt the baiting of bears and the use of hounds to hunt bears and cougars. How significant is it that in the midst of what seemed a conservative onslaught, these wildlife-protection ballot initiatives succeeded in Arizona and Oregon? [The Arizona initiative bans the use of leghold traps, body-gripping traps, snares, and poisons on public lands.]
The success of ballot initiatives in two Western states that are supposed to be strongholds for the wise-use movement, states where the hunting and trapping community historically has had a strong grip on policy making, is a tremendous indication of the strength of the animal protection movement. Pro-hunting forces devoted more than $1 million to defeating those measures. We were outspent three to one in Oregon, and we were outspent in Arizona.

Since 1990 we have won four out of five ballot measures, and the only one we lost, which was the 1992 Arizona trapping campaign, was resoundingly reversed in 1994. We've been saying all along that state fish and game agencies and state legislators who set hunting and trapping regulations have been out of touch with prevailing public sentiment, and here we have two very clear examples of that.

Where will the next initiative be?
We don't know yet, but we're thinking of several for 1996. We're going to continue the Western focus while expanding to the upper Midwest and, perhaps, to an Eastern state. [*See Editor's note on page 87.*]

Is the campaign to get a ballot initiative passed much different from any other political campaign?
Ballot initiatives are basically statewide political campaigns that are not different from a governor's race or a senator's race in terms of what needs to be done to get the message out: polling, organizing, advertising, fund raising, conducting focus groups, everything. I'm very attracted to the political aspect of ballot initiatives.

Will that experience stand you in good stead when you run for office?
That's funny. Certainly, I have learned to run statewide campaigns, but I'm very satisfied with my place at HSUS. I think HSUS is going to be a major force for social change in this country, and that's where my energies are best directed at this time.

So you don't have even tentative political ambitions?
Not at the moment. It certainly creeps into my thoughts every once in a while, but my present job allows me to devote my complete attention to animal and environmental protection issues.

What problems will the GATT [General Agreement on Tariffs and Trade] create in the struggle for better treatment of animals?
In some cases we'll see a least-common-denominator approach to environmental and animal protection laws. If one country has a strong law and another country has a weak law on the same topic, we'll see a weak standard across the board. For example, the United States previously did not allow the importation of Mexican cattle that had not been slaughtered in ways consistent with the U.S. Humane Slaughter Act, but now we may not be able to exclude those cattle. There are many other laws that will be affected, too. It's a whole new day and a

whole new economic world, and the concerns of animal protection and environmental groups are well justified.

What is HSUS's relationship with the environmental movement? And how important to the cause of helping animals is cooperation between the two movements?
Concern for animals and concern for the environment are inextricably linked. HSUS has, in my opinion, deeper connections to the environmental movement than does any other animal protection group. We have an environmental arm called Earth Kind. We have a wildlife- and habitat-protection department. We have an education arm that includes the Center for the Respect of Life and the Environment, and the National Association for the Advancement of Humane and Environmental Education. We recently established The HSUS Wildlife Land Trust in order to redress the inconsistency in existing land trusts: the land is protected, but the welfare of individual animals that live on that land is not. The HSUS Wildlife Land Trust is designed to protect habitat, to preserve the integrity of the ecological system, and to assure people that no hunting, trapping, or other forms of animal abuse will be permitted on protected land.

Will the Wildlife Land Trust compete in any way with the Nature Conservancy's activities?
Yes, it may, but we are opening a dialogue with the Nature Conservancy. In the final analysis The HSUS Wildlife Land Trust is an animal protection initiative, whereas the Nature Conservancy is a land protection organization. The ultimate wildlife cruelty is the destruction of an animal's habitat.

There is increasing discussion about ethics in the animal rights movement with respect to how organizations manage their financial resources, supervise their staffs, and interact with other national groups and local organizations. How do you rate HSUS in those areas?

There's a perception among some segments of the animal protection community that HSUS is not very aggressive in spending its money, but that is not the case. We are not sitting on a huge account. We do not have an endowment in the traditional sense, but HSUS does maintain fund balances that will carry the organization for a year. Some authorities say that a charity should rightfully have a three-year cushion.

As far as working with other groups is concerned, when we agree on issues, we will work with other groups. There are times when we don't work with other groups, but that's not a sign of dysfunction; that's a sign of diversity. Different groups have different agendas and utilize different tactics. That is healthy for our movement. Just like an ecological system is stronger when it contains maximum diversity, so, too, is our movement.

Do you agree that HSUS has, at times, had a reputation for keeping itself removed from the rest of the animal advocacy movement?
Among some people it has that reputation, but I think the opinion is overstated. We don't see it as a major problem at HSUS. I dealt with HSUS when I worked for other groups, and I never really saw [HSUS] as a problem when I was looking from the outside in.

HSUS is uniquely placed in the movement to advance the cause of animals in the political realm. We have more than two million members now and projections of five million members in five years. With the credibility that HSUS has, with the professional staff, and with the pragmatic approach that HSUS has adopted, we are uniquely suited to be a major political player.

What are the main positive and negative developments in the campaign for animal rights that have occurred since you signed on with *Agenda* in September 1987?
The movement's profile is certainly higher. The term "animal rights" has become common parlance. There have been a number of tangible victories and measurable gains as well. The campaign against fur has

had a great impact; a number of hunts have been stopped; hundreds of companies no longer use animals in product testing; many laws have been passed at the state level to protect animals; there are a number of dog and cat breeding-control ordinances at the county or municipal level; and with the passing of four out of five ballot initiatives we have seen the resurrection of that tool as an effective means of accomplishing meaningful change.

One of the major changes that has occurred since 1987 is the diminishing of the historical dominance of the vivisection issue in the animal protection movement. In the early and mid-1980s, vivisection was a major issue, in part because of the publicity generated by the Silver Spring monkeys and the Gennarelli case. [*See Editor's note on page 87.*] The vivisection discussion has become bogged down, however, in unproductive debates over the worth of animal versus human life. At the same time, though, there's been a fuller and broader examination of other issues. The animal agriculture issue, which is ultimately the biggest of all animal issues in terms of units of animal suffering, has received greater attention.

Another major development that has occurred since 1987 is the backlash from the animal-use community. We have seen better organized corporate activism from the forces we're opposing. The medical lobby, the farm lobby, the hunting lobby, just to name a few, are far more conscious of our activities and are increasingly proactive. It used to be they reacted to our advances; now they're taking the initiative to thwart our efforts.

Where do you expect to be in ten years?
I certainly don't know. I hope the political landscape in this country will have changed dramatically with respect to animals by then. I hope that animal protection will be a major issue for both parties. If I have any role during the next decade, that would be it: to make animal protection, animal rights, a major national issue in a positive way. For the sake of the planet, these issues have to be addressed more substan-

tively by policy makers. We are tampering with the life-support system of this planet.

☙

Editor's note: This interview took place in 1994.

The Canned Hunt legislation is still under consideration in Congress. The HSUS has worked to ban canned hunts at the state level, for example, Oregon and Montana have banned canned hunts. There is no progress to report on the Freedom of Information Bill for animals in research. The horse slaughter effort has been refocused to the state level. Efforts in the U.S. Congress to ban pet theft continue. Wayne Pacelle has helped to found the Political Action Committee, Humane USA.

In 1996, voters in Colorado and Massachusetts approved bans on the use of leghold traps and body-gripping traps. Washington voters approved a measure to ban bear baiting and hounding. Alaska voters barred the same-day airborne hunting of wolves and other predators. Idaho and Michigan voters rejected initiatives to restrict bear hunting. In 2000, voters around the country sided in favor of animals in five out of nine ballot measures addressing animal protection.

The final round of negotiations in 1995 on the General Agreement on Tariffs and Trade (GATT) resulted in the formation of the World Trade Organization. The WTO is responsible for monitoring national trading policies, handling trade disputes, and enforcing GATT agreements.

On May 28, 1984, the Animal Liberation Front raided the University of Pennsylvania Head Injury Lab that was led by Thomas Gennarelli, removing about sixty hours of videotape shot by the researchers themselves. The tapes were handed over to People for the Ethical Treatment of Animals (PETA), who distributed a thirty-minute compilation that led to the suspension of public funding for the Gennarelli laboratory in 1985.

HSUS reached five million members in 1997.

A Conversation
with Tatyana Pavlova

MARTIN ROWE

I N A COUNTRY LIKE RUSSIA, WHERE CAPS MADE OF DOG
fur are popular and most people cannot afford to have their
companion animals sterilized, animal rights can be a tough sell.
That has not kept Tatyana Pavlova from trying. A vegetarian and
animal activist, Pavlova has a master's degree in biology and teaches
English part-time in an engineering college. She has been president of
the Vegetarian Society in Russia since 1990, the year after it was
formed. She is also a co-founder and the director of the first Russian
animal rights society, the Center for the Ethical Treatment of Animals
(CETA), established in 1991. Both organizations are based in Moscow.
The Animals' Agenda spoke with Pavlova in the summer of 1995 when
she visited Ethel Thurston, president of the American Fund for Alternatives to Animal Research (AFAAR), in New York City. This
interview took place in 1995.

How did you become interested in animal rights and vegetarianism?
I became a vegetarian in 1969. I had often thought about doing so, and
finally the example of some of my friends who had become vegetarian
made me give up meat. A few months after that, one of my friends who
was acquainted with animal welfare people told me a few things about
the way animals were being treated. I was so horrified by what I heard
that I decided to go to the Animal Protection Society (APS) and offer
my help. I was involved with the APS until it folded a few years ago,
when new animal protection groups were formed in Moscow and
other cities in Russia.

Is there a tradition of vegetarianism in Russian?
Yes, but tradition would be a strong word. There were some religious sects in Russia that abstained from meat—the Khaborers, for example—and other people who did, too. They were often persecuted for their beliefs.

In addition to religious vegetarians, there are people like Tolstoy who became vegetarian for ethical reasons. And now there is a third group of people, who are interested in vegetarianism for health reasons. These are people who are also involved in yoga and Oriental medicine. They are the largest group of vegetarians. As far as the vegetarian movement is concerned, the Vegetarian Society has branches in different cities: St. Petersburg, Western Siberia, and in the south on the Volga.

Is there a growing awareness of animal rights in Russia?
People in Russia don't know much about animal rights. There has been no legislation protecting animals from cruelty in Russia since 1954. The concepts of mercy and compassion toward animals were not promoted. CETA is the first organization to promote animal rights on television, in talks, and in books.

Do you find when you talk to people on the streets that they are sympathetic to your cause?
I never try to talk to people on the street because they are always in a great hurry. I did talk to people on the street when we had the Meat-Out show last year. Some people praised us. Others said we had no right to ask people to give up eating meat, even for one day.

How many members are in CETA?
Actually, we don't have any membership. I spent twenty years with the APS trying to organize the activities of amateurs and volunteers. As a result, I now prefer to pay people, however little, and make them work. CETA's organizers are involved with projects that don't demand going about waving banners and such. Our work is conducting scien-

tific experiments and holding discussions with various groups and government officials.

How is the campaign against fur going?
Badly. I know very few people who have given up wearing fur. There is new legislation that forbids using leghold traps. I saw the legislation before my departure for New York. It says that cruel ways of hunting, including leghold traps are forbidden—except in cases where legislation allows it.

That's a success, no?
Well, they say "except" and "but," which provides a loophole for anybody who can get permission to use leghold traps from local legislation. I believe they made this bill sound as though it's more strict than it is because they didn't want to quarrel with the European Council, which bans furs from countries that use these kinds of traps.

Editor's note: In 1991, the European Union agreed to prohibit the use of leghold traps in the EU from 1995 and ban the import of pelts from thirteen species of wild fur-bearing animals caught by leghold traps or methods that do not meet international trapping standards. However, the EU law was modified and postponed to prevent a challenge at the World Trade Organization. International standards were subsequently set, which are considerably weaker than the original EU law.

Have you had any specific successes in your campaigns?
We have had some success in humane education. For example, I have prepared a textbook on ethics for grades one through three and six through eight. It will be used first as an experimental textbook, and then, I hope, it will become part of the school curriculum.

We have also prepared a book called *Bioethics at School*, and we have been promised that it will be used with college students. If that happens, it will be something of a revolution because the book promotes vegetarianism, respect for life and animals, and the anti-vivisection and anti-fur campaigns.

In addition, we have also organized lectures on bioethics for students at the Moscow University Biology Department. These have been going on for five years. The lectures last ten weeks and comprise twenty academic hours. Students are tested at the end of the lectures.

Finally, we have presented a seminar in each of the last two years for teachers in biology departments in teacher-training colleges and universities.

Is there a growing animal rights movement within the philosophical tradition in Russia?
I wouldn't say movement; I would say interest, but not with many people. There has been some progress in high schools, where administrators decided that students in biology departments could have an alternative to dissection as of September 1995.

There has also been some progress regarding alternatives to animal experimentation. CETA is taking part in the big international project, headed by AFAAR. This is the second year we've been part of that project. We have conducted experiments that show that it is possible to use human cells and protozoa for toxicity testing. We are now trying to validate these methods for the government ministries.

We are trying to substitute biosterilization for catching stray dogs and stray cats. In 1994 we carried out an experiment with stray dogs and to a certain extent with stray cats. We put drugs that would render the animals sterile into their food. We presented the results of this experiment to the Moscow administration. They accepted the results, and they will carry on an experiment of their own this autumn to validate our findings. Maybe they will stop catching dogs and cats eventually.

How serious is the problem with stray dogs and cats in Moscow?
Current methods of capturing stray animals do little to keep the number down because real strays are never caught by those methods. Most of the dogs and cats running loose are pets, which is typical for Moscow. And the dogs in the countryside are no better off. They are

often kept on short chains, isolated by a fence, unprotected from cold, without drinking water, sometimes half starved.

What do city officials do when they catch dogs and cats?
They sell some to research laboratories, and the rest are put to death, often by beatings. We are pressing the veterinary department to give up those cruel methods and to switch to barbiturates. Preferably, we would like to see the Moscow administration keep the numbers down by sterilizing female dogs and cats.

Animal Passions
Jeffrey Masson

KIM STURLA

W HEN JEFFREY MASSON WANTED TO READ A BOOK on animal emotions, he discovered that he would have to write it himself. The resulting book, *When Elephants Weep*, which Masson co-authored with Susan McCarthy in 1995, became an instant best seller. The book is in its fifteenth printing and it has been translated into eighteen languages. In 1997 Crown Books published Masson's sequel, *Dogs Never Lie About Love*, which examines the emotional world of dogs.

What was the catalyst for writing *When Elephants Weep*?
I wrote this book because I wanted to learn about animal emotions. And there was no place I could go. There wasn't a book, not even an article, devoted to animal emotions.

The question was why has this topic been avoided. And I think the reason is that we humans do not want to be displaced. It is possible, and I suggest this in the book, that some animals have some feelings that are more intense than ours. Any number of animals can do things we can't do. I think we agree that there isn't anything unique about humans except they think they are uniquely unique. And we're not. Every animal is unique and can do things, whether it's a pig, a dog, or a toad, or any other animal [that] has certain skills, certain sensibilities, certain sensory capacities. But we don't like to think— especially when they are connected with anything to do with the mind—that our capacities might be inferior. It would be unbearably humiliating for humans to think that an animal can be more intelligent. Obviously certain animals are more intelligent than humans about certain kinds of things. I think the same thing is true with the emotions. We like to think that profound emotions—like love, loneliness, or sadness—are uniquely human. But they are really not.

Why do you think the book has been such a success?
I'm not sure I understand why, but I think it has something to do with the really immense change that we are undergoing in the United States and pretty much around the world about our attitudes toward animals. There are more vegetarians now than there ever have been. There are more people who are aware of what it means, why one should be a vegan. And this was a word no one had even heard of ten to fifteen years ago. More people are opposed to using animals in any kind of experimentation. That's also very new.

I think a lot of people have a very bad conscience when it comes to animals. Almost everybody has been horrible to some animal at some point in their life. To suddenly realize that these animals are capable of profound emotions makes you really reflect about the way you've behaved.

Do you believe your book has convinced scientists that all animals do have emotions?
No, I'm afraid not. I'm afraid very few of the 280,000 books sold went to scientists. Somebody sent me an e-mail in which someone had proposed a scientific symposium on what's wrong with my book. By and large, scientists who work with animals do not like this book, with the exception of scientists like Marc Bekoff [who teaches a course on animal awareness and cognitive ethology at the University of Colorado] and Jane Goodall [author of *The Chimpanzees of Gombe*]. The ordinary scientists working in the university having anything to do with animal laboratories, they don't like this book. They don't feel it is scientific, they don't feel they've been convinced; some refuse even to read it. However, no scientist has ever said [he or she] can prove

that animals don't have emotions. It is just a subject they have never wanted to take up because they do not feel it can be scientifically investigated.

Have your views about nonhuman animals changed after researching and writing your book?
Yes they did. I was raised a vegetarian, but when I was eighteen, I gave it up. When I started to do research for this book, I was eating meat. And by the time I finished, I could no longer bring myself to do it. And if I had the strength and will I would be a total vegan. I really believe in it. I find it very hard. I'm so used to cheese. But I see we are producing more and more sophisticated replacement products. People love it. Soy milk is marvelous—much better tasting than regular milk.

After conducting extensive research on animal emotions, do you find yourself more intrigued with one species in particular?
I have a tendency to beatify certain species, to think of certain species as almost saintlike. I always thought of dolphins as marvelous creatures, and then my co-author sent me some research showing that adolescent male dolphins will sometimes form these gangs and gang rape reluctant females. Reading that was a little bit disheartening. And Jane Goodall pointed out to me that chimpanzees not only do that but they will sometimes go to war in a limited way and will kill baby baboons.

There is something about elephants that fascinates me—and dogs. I think it is the fact that they are so social, that they love one another so much. And that they can be so friendly to one another—that fascinates me. But what I am really intrigued by is interspecies compassion. That's what really gets to me. I don't know what animal has the greatest capacity for that. I would suspect that maybe dogs, just because they treat us with such compassion.

Tell me about *Dogs Never Lie About Love: Reflections on the Emotional World of Our Best Friends*.

It's a natural sequel to *When Elephants Weep*, because originally I wanted to include domestic animals, but my publisher persuaded me that I shouldn't for many reasons. The most persuasive argument was: How can we be certain that dogs haven't been contaminated? That's a strong word, but [means] that they've taken from us because of 10,000 years of living with humans, that they imitate our emotions....And I didn't entirely succeed, but I thought it would be interesting to do an entire book on dogs.

They are right there, they're in your face. And they have an intensity of emotions. I mean, can any animal be more joyous than a dog when you tell them we are going for a walk? Or disappointed when you tell them, no we're not? And they throw themselves down on the floor. Their ears go down, their eyes drooping. They just show it. They are pure emotion, in a way. That's what fascinates me about them. And I also envy them. I think their capacity to live in the moment is greater than ours—certainly than mine.

Tell us a little more about what's included in your book on dogs.

I have questions about why we love them so, and questions why they love us, why dogs are capable of this type of fidelity to humans. I look at things like gratitude, compassion toward other dogs, humans, and other species that fascinates me. It's amazing the close relationship dogs will form with other animals.

I look at loneliness. And then I have to look at, reluctantly because it is so awful for me, experiments that are done on dogs. I am really opposed to them. I am opposed to experiments on any animal. But there is something particularly appalling about taking this animal that trusts us so much and doing these horrendous experiments that they do. It was very hard for me. I couldn't get any first-hand information because people would just hang up. I would call the university; UC Berkeley would not reveal to me what they are doing. Finally I got somebody who was doing some research with dogs, and when they heard my name they said, "Didn't you write that book, *When Elephants Weep*?" and then just hung up the phone. They weren't going to talk to me. So they do research still on dogs. I was appalled.

At least 200,000 to 300,000 dogs a year are experimented upon— not for their own good. So it still goes on. But nobody likes that. There is not a dog owner in this country—and there are forty million of them—who would say "Yeah, that's fine, take my dog and do some experiment on it." So this is an area where...I'm just hoping that people might realize, "Well, we don't want our dogs experimented on and so we don't want any dog experimented on, and why should we want any animal experimented on?"

Ahimsa with Attitude
An Interview with Maneka Gandhi

MIA MACDONALD

M ANEKA GANDHI IS A MEMBER OF ONE OF THE MOST
famous families in the world. Her husband, Sanjay Gandhi,
died in a plane crash in 1980. Sanjay was the youngest son
of India's prime minister, Indira Gandhi, and the brother of Rajiv
Gandhi, who also was a prime minister of India and was assassinated
in 1991. But it is Maneka Gandhi's work, not her name, that makes her
remarkable. Gandhi is an animal rights and environmental activist
who sees no difference between the two movements. Based in New
Delhi, India, she spoke with Mia MacDonald, an animal activist and
writer in Brooklyn, New York.

How did you get interested in animals and the environment?
I actually started by losing an election. Until then I was an ordinary
person. I fought an election and lost at the age of twenty-eight [in
1984]. So when I lost, I started thinking to myself, suppose I'd won?
What would I have given to India? Why was I fighting this election to
begin with? To give something, not to take something. I came to the
thought that I should do what was important for me, and what was
important for me was my son. What was I doing for him? I was putting
away all the material possessions for him, his cutlery, his crockery, his
linen, his school, his education, his marital life, his jewelry. But, the
essentials [were]: If I couldn't leave him a glass of water, what was the
point of all this? Or, if I couldn't let him cross the street, or if he never
saw a park to play in, or if he couldn't breathe without wheezing, or if
he was ill every second day, I thought that I must do something.

So I started traveling in India and I said, "Let me not impose my views." I started seeing: What is it that people want? How have they developed? What should happen? And from there I came into the environment. I discovered the word "environment" for myself, and studied and learned, and read a lot, traveled a lot. Then I became the Minister for Environment (1989–91), and found that the word "environment" was misspelled in the Ministry's letterhead! When I became Minister, India had no laws for the environment—none.

How did animals become central to your ideas about environment?
I'd always been an animal person, and when my husband died, I opened an [animal] hospital in the same year in his memory. But I'd never thought of fitting it into an agenda. For me it was something I did because I loved animals. But the more I studied in the environment movement, the more I thought, "Why should animals be separate, and especially in a country where animals run the country?" If I remove the cow, we're all dead. It's a cow dung economy; it's not an open or closed or democratic or communist economy. If you remove the cattle from it, you might as well pack it all in, because there's nothing else.

If you remove the cow, you need buses to bring things to market and you don't have them. If you remove the cow, you need gas cylinders to cook on, which you don't have. If you remove the cow, you need pesticide and fertilizer. If you remove the cow, you need something other than milk. Everything ties right back to the cow, the buffalo, the bullock, the horse, the camel, the elephant, the dog—which is one of the biggest scavengers of the city—[and] the vulture, another big scavenger. Everything has its place, except man. So then I thought that since nobody else is going to do it, I must bring animals into the environment movement.

Can you describe the scope of the work you do?
I run an NGO [non-governmental organization] called People for Animals, which is an umbrella organization for practically all the animal work in India. We make shelters ourselves and fund other

shelters. I also go around India and set up shelters. I get land from state governments and try and arrange money; I get animal groups organized to run the shelters. We have shelters coming up in lots of parts of India. We also put cases in court against animal cruelties. For instance, I have a case in court now against using animals in the circus, which is coming up for a hearing next month. And I have another one for zoos selling animals to the circus. We just won a case against the slaughterhouse in Delhi, which had to shut down because it was perpetuating so much cruelty. I'm the chairperson of the SPCA, and that involves inspections. I have seventy-five inspectors who patrol Delhi and have the power to give summonses. We prevent cruelties. We catch trucks, which are overloading meat animals. And I run a hospital of my own in Delhi, a shelter called the Sanjay Gandhi Animal Care Center. I'm setting up another one for People for Animals, which is the biggest goshala, or cow shelter, in India. It will have about 10,000 cows. It's already got about 600 cows, the stray cows of Delhi.

What are some of your current campaigns?
We are working on something called "Artists for Animals" where we're making every film star sign a pledge that they won't work with animals. It's getting to be too much—they're shooting pigeons on screen, tripping horses, and they have tigers with their mouths sewn up, fighting with these macho stars. Then I have taken on the stopping of dog killing. About two to three million dogs are being killed every year in India because they are strays, supposedly to stop rabies. It has no effect whatsoever. So now we are trying to stop that program and replace it with sterilization and vaccination.

You are a very well-known person in India. How do you use that notoriety to further your causes?
I do a column called "Heads & Tails" every week for about thirty newspapers, and that's been collected into a book. I have two TV shows. One is called *Heads & Tails*. It's the Ahimsa show, in the sense

that it shows animal cruelties, and shows people who are doing good work. It shows what you can do.

I have another TV show on environment, a six-minute show every week after the news on Sunday, which says that, for instance, when you use aluminum foil, you kill the tiger. The bauxite is mined in the Bihar forest. The Bihar forest houses the tigers [and] the big cat is killed first when mining starts. It shows you the inter-relationships, the "house of cards" effect—how the aluminum was mined and where.

Was it hard to start work on these issues in a developing country, where there are so many pressing human needs?
For me, it wasn't a decision that was made looking at anything except the need and whose need was greater? And then who would take it up? You know, it's very easy to do [work with] children, because that's politically correct. If I hadn't come into it [animals and environment], quite honestly, nobody would have. It has to be one person who's confident enough to say, "I don't care what you say, it has to be what I know to be true." People in politics say, "You don't do it for people, you do it for animals? Where will your votes come from?" Really, it [the work] has a vote multiplier effect, because you're seen as good.

What do you think about the term "animal rights"?
I think it's very important. But it shouldn't be separated from animal welfare. In America, because you're so rich and you're so bored, you invent debates, for instance the debate about abortion. It's so nonsensical. We're amazed that you people should be burning abortion clinics and killing abortion people. The debate is so irrelevant to the rest of the world. If you want to have an abortion, have it. If you don't want to have it, don't have it. Why do you make a thing about it? And why lobby, and why go to Congress? The right of a person to their own body is the first right, before anything else. So, the same way, now you've invented the debate between animal rights and animal welfare. How can we separate the two?

My child's right is to live, therefore I must look after the child. So, welfare is tied into rights. If I were to leave a one-day-old baby and say, "Right, now it's your life's right to live, bye, bye," it doesn't mean anything. So, welfare is tied into rights. What I'm trying to do in India is start from a position of welfare: first welfare, then rights.

If I look at a donkey on the road and it's been run down, I can't take it home. If I don't have an animal shelter, the next time I won't even look; I'll just turn my eyes away because I'm ashamed. So, if I'm to further nurture it, then I must first have the shelter, then I have the rights—I see no debate.

Editor's note: This interview is adapted from an interview that was first published in Satya *magazine (see resources).*

∾

Pacheco After PETA
Seeking a Humane America

JILL HOWARD CHURCH

IT'S BEEN NINETEEN YEARS SINCE A COLLEGE STUDENT named Alex Pacheco walked into a Silver Spring, Maryland, laboratory as a novice animal activist and came out as the co-founder of what is now the most high-profile animal rights organization in the world. The landmark Silver Spring Monkeys case put People for the Ethical Treatment of Animals (PETA) on the front page of major newspapers, and the group has been making headlines—and thousands of friends, enemies, and dollars—ever since.

So it may surprise many people to learn that Pacheco quietly left PETA late in 1999 to embark on a voyage into new territory. He is now president of the nonprofit Humane America Animal Foundation as well as the founder of a for-profit venture called All-American Animals. The move comes at what he considers a pivotal point in his life, looking ahead rather than behind.

Why did he leave PETA? "Well, [for] a whole series of reasons," Pacheco explains. "Everything from differences of opinion on the direction of the organization to wanting to branch out and take on new projects in a new way." He says that his desire to expand PETA's programs to include business ventures and other programs with "a more direct payoff for the animals" was not shared by PETA co-founder and president Ingrid Newkirk, so he was faced with a tough decision. "I could've stayed at PETA and fought, but I don't like to fight," he says. While Newkirk had directed the group's high-profile campaigns, Pacheco had concentrated on legislative issues and the organization's infrastructure.

"Program-wise, I feel like the last twenty years I've been doing a variety of things, and I know now that I've sort of reached that turning midpoint in life and I'm looking at things in terms of 'What am I going to do for the rest of my life?'," he says. "Getting older definitely makes you look at things more closely....Now that I'm forty-one, I pick my fights more selectively." He calls PETA's often sensational and confrontational campaigns "good fights, valuable fights, and important fights," but was concerned that such tactics didn't immediately result in saving large numbers of animals.

"I could've stayed and argued my case, but I stopped when things started flying across the room. I didn't want to cause a civil war," Pacheco says.

So in the fall of 1999, he walked away. "It gave me pause," he recalls thoughtfully. "It felt like a divorce. Ingrid was the mom and I was the dad. We didn't have any kids, but the baby is PETA."

He expresses no ill will toward Newkirk. "I learned a lot from her," he says. "We were very much equal in different ways...a very nice combination."

Newkirk acknowledges that she and Pacheco "had rows because I wanted PETA to be true to its original purpose: to push the envelope...." She says of their partnership, "Relationships change, people change, and you have to accept that. I've always been a hardhead, Alex is a conciliator....I was very sorry to see Alex leave, but it is good for the organization."

When PETA moved its headquarters from Rockville, Maryland, to Norfolk, Virginia, in 1996, Pacheco didn't go to the new site, choosing instead to work from Los Angeles. He moved to Florida in 1998. California is the headquarters of both Humane America and All-American Animals, and he plans to relocate there in the coming year. And what a year he has planned!

On June 3, 2000, Humane America will hold its coming-out party at the New York City studio of artist Peter Max, who serves as the group's creative director. David Meyer, formerly of Last Chance for Animals, is the executive director; Amy Luwis and Doug Mckee are the art and research directors, respectively. Two major donors have provided the group's seed money, but Pacheco will be aggressively fundraising to support Humane America's first major project: 1-800-SAVE-A-PET, a coordinated effort among a variety of groups and individuals working to solve the companion animal overpopulation problem nationwide, starting in Los Angeles. Pacheco notes that for the past three years the city's euthanasia rates have gone up while its adoption rates have gone down, so the goal is to reduce the animal supply while increasing the demand. "Instead of saying we're going to have a no-kill shelter," he explains, "we're going to have a no-kill region."

Using what he calls a "customer service approach," 1-800-SAVE-A-PET programs will use demographic data to target some areas for promoting adoptions and other areas for aggressive spay/neuter programs. Mobile adoption units will be brought to shopping centers with available animals and a computer system that can match potential adopters with animals housed elsewhere. The group will also provide pick-up, spay/neuter, and drop-off services to low-income areas, even going so far as to pay individuals $5–$10 for each animal altered. Humane America's "Females First" program will focus special attention on spaying as a means of stemming the reproductive tide. This year the group aims to place 9,000 animals and perform 33,000 surgeries more than are currently done in Los Angeles. A similar program is in the works for the San Diego area.

Humane America's companion animal program is being supported by corporate and private funding, and will be publicized through media advertising, sporting events, and public service announcements. Actress Alicia Silverstone will appear in the first series of ads to promote it.

Pacheco's second group, All-American Animals, is much different. It is a lower-profile, profit-sharing venture aimed at channeling money from vegan products and services back into animal-saving programs. "We're going to be doing partnerships with businesses," Pacheco explains, although many details are not yet ready for public announcement. He raves about a convenient and economical "vegan meat" product that will be marketed for use in large-scale institutional programs such as disaster relief, the military, and school systems, as well as home products. "It absolutely knocks any other protein out of the water," he says.

Among the projects to be financed from business profits will be two strategies close to Pacheco's heart: undercover investigations and helping smaller animal protection organizations grow. He reveals only that the investigations will target "all the bad guys," but is much more explicit about his desire to empower other groups.

"It just kills me to see so many dedicated, good people struggling because they don't have the proper power structure around them that would allow them to be effective," he says. His hope is for smaller groups to function less as independent "cells" and more as part of a larger, cooperative effort. "Some people are really good at what they do, and very effective at it, but what needs to happen is for that person to be training people in other organizations." Toward that end, Pacheco is making himself available to individual organizations interested in making themselves more professional, which in his definition means having a plan for such things as campaigning, lobbying, and fundraising. "The plans are pretty simple, and it's all stuff that I've done myself," he says. For example, he claims to be able to teach an all-volunteer group how to expand and be able to afford a paid staff within a year's time.

He admits his high ambitions are not yet matched by a high budget, and operating with far fewer resources than he was used to at PETA is challenging. He points out that none of the new groups' projects competes or overlaps with PETA's programs. He says he is encouraged by a growing group of supporters, and isn't daunted by starting fresh. "It's quite exciting....Everything's new, from top to bottom, from the projects to the people involved in them," he says. "It's keeping me busy, very busy."

Alex Pacheco is in perpetual motion, and has one simple prediction: "These programs are going to succeed."

⬿

Something to Believe In
Rikki Rockett

KIRSTEN ROSENBERG

OW COULD RIKKI ROCKETT, DRUMMER FOR POISON—
a multiplatinum pop metal band that's sold more than
twenty-one million records, scored fifteen Top Ten singles,
and played to sold-out arenas around the world—be an "unsung
hero"? Because although millions have seen and heard him play live
or on MTV, most people don't know that this rocker is a committed
and very active animal rights advocate.

I caught up with Rikki in July 1999 as Poison's summer tour
visited Virginia. Sitting in his dressing room, discussing such topics as
the Animal Liberation Front, "pet" theft, and his vegan lifestyle (down
to the nonleather shoes), I could have been talking to any seasoned
activist—except for the steady interruption of band members, roadies,
and a few groupies passing through.

Whether he's arranging for animal groups to set up information
tables at Poison's concerts, marching at protests, speaking at events, or
designing groups' Web pages (such as Last Chance for Animals'
www.AnimalCruelty.com), Rikki's commitment to the cause comes
through as loudly as the pounding of his bass drum.

How long have you been involved in animal rights?
When I was in eighth grade there was a movie called *Willard*, about a
rat, and I fell in love with rats. I wanted one and there were no pet
stores where you could buy rats, so one guy suggested that I call
Hershey Medical Center 'cause they use rats and maybe I could get one
of those. So I called and they said, "What kind of rat?", and I said, "I

don't know, a white one would do just fine." And they said, "Okay, what experiment's it for?" I said, "I don't wanna experiment on it, I just want it for a pet!" And they said, "Well, we can't do that. You have to have a note from your teacher that explains what the experiment's gonna be or we can't sell you the rat."

So, it was weird how things come full circle. About two weeks later, I go out to the mailbox, and there's this thing from the [American Anti-Vivisection Society]. Lo and behold, I'm looking through all these different experiments and I see a rat there, spread wide open, and it said some of the experiments [were] done at Hershey Med Center. So—boom!—I put two and two together, and I decided to do a report in school about it. I took advanced bio and you had to dissect cats, and I started [asking] questions, "Where'd the cat come from?", and that really ruffled some feathers. "I'm not gonna do this, you know." So basically I got thrown out of advanced bio. From that point on I became an antivivisectionist.

But I never put two and two together with anything else. I never put vegetarianism or any of that stuff together. I'm from Pennsylvania, "meat and potatoes" part of the country. That's how I grew up, that's how it was. I didn't think about leather, I didn't think about any of that kind of stuff.

And then when we moved out to California in 1984, I met a girl [who] wanted me to do a benefit [show] for the animal stuff—this was probably '87 or something like that, after we'd had our first record come out. And we started talking about all this stuff and she goes, "Is there a good vegetarian restaurant around here we could go to?" And I looked at her, "I don't know! I'm just a vivisection guy." "Oh really! Well how could you?"— we get into it. I told her she was crazy for all this other stuff. I hit her with every question in the book, and she never, ever once got mad at me. And the next day, everything hit me. So I was this insensitive asshole about everything except the vivisection issue, which I think makes me a better activist because there isn't an argument you can throw at me that I haven't thrown somewhere along the line.

At what point did you actually become "active"?

Well I would write [Gillette] letters all the time, you know. I'd say stuff like, "We're gonna be touring this year and I'm gonna be sticking it to you guys [in the press]!" So I would write this mean stuff like I was this violent person, which wasn't really the right way to say it.

And my girlfriend kept saying, "Well, you should meet Chris from [Last Chance for Animals]." Chris didn't want to meet me because he hates celebrities—I shouldn't say that, he's suspicious of celebrities. And I'm suspicious of people who run animal rights groups, you know what I mean? [*laughs*] I said, "No, I don't wanna meet the guy." I'm envisioning this wacky person. And then I was at the Pegasus horse foundation dinner, and I walk outside to smoke a cigarette and Chris was standing outside, and we're just talking about stuff. At the end of the conversation, he goes, "I'm Chris DeRose." And I said, "You're Chris DeRose?" And he goes, "You're Rikki Rockett? They're right about you, you're okay." I was like, "Yeah, you're alright, too." So he said, "Why don't you come down to the office some day," and so I did.

Okay, now for a dumb question: I know the drummer plays the "skins" but drumheads aren't really made of skins, right?

No, they're [synthetic]. There haven't been calfskins used for years. There is a company that makes calfskins for vintage drums. On some of the vintage drums the newer heads don't fit, so they make calfskin for the people that wanna collect or whatever.

Is it difficult being vegan when you're on tour?

I've had a couple problems getting food at certain gigs. Usually if I yell enough I get something, but I horde stuff on good days. I get the Phony Baloney and all that stuff.

[Things] are changing. When I went vegetarian it was really hard on the road, and that was just eight years ago. And I see people doing it twenty, twenty-five years, traveling, and it's like, wow! Like the guy in Lynyrd Skynyrd, he was vegetarian way back; on the cover of the *Nuthin' Fancy* album, there's a shirt that says "vegetarian." There's quite a few people that you don't know [are vegetarian]. Joan Jett, I just discovered. I went to see Joan [perform] in North Dakota and afterwards we hung out and had veggie burgers together. She's not vegan but she's vegetarian. I was tickled to death when I found that out.

Do you feel your beliefs are respected by the band and the crew?
I've taken issue with very few people on this tour. Part of the reason is I don't want to get fired [*laughs*], but as far as the band, they've been great. There was even one day where some of the road crew had, I think, some Burger King™ and Bret [Michaels, lead singer] said—and I'm sitting there—"Can you please move that stuff out of respect for Rikki," which I thought was really cool. Bobby [Dall, bassist] has been great about it. C.C. [DeVille, guitarist] is learning more and more all the time. But I'm the only one right now.

When is Poison going to do an animal rights song?
As a general rule, we haven't been a political band. There's some messages in there from time to time, like in "Something to Believe In" and stuff like that, but if you can't get into feeling the same way, you're not going to write a song together. And that's just one issue I haven't been able to get everyone to feel the same way.

How was it personally between you and [pro-hunting rocker] Ted Nugent when you toured with the Damn Yankees?
We went at it a few times. We didn't fight, but what he does is gives his long string of soundbites and walks away and I went, okay, I can play that game, too. He'd go, "If you really want to sit down and talk, I'll change your mind." I said, "If you wanna sit down and talk, I'll change *your* mind." Well, neither of us are gonna change our minds so what's the point of us sitting down?! [*laughs*]
Then one day when we were off tour he was in L.A. for some reason. I went into Jerry's Deli and he goes, "Hey, Rikki," and I look over and it's him and his family, and he's eating some roast beef or

something. And he goes, "I told you if you ever want to talk about some stuff...." I said, "Ted, I've been there, I know, I was in the hunter safety course, I went out and shot guns. I'm from Pennsylvania. We have three days allowed off from school to go hunting! I didn't grow up in the city, I grew up in the country. I've been there and I've made my decision." I don't hate Ted. I hate his politics. As a person, he's actually been relatively respectful towards me, to tell you the truth. Even after the tour was over and he didn't have to watch himself, because they were in an opening slot—I just need to shove that in [*laughs*]—he was still cool.

Is your family supportive?
Yes. I learned a lot of compassion from my mother. My parents are not vegetarian; it drives me crazy because I know they'd be healthier. But, yeah, they're very supportive. I've shown them videos, I've shown them all kinds of stuff.

How do you think the movement could be more effective in reaching people?
I'd love to have more men in the movement. There's a lot of women in the movement—I love that they're in the movement, don't get me wrong—but I'd like to have more men in the movement because they're more convincing to other men. It's very difficult to get a woman to convince a man a lot of times if the guy has this macho problem. So get a guy with a macho problem that supports this to talk to another guy with a macho problem.

When [groups] were doing the tabling [during a Poison tour], just as a goof, I went out with a hat on and the people who were tabling had no idea who I was. I went up to the person standing in the front and I go, "I want to talk about bowhunting," to just piss 'em off. This guy walked over to me and goes, "If you're gonna talk to anybody you talk to me. I was a prisoner of war and I know what the f—k it feels like to be in a cage, so if you got something to say you say it to me!" I was like, "Let me order one million of you guys!" [*laughs*]

I don't have a bitter view of people. I think on a very basic level people wanna do the right thing. And if we continue to focus on that part of them that wants to do the right thing, we can win maybe at the next generation or the one after that.

≈

P
**************6079

Speaking out for...
anf
33305016454484

9/3/2016 10:18 AM

A New Order in Court
Steven Wise

JILL HOWARD CHURCH
AND
KIRSTEN ROSENBERG

J ANE GOODALL CALLS STEVEN WISE'S BOOK, *RATTLING THE Cage*, published in paperback in 2001, "a major stepping-stone along a road that is gradually leading to a new legal relationship between humans and other sentient, sapient life forms." Wise, an accomplished attorney and legal scholar who formerly headed the Animal Legal Defense Fund, currently teaches at Harvard Law School, Vermont Law School, and John Marshall Law School. He is also the founder and president of the Center for the Expansion of Fundamental Rights, Inc.

Rattling the Cage has created quite a murmur in the often hushed halls of the legal world. Its advocacy of greater legal rights for nonhuman animals has been hailed by supporters as progressive and by opponents as heretical. Wise told *The Animals' Agenda* about how much "rattling" his work has caused.

What kind of impact do you think your book has had thus far?
That is hard to tell. It's only been five months since publication, while the legal "thinghood" of nonhuman animals has been in place for thousands of years. At the least it has stirred up discussion inside the legal arena. I have had the opportunity to publicly debate such legal luminaries as Richard Epstein and Judge Richard Posner, while such respected constitutional law professors as Harvard's Laurence Tribe and the University of Chicago's Cass Sunstein have just as publicly come out in support of legal rights for nonhuman animals.

This legal debate is something new. Philosophical disputes over whether nonhuman animals should have moral rights have been raging for decades. But it took me years to understand fully that judges and philosophers inhabit parallel universes.

I think that when people demand "animal rights," they mean legal rights. But philosophers are not generally trained in law, and judges are generally not trained in philosophy. The main reason I wrote *Rattling the Cage* was because no one had ever made the case for legal—as opposed to the moral—rights of nonhuman animals. I hoped to persuade lawyers and judges that a powerful case for the legal rights of at least some nonhuman animals already exists, and that it is grounded upon our highest legal principles and values. I wanted those who exploit nonhuman animals to see that a strong case could be built. And I hoped to help nonlawyers understand how to fashion powerful arguments for the legal rights of nonhuman animals in terms that lawyers and judges will respect. I also hoped that *Rattling the Cage* might act as a jumping-off point for others who might use it to say "He's wrong and I'll tell you why." In this, I have been wildly successful.

What kind of cases need to be brought before the courts in order to establish common law favorable to animals?
Lawyers must bring cases in which they seek to represent nonhuman animals directly and to establish their legal personhood and basic legal rights. One possibility might be to intervene in a situation when an ape is scheduled to suffer some potentially fatal biomedical procedure, as in the case of Jerom, the chimpanzee to whom I dedicated *Rattling the Cage*. In the United States there exist more than fifty separate legal jurisdictions. The decisions as to which jurisdictions are likely to be the most favorable in which to bring these initial cases are staggeringly complex. They have to be made carefully and wisely, for the initial cases will be very expensive and the first decisions that appellate courts hand down are likely to influence the decisions of later courts.

By the same principle, is there a danger that animals' legal status could be worsened by an unfavorable ruling that would set a harmful precedent?

Even the best seed will not sprout on stony ground. There is a great danger that over-eager lawyers and activists will demand legal rights for nonhuman animals in the courts before any realistic chance exists that judges will give them. They will lose. If that happens, the legal struggle for the rights of nonhuman animals will be set back decades. The responsible course is to spend whatever time is necessary to do whatever it takes to win. If that means digging up the rocks and plowing ourselves, then we do it. Judges and lawyers must be educated about why justice demands basic legal rights for nonhuman animals. We are on that course. Books and articles are being written. An increasing number of animal law or animal rights law courses are being offered at law schools. The first casebook on animal law has been published. Legal conferences are beginning. *Rattling the Cage* was even reviewed in the *Journal of the American Bar Association*!

Has there been a significant change in the number or types of legal cases involving animal cruelty that would indicate a shift in mainstream attitudes toward animals' rights?

While important, animal cruelty cases have little in common legally with animal rights. Someone can easily think that humans should not be cruel to nonhuman animals, but that they should remain legal things who are not entitled to rights. That has been true in Western law for nearly 200 years. American anti-cruelty statutes are so riddled with exceptions that they generally apply only in the rare instances of someone setting his cat afire or starving her dog to death. One of the most troubling trends in animal law in the United States, as opposed to Europe, over the past decade has seen legislatures exempting factory-farming practices or the billions of nonhuman animals raised on factory farms from anti-cruelty statutes.

How have both your law students and your peers reacted to your courses on animal law?

I actually teach "Animal Rights Law." We spend much of the class discussing what legal rights are, how and why humans got them, where they come from, whether nonhumans are entitled to them, and if they are, which ones are entitled to them, and to what rights they are entitled. Many of my students are surprised at how wide-ranging and difficult the course is, but they get over it and jump in. And they often expect me to be one-sided and judgmental. When they realize that I strongly encourage discussion of every aspect of every issue we discuss, they respond enthusiastically. Eleven years of student evaluations at three law schools have been extremely positive.

When I began teaching in 1990, many lawyers, judges, and law professors saw the course as being lightweight, eccentric, and temporary. As these have not been true, their interest has greatly increased.

Has the issue of greater legal protection for apes been introduced in their African and Asian homelands?

Many primatologists and others who care deeply about the plight of apes are working tirelessly in Africa and Asia to stem the slaughter of the apes and to preserve what habitat remains. When I suggested to Jane Goodall that perhaps I should try to focus the argument for the legal rights of the great apes on their native lands, she told me not to waste my time. So I am focusing it on the Western countries and hoping that when legal rights for apes are achieved anywhere, their protection will increase everywhere.

You've been criticized for drawing the line with chimps and bonobos (based on the principle of "autonomy") while leaving out other sentient and highly intelligent animals, such as dolphins or elephants. How do you respond?

Those who criticize me for drawing a line at chimpanzees and bonobos based on the principle of autonomy have not read *Rattling the*

Cage very closely or didn't make it to the final chapter. On page 268 I wrote that "I also never meant to imply that chimpanzees and bonobos are the only nonhuman animals who might be entitled to the fundamental legal rights to bodily integrity and bodily liberty." I don't draw any lines.

Rattling the Cage is not a discussion of how I think a legal system ought to treat nonhuman animals. Nor do I argue that autonomy is necessary for legal rights. I argue that judges believe that a low-level or practical autonomy is sufficient for entitlement to basic legal rights as a matter of fundamental liberty, which is one of the principle values of our legal system. Then I argue that the autonomy of chimpanzees and bonobos far exceeds the necessary minimum. I also argue that chimpanzees and bonobos are entitled to basic legal rights as a matter of equality, another of our major values. I am in the middle of a second book in which I discuss whether such nonhuman animals as gorillas, orangutans, capuchin monkeys, dolphins, elephants, African gray parrots, and dogs are entitled to basic legal rights.

I am not a revolutionary. Lawyers never are. But we know how to demand justice within an existing legal framework. So I look at our basic legal values and principles and show that justice demands that they not be applied only to human beings, but to every animal to whom they can be applied.

What's your take on the growing field of "animal law"? Do you think it's turned a corner and is going to really take off now?
I agree with the authors of the legal casebook *Animal Law* that "animal law" incorporates "statutory and decisional law in which the nature— legal, social, or biological—of nonhuman animals is an important factor." I argue that the term is neutral, that animal law can be wielded by those working either for or against the interests of nonhuman animals. In a lawsuit that involves nonhuman animals, both sides might be practicing animal law. Animal law has been around for many hundreds of years. I define "animal protection law" as the law that lawyers use to advance the interests of nonhuman animals within a

legal system that considers them to be legal things. In a lawsuit, usually only one side practices animal protection law; the other practices animal law. That is what has really begun to explode and its momentum is increasing daily. "Animal rights law" involves judges recognizing that at least some nonhuman animals possess at least some basic legal rights. It does not yet exist. But the groundwork for it is being laid. If we play our cards carefully and correctly, one day it will take off, too.

2: Happy Endings ✌

Introduction ✌ KIM W. STALLWOOD

ANYONE WHO WORKS TO RESCUE ANIMALS KNOWS— or will tell you—heartbreaking stories of cruelty, suffering, and neglect. These are not those stories; or rather, that is not where these stories end. Here, from *The Animals' Agenda*, are heart-warming tales of hope that prove that no matter how hopeless a situation may be, the right amount of effort, faith, and luck can make all the difference.

Surely all animals deserve to have a life with a happy ending. Isn't this also what we would like to see for our family and friends? Sadly, however, billions of animals worldwide exist in the most miserable conditions, experiencing the most horrific of cruelties so that their bodies can be transformed into products for human consumption. Consequently, the single most important action that anyone can take to help animals is to become a vegetarian, or better still, a vegan, and shun all animal products.

What could be a more perfect happy ending to every day than the satisfaction of knowing you saved animals from abuse by choosing a cruelty-free lifestyle?

✌

The Ties That Bind

LAURA A. MORETTI

" He's beautiful." And by "he" they mean Shilo, the horse I rescued from the killers four years ago. I paid the horse trader $50 more than the slaughterhouse would have paid him to keep him from putting that little gray Arabian onto the livestock truck bound for Texas.

I liken it to the way Oskar Schindler bought freedom for 1,100 Jews.

I don't know how to respond to "He's beautiful." "Thank you"? For what? I didn't make him. I didn't create him. I can't take credit for his grace, his spirit, his fire. Such questions leave me feeling awkward and speechless.

There's a fine line among us. We recognize that animals have interests in their own lives, that they feel, think, reason, sleep, eat, drink, play, mate, dream, and die. But to whom do they belong?

They belong to no one, just as you and I belong to no one. But under the law, animals "belong" to those who have bred, raised, possessed, or purchased them. They are, legally speaking, our property. And we, legally speaking, are their owners.

Except in rare cases, injuring or killing a dog or a cat is a violation not of the rights of the victim but of the animal's "owner." In other words, the wrong wasn't committed to the animal involved, but to the property of the human being who owned that animal. Damages are paid by the violator to the owner, and the value is determined as to the monetary "cost" of the injured or killed animal.

So I find myself, in those moments when visitors are admiring Shilo, unable to respond accordingly. I feel foolish thinking what they would think if they knew I didn't consider Shilo mine, even though I've paid to rescue him, pay to feed and house him, to train and groom him, to transport and medically care for him, and even though I have the receipt from the kill buyer proving that Shilo, under the law, belongs to me.

It is difficult in those moments because I recognize that the law of the land is speaking a completely different language than I am. At the risk of appearing the fool, on occasion, I've found myself appealing to the sensitivities of others.

"He's beautiful."

"Thank you," I say.

On second thought, however, our community has risen quite well above the semantics of language. Animal shelters don't encourage the general public to come in and "buy" a dog or cat; they encourage them to "adopt" an animal. It isn't until the cash is exchanged and the documents are drawn that the word "owner" appears in the dialogue.

For as long as we regard other creatures as property to be bought and sold, to be owned or mastered, we humans will forever distance ourselves from the essence of our species: our ability to hold sacred the natural world, to view the other lives around us as gifts given to us by a great spirit, and in so doing, regain our empathy.

If we cannot relinquish our rights to animal ownership, animals will continue to suffer immeasurably—as did African slaves in the grip of human bondage—because their suffering will never be weighed for what it is, but only for what it costs their legal "owners" in terms of "property" damages.

But until we liberate our language, we will never liberate animals. It begins by removing the words "owner" and "property" (and any variation of those words) from our vocabulary, no matter the social consequences. Until we take that step, the court systems cannot follow.

"The law may tell us we can own animals," says Jeffrey M. Masson, author of the groundbreaking book, *When Elephants Weep: The Emotional Lives of Animals*, [see page 93] "but the law also told us in the past that men owned their wives, and parents owned their children. We know this was wrong." Masson is also co-chair of the newly founded international campaign, "They Are Not Our Property;

We Are Not Their Owners," spearheaded by In Defense of Animals (IDA). "We can be animals' friends," Masson adds, "their companions, their helpers, stewards, and caretakers."

Even their saviors.

But we are not their owners.

The IDA pledge is simple: "Whereas, I believe that all animals deserve to be treated and respected as individuals with feelings, needs, and interests of their own, and whereas I believe that animals are not commodities or property to be bought or sold, disposed of, exploited or killed, I hereby pledge always: a) to live my life with an ethic of respect and consideration for all animals, rather than one of ownership in which animals are considered mere property; b) to adopt and rescue rather than buy or sell animals; c) to represent myself as a caretaker, guardian, companion, protector, and friend of animals rather than their owner or master; d) to strive at all times to make the world a more just and compassionate place for all beings, human and nonhuman alike."

Shilo paws the ground and dances in place, arching his neck, as if he knows he's being admired. And then the inevitable remark: "He's beautiful."

I have found a new answer.

"Yes," I say, "he is."

Keep fighting the good fight.

Keiko Goes Home

MARK BERMAN

The dream of returning the orca whale Keiko, star of the *Free Willy* movies, to his home territory has finally come true. As of 1998, Keiko is safely back in his native Icelandic waters nearly five years after he first captured the world's attention while still captive in a Mexico City aquarium.

In 1996, Keiko was transferred from Mexico to the Oregon Coast Aquarium, where he underwent two years of successful rehabilitation. Keiko left Oregon on September 9, 1998 amid cheers from local children and other whale conservationists. The twenty-one-foot whale was accompanied on his ten-hour flight aboard an Air Force C-17 by a team of veterinarians, animal care staff, and representatives of the Free Willy Keiko Foundation. Keiko arrived in the tiny volcanic Westman Islands of Iceland on September 10, and was warmly received by more than 4,000 children and adults waving signs and banners and sporting T-shirts saying, "Velkommen Keiko" ("Welcome Keiko"). He was released into a spacious sea pen where he will become reacquainted with his natural surroundings and studied for possible release into the open ocean.

For the first time since 1979, when he was captured at the age of two, Keiko felt his native waters and immediately slapped the surface with his tail fluke. Keiko then dove and swam several laps around the entire pen, reveling in his new surroundings. He then quickly began accepting his normal feeding routine.

Only two hours after his arrival, Keiko had an interaction with a wild cetacean, a pilot whale who visited outside his sea pen. Keiko's vocalizations intensified as he and the pilot whale checked each other out. Since then, he has had encounters with harbor porpoises and a minke whale. He also has been vocalizing more than at any time in his past nineteen years of captivity.

Keiko's vets have been extremely pleased by his level of activity and interest in exploring his new environment. Nolan Harvey, the director of animal care for the Free Willy Keiko Foundation, reports that "[h]is activity level is very high, certainly higher than it was in Oregon." The sea pen site is rimmed by breath-taking cliffs that are the homes to millions of puffins and other sea birds. The pen allows for a variety of fish and other marine life to swim with Keiko, and he has already begun chasing and catching live fish.

Keiko's return to Iceland continues the amazing story. The next year will provide crucial information as to whether Keiko can be successfully integrated back into the wild orca population.

Not surprisingly, such a release would set an unwelcome precedent for the aquarium/marine park industry. Brad Andrews believes the twenty orcas under his care at Sea World's four parks enjoy their life in captivity, entertaining audiences. "If they didn't, they wouldn't do it," he claims. The industry's concern is understandable because if Keiko is set free, says whale researcher Paul Spong, "more people will find it objectionable to watch these orcas perform tricks."

Keiko's arrival is also spurring a dramatic increase in scientific research on wild orcas, which will likely lead to a new understanding in Iceland of the value of watching whales, studying them, and protecting them.

Editor's note: In 2000, Keiko enjoyed supervised swims in the open ocean off Iceland, where he mingled with the wild orca pods he may someday rejoin.

Hope, the Pig and Ivan, the Gorilla
THE ANIMALS' AGENDA

Hope, an eighteen-month-old Vietnamese potbellied pig, has officially moved into the PIGS sanctuary in Charles Town, West Virginia. Hope was confiscated by an animal control officer when a neighbor reported that Hope had been attacked by her owner's dogs. Upon arriving at the owner's residence in Prince George's County, Maryland, the animal control officer immediately confiscated Hope and the malnourished dogs. Hope's wounds were extensive. Her right ear was totally ripped off. George Whiting, Prince George's County animal control director, recommended that Hope not be returned to her owner, but the commission for animal control believed otherwise. After hearings and meetings had been held and many protest letters had been written, Hope's owner signed a release form giving up all rights to Hope and relinquishing her to the PIGS sanctuary. Hope has since recovered and settled into her new home.

Ivan, a 450-pound silverback lowland gorilla, saw other members of his species for the first time in nearly thirty years on January 20, 1995.

Captured as an infant in Congo in 1964, Ivan was raised by a Tacoma, Washington, family until he was four. He was then put on display at the B&I discount store in Tacoma, where he remained until October 1994. From 1977 until his liberation, when he was sent to Zoo Atlanta, Ivan languished in a forty by forty-foot concrete enclosure. His release was the consequence of a seven-year campaign led by the Progressive Animal Welfare Society (PAWS) in conjunction with zoos in Seattle and Atlanta.

After arriving at Zoo Atlanta, Ivan spent three months in quarantine. During that time he lived in a two-room suite next to the gorilla holding facility so that he could be socialized progressively. That process included, among other things, engaging in quarantine-enrichment activities such as licking peanut butter off a wooden dowel and watching keepers perform their daily tasks.

His quarantine over, Ivan was moved to a room with a wall of iron-mesh netting through which he was able to see three females and two young males in a hallway a few feet distant. Although Ivan and the prospective members of his new family can see and smell each other, they cannot touch.

As a crowd of Ivan's human cousins looked on, he eyed one of the female gorillas, named Molly; but he seemed more interested in watching the people who were watching him and in laying claim to his new closure, which he did by grunting and jumping around a bit. These behaviors are more territorial than sexual, zoo experts explain. Then, while Ivan ate some peanuts, Molly tapped the mesh.

Zoo Atlanta hopes that by springtime Ivan will be residing in the Ford African Rain Forest, the zoo's four-and-one-half-acre naturalistic habitat for gorillas.

Editor's note: Ivan is fully socialized and living in a family group with other gorillas at Zoo Atlanta.

Annabelle, The Baby Broiler Hen
KAREN DAVIS

Annabelle was a heap of soaking wet chicken when Donna Minor picked her off Interstate 20 near Anniston, Alabama, at 7:30 in the morning on Friday, February 24, 1995. So many chickens fall off trucks on this highway on the way to the slaughterhouse that the sight was not unusual. But this time, Minor said, "the little heap raised its head" as though struggling to keep alive. Seeing this, Minor got off at the next exit and went back to find the soggy bundle of feathers—wet, wounded, and bloody—that would soon be Annabelle.

After gathering up Annabelle, Minor drove to her friend Julie Beckham's in Atlanta, where she had been headed for the weekend. After she arrived, they called United Poultry Concerns to find out what they should feed Annabelle, how they should treat her wounds, and where they should take her if she survived. Her survival was doubtful. She looked, a veterinarian would say later, "like somebody beat her up and banged her around a lot." Even her beak was bleeding from the debeaking she had received.

...lle ("Anna" is for Anniston and "belle" for her Southern ...defeated and exhausted little bird with her head hanging ...her first twenty-four hours in Atlanta. Minor and ...her pieces of fresh corn from the cob and cooked brown rice. They soothed her injured legs and wings with hydrogen peroxide. By Sunday she had progressed to a wobbly patient perching on the edge of her carrier. Then she started peeping—a hopeful sign!

On Tuesday, Beckham's friend Ricardo Ferreira drove Annabelle from Atlanta to United Poultry Concerns in Potomac, Maryland, near Washington, D.C. I was not prepared for such a little bird, giving out tiny peeps, looking like a plump white partridge. Annabelle, who weighed just two pounds, must have been one of those month-old broiler chickens sold as Cornish game hens.

The next day, I took Annabelle to the veterinarian, who treated her fractured beak with surgical glue and explained that the outer bones in both her wings were dislocated and that she must have rest and medication. Luckily for Annabelle, our hen Petal was recovering from mouth surgery and had to stay in the house and eat wet mash. Annabelle insisted that Petal become her foster mother. At first Petal did not seem thrilled at having this eager stranger snuggling up to her, crawling over her back, and butting against her head at the food dish. But to see them now, sitting side by side under the kitchen table, you would say they are family, especially when Annabelle preens Petal and Petal closes her eyes looking for all the world as if she were blessed with the only child she ever had.

❧

A Dog Named Bear and the Calico Cat
JANE EHRHARDT

In January, prodigious rains turned California's Ventura River, normally a docile trickle of water, into a seething torrent. Among the many animals affected by this uprising was an eighty-pound, mixed-breed dog named Bear, who became stranded after his homeless human companion, unaware of the escalating water, had left

Bear at their campsite and had gone to help some friends up river. When the owner returned a few hours later, the swollen river had turned his campsite into an island.

The now mighty Ventura, filled with debris, was impossible to cross. While television cameras and onlookers watched, Bear settled on top of a ramshackle shed and waited as the river soaked up more and more of his island. When the Ventura County Department of Animal Regulation heard about Bear, it appealed to the emergency animal relief program of the American Humane Association (AHA) for the funds needed to rescue him. The AHA granted the request, and the department quickly found a helicopter and an experienced pilot to fly staff veterinarian Craig Koerner to Bear's tiny island.

Koerner and Robert Sherzinger, the pilot, were unable to see the dog from the air. They located the right island by following the signals of staff members on the ground. After Sherzinger had landed on a nearby sandbar near Bear's island, Koerner struggled through dense undergrowth and mounds of debris to reach the dog, calling Bear's name as he went. Bear did not answer, but above the roaring of the river, the drumming of the rain, and the whirring of the helicopter Koerner heard meowing. He followed the persistent cries until he found a calico cat huddled in the timbers of a shack. He reached up, grabbed her, and, cradling her in his arms, made his way back through the undergrowth to a place from which he could flag the helicopter.

After getting the sopping cat to shore, Koerner wanted to return to search for the dog. The fire department warned him about the danger posed by the rising waters, the wind, and the coming darkness. Koerner and Sherzinger decided to go back in search of Bear nevertheless. The fire chief sent some of the crew with special rescue equipment to a bridge down river in case Koerner got swept away.

When Koerner got back to the island, he began the laborious search again. Following directions from bystanders on shore, he found the dog perched on some debris. Koerner knew that a dog this size would have to be completely calm in order to be carried, so he gave

Bear a light tranquilizer. Then Koerner lugged the eighty pounds of wet but serene dog to the waiting helicopter.

Once they had reached the Ventura County Animal Shelter, Bear and the calico cat were dried, cuddled, fed, and examined. Both had weathered their adventure well, and within a few days they were transferred to new, loving, and dry homes.

❧

Arthur and Annie
CATHY C. GAYNOR

In April 1992, I met Arthur and Annie, two Suffolk lambs less than eight weeks old. They were living on a farm in Baltimore County, Maryland, in a small, dark, makeshift shed no larger than a pair of veal crates. Purchased a few weeks earlier at a livestock sale, the lambs were being fattened for slaughter. Several times a day the door to the sunless shed would be opened long enough for someone to stuff a bottle into their mouths. Otherwise, they never glimpsed daylight. At one of those feedings I first saw their faces.

In a field adjacent to the lambs' shed, ten geldings sniffed the air nervously and raced about their pasture. They could smell but could not see what was making the unfamiliar bleating noises. The people who boarded these horses at the farm began to complain because they could not catch their animals in order to ride them. My horse was one of those boarders. As I saw the tension mounting, I also saw a chance to save the lambs.

Paying, I am sure, far more than the "expected" market price, I acquired Arthur and Annie with little fuss. I had no idea what I was going to do with them because our twenty-five acres were not fenced at the time, but when I let them out of the shed and watched them run and hop and turn their faces to feel the sun, I knew that somehow I would manage.

That was more than three years ago. Since then I have established Heron Run Refuge Inc., a nonprofit organization devoted to saving and caring for unwanted and abused large animals. In addition to numerous horses, goats, and potbellied pigs, three more sheep previously destined for slaughter have joined Arthur and Annie at Heron Run.

Last summer Annie developed a chronic hoof infection that did not respond to treatment. I called Carroll Thumel, D.V.M., who consulted someone at the veterinary school from which he graduated and learned about a procedure that had been performed on a "valuable" dairy cow who had suffered from the same hoof problem as Annie. With the help of Thumel's partner, Barbara Reitzloff, D.V.M., and some staff from Countryside Veterinary Clinic, we tranquilized Annie, loaded her into the back of our pickup truck, and drove her to Countryside. There we lifted the 200-pound ewe onto the X-ray table.

When the veterinarians determined that Annie's infection had spread into the bone, she was taken straight to the operating room. The mask that provided her with halothane gas covered her muzzle, making her look like a strange sort of dog. Thumel drilled out the remaining infection while carefully monitoring Annie's respiration. Amazingly, she regained consciousness two minutes after the surgery had been completed. Soon after, she was back in the truck and on her way home to her friends.

Annie's recuperation was short and complete. She spends her days with Arthur and the other sheep at Heron Run. The vets who saved her life will always have my gratitude and respect.

New Life for Elephants

KIRSTEN ROSENBERG

For Tammie and Annie, October 3, 1995 marked a profound change in their lives. This was the day that the two Asian elephants arrived at the Performing Animal Welfare Society's (PAWS) captive wildlife sanctuary in Galt, California. Tammie, forty-three, and Annie, thirty-seven, will spend the remainder of their lives roaming over a full acre, enjoying a custom-built swimming pool, and sleeping in an enormous heated barn. "We have spent the last year anticipating this very special moment," said Pat Derby, founder of PAWS. The Milwaukee County Zoo in Wisconsin, the only home the elephants had ever known since being taken from the wild as babies, decided to retire them to PAWS in order to create more room for other animals living at the zoo.

For Annie and Tammie, life at the sanctuary is a far cry from their previous existence at the zoo. The Milwaukee climate, unsuitable for Asian elephants, forced them to endure long and cold winter months chained in a barn with damp, unheated floors. Like so many wild animals in captivity, they exhibited stereotypic behaviors. For hours on end, Annie would step from side to side, swinging her head back and forth. Tammie's movements were even more bizarre: while swinging her head in a rotating motion, she would lurch forward then backward, again and again.

Now that they have been relieved from the tedium of zoo life, the elephants' mental health has improved tremendously due to the enriched environment of their new home, and their physical ailments are responding well to constant medical attention, improved diet, and a warmer, drier climate. Tammie's chronically infected feet (exacerbated, if not caused, by endless hours on a cold, damp floor) and Annie's hip arthritis (a result of an injury sustained during a breeding attempt at the zoo) are improving.

Yet one of the most amazing changes is that the elephants are now displaying the normal range of elephant vocalizations. They express themselves with a repertoire of squeaks, chirps, and rumbles—sounds that were not heard at the zoo.

When Tammie and Annie arrived at the sanctuary, their eyes had a "dead, glassy" look, said sanctuary keeper Stephanie Taylor. Today their eyes sparkle, they take interest in their surroundings, and "actually look at things." A stimulating environment is something to which Annie and Tammie were unaccustomed. "They've come alive," said Taylor. "For the first time in thirty years, they get to take a dip in the pool in January!"

Abandoned Pigs Find the Good Life

KIRSTEN ROSENBERG

For eighty-nine Vietnamese pot-bellied pigs, life isn't so bad anymore. In fact, life is good, very good, now that they reside at PIGS, a sanctuary, in Charles Town, West Virginia.

Before coming to PIGS, created specifically for potbellied pigs, life for the animals was bad indeed. Like so many other potbellied pigs, these animals had become castoffs after the novelty of having an exotic "pet" was gone. They had been living at a potbellied pig "sanctuary" in Colorado when they were abandoned last October after the operator, overwhelmed by the demands of caring for the animals, simply quit. Investigators from Wilderness Ranch Sanctuary for Farm Animals near Loveland, Colorado, discovered 114 pigs and piglets on the premises, all without adequate shelter, and with virtually no water or food. Some were starving to death; others were found huddled together in a ditch for protection against the cold Colorado weather. Said Wilderness Ranch President Jan Hamilton, "When I looked into the first plywood box and saw twelve shivering piglets huddled around their dead sibling, I knew it was worse than I feared." The Humane Society of Boulder Valley agreed to take twenty-five of the pigs, while PIGS agreed to take the remaining animals. Wilderness Ranch Sanctuary for Farm Animals served as an interim home for the pigs while funds were raised and arrangements were made to transport them to West Virginia. In the meantime, the bristly-haired pigs were restored to good health. They were wormed, vaccinated, spayed, and neutered, their hooves and tusks were trimmed, and they were lavished with love and attention.

On Thanksgiving, four heated trucks carrying sixty-four pigs nestled in thick beds of straw and blankets began the 1,705-mile, two-day trek across nine states to reach PIGS and a new life. A crowd of anxious volunteers was on hand to help unload the porcine travelers and usher them into their new living quarters. A custom-built barn had just been completed by the time the remaining twenty-five Colorado pigs joined their companions on January 19.

The fast-paced life is not for these pigs: they are content spending most of their time in the barn, asleep in deep straw or snuggled under heat lamps, according to Jim Brewer, PIGS co-founder. But on sunny days, they can be found outside, lazily basking in the sun.

The contributions and support of several organizations, foundations, and dedicated volunteers made all the difference in the world for these castoff pigs. Now safe and secure, with warm beds and full potbellies, these once forlorn, abandoned pigs have found the good life.

Putting a Face on Meat
Kirsten Rosenberg

Emily loves life. This comes as no revelation to those who already know that cows are sensitive, self-aware, unique individuals. But for many, the story of Emily's fight for life was a spiritual awakening.

Emily is really no different from the millions of dairy cows who are slaughtered annually once their output wanes. She was headed for a violent death when she arrived at the slaughterhouse in Hopkinton, Massachusetts, on November 14, 1995. Like the other frightened cows, Emily sensed the horror that lay ahead, but rather than succumb in confused and helpless terror, she propelled all 1,400 pounds of herself over a five-foot-high fence and escaped into the surrounding woods.

Reminiscent of a biblical odyssey, for forty days and forty nights this courageous cow eluded her captors, enduring severe snowstorms and freezing temperatures, all the while foraging for sustenance. Local media began chronicling daily the Holstein's plight, prompting sympathizers to leave secret stashes of hay in back yards and woods. When vegetarians Meg and Lewis Randa heard about Emily, they convinced the slaughterhouse owner to sell the brave bovine to them for $1. Then on Christmas Eve, after days of trying, the Randas finally coaxed a frightened but tired Emily into a trailer for the ride to the sanctuary at Peace Abbey, a part of the Randas' school for children with special needs.

Now settled into her new home, tender loving care has done wonders for Emily, who is up to 1,800 pounds after losing 500 pounds during her fugitive days. Lewis Randa says that Emily appears happy and at peace, and despite her ordeal at the hands of humans, she prefers the company of people to her two horse companions. Still, the Randas plan to adopt a bovine buddy for Emily.

Emily's influence and circle of friends continues to grow. Hundreds of well-wishers have come to visit the now-famous cow. She welcomes a good head scratch, loves carrots and other treats offered from outstretched palms, and freely gives away kisses in the form of a giant lick. According to the Randas, her effect on people is powerful: many swear off red meat or become vegetarian after meeting her. She has even been a "bridesmaid" at a wedding held in the Randas' barn.

Serving as a compelling ambassador for vegetarianism, Emily has garnered national media attention, including a full-page profile in *People* magazine. A motion picture about Emily's story is in the works.

Why have people been so moved by one cow's courageous effort to avoid death? Perhaps it is because for the first time, they see that "meat" has a face.

~

In Emily's Hoofprints
Kit Paraventi

Emily may have begun a trend. In August 1996, Hopkinton resident Diane Larocque was bewildered to hear someone pounding frantically on her front door late one afternoon. She was even more startled to find that the visitor was a wild-eyed brown goat. It was a little like a Walt Disney cartoon unfolding on her front porch. When she opened the screen door, the goat bounded past her into her kitchen and headed for her dog's water bowl.

"I figured she was a missing pet," says Larocque. However, a phone call to the police brought a slaughterhouse livestock truck, which prowled Larocque's sidestreets with predatory stealth. Larocque quickly closed her front door and tried to keep the goat quiet for the night, which was no easy task. Like Emily in the above story, Belle the goat was another slaughter-bound escapee. Frantically, Larocque made several more phone calls, finally reaching the Peace Abbey. "Do you think you can save this one?" she asked. While waiting for Meg Randa, Larocque coaxed Belle out to her back yard and into a large dog kennel.

By the time Randa arrived, the emaciated Belle had made short work of Larocque's grass, then somehow managed to make a den for herself inside the igloo-shaped dog shelter. It was clear that Belle was very sick; her body was emaciated and she had a runny discharge and festering blisters smearing her nose and mouth. Belle had a contagious and often fatal form of hoof-and-mouth disease. Quarantine was mandatory, and Larocque was up to the task. She converted the dog pen into a sterilized sick ward for the next three months, giving Belle aspirin hidden in peanut butter.

When Belle finally arrived at the Peace Abbey in time for the annual vegan New Year's Eve celebration, another diagnosis became clear: Belle was pregnant. A month later, two frolicsome brown-and-white kids named Joshua and Jacob were born.

But the story wasn't over.

Early in June 1997, Gloria, a Holstein who spent eight years on a dairy farm, caught the stockyard wranglers off-guard when she came bursting off a truck and lumbered away. Neighbors who spotted the escaped cow munching grass in their back yards called the Peace Abbey. "Do you think you can save this one, too?" they asked, with a hint of conspiracy. Once more, Meg Randa contacted the slaughter-house owner and negotiated the sale.

At Peace Abbey, Gloria became a changed cow with the arrival of Albert and Gabriel, two motherless former veal calves adopted from other rescuers. She immediately fixated on Albert, studying him as if he might be one of her possibly seven or eight calves who were loaded into crates and trucked away. Now she's the typically adoring, doting mother, slathering Albert with lavish kisses at every opportunity. "He's usually soaked," laughs Meg Randa.

Something has changed in Hopkinton. There's a quiet air of insurrection invading its streets, filtering into its conversations, toying with its thought patterns. The town has become a sort of underground railroad for slaughter refugees. Says Meg Randa, "It's as if Emily has sent out some sort of silent signal." Together with turkeys, a pony, and a pair of rabbits from an animal lab at Northeastern University, the runaway cows and goat live peacefully with their newfound families. "Gloria and Emily are so close," says Meg. "Hardly ever apart."

Perhaps this story isn't over yet.

⋙

Popcorn Ponies

KIRSTEN ROSENBERG

Grandpa and Granny have reached their golden years. Grandpa, a thirty-four-year-old miniature horse, and Granny, a pony more than twenty years old, are living out the rest of their lives in peace, comfort, and safety at the Popcorn Park Zoo in Forked River, New Jersey. The seven-acre sanctuary, run by Associated Humane Societies, is home to nearly 300 formerly abused, abandoned, or injured animals.

Too old to breed and no longer useful, Grandpa was put up for sale for $100 by his Pennsylvania caretaker. Zoo general manager John Bergmann intervened after being contacted by someone who was concerned Grandpa would end up going to slaughter. Bergmann was able to acquire Grandpa and his close companion, Granny.

Years of neglect had taken its toll on the two old-timers. Both animals had gone blind; Grandpa was emaciated, and Granny had bare patches on her shoulders from chronically chewing on herself out of boredom and frustration. They had spent long periods confined in a filthy stall.

The inseparable equines adjusted immediately to life at Popcorn Park, where they share a clean barn with an adjoining paddock. Veterinary care and ample, nutritious feed have allowed Granny and Grandpa to gain weight. Their coats, once ragged and dull, are smooth and shiny. Volunteers lavish the seniors with love and attention. When Granny and Grandpa hear visitors, they come to the fence to accept popcorn and other favorite treats.

"They are so trusting," says Bergmann, describing how the blind equines confidently run with the caretakers, attached by a leadrope, for daily exercise through the park grounds. "I feel good when I see them running."

Birdman of Puerto Rico

PAT VALLS-TRELLES

Despite the billions of dollars in aid the United States gives to its territory of Puerto Rico, dogs of every breed and size can be seen dying of starvation and disease on Puerto Rico's streets. The street dogs live slow deaths, succumbing to a combination of parasites, malnutrition, injuries, infections, and a host of gruesome diseases. Local municipalities do not provide animal control services. Animal shelters on the island have consistently limited their services amidst the ever-increasing problem. Conditions at the shelter in Ponce have been described in the press as deplorable.

In response to pressure from animal activists, the San Juan shelter has recently made some positive changes. But then there is the Humane Society of Puerto Rico in Guaynabo.

On November 14, 1996, members of Save a Sato, a small, all-volunteer Puerto Rican animal rescue group, took friends from a Boston shelter to Guaynabo to show them the conditions. No one expected what they found. Each fenced run contained ten or more dogs lying or sitting listlessly in filth and slime. There was no fecal matter because the animals had not been fed. Broken water bowls spilled constantly, flooding the cement floors and adding to the animals' misery. Too weak to bark, the dogs shivered, their eyes vacant as they waited to die.

A week later, Karen Fehrenbach, one of the founders of Save a Sato, returned to the shelter. She followed what sounded like puppies screaming to the rear of the facility. There, as she knelt down to count the number of animals crowded into one small cage, a small, determined puppy about five weeks old squeezed through a small hole in the fence and jumped onto her lap. Covered with mange and weighing less than three pounds, every ounce of him told Karen, "I want to live."

Christening him Birdman (after the film *Birdman of Alcatraz*), Fehrenbach brought him to a veterinary clinic for his mange and parasites, and to make sure he didn't have distemper, which had killed some of his cagemates. Birdman, now in foster care before leaving for a loving home in the United States, is delighting in the glories of puppyhood. "He's a typical puppy, constantly in motion—playing, biting, chewing," said Fehrenbach, calling him "a real lover." No longer scrawny, hairless, and grayish-pink, this "purebred Puerto Rico sato [mixed-breed, street dog]," as Fehrenbach puts it, has blossomed into a striking black-and-white, exuberant puppy. He is, she says, "the happiest puppy in the world."

An Angel with a Wagging Tail
DAWN WILLIS SOLERO

Bitter, lonely, and bordering on reclusiveness after an industrial accident left him disabled, Philip Gonzalez was persuaded by a friend to adopt a dog from a local animal shelter. His determination not to be swayed by the face of a needy animal crumbled after a brief walk with a little Siberian husky/schnauzer mix soon to be known as Ginny. Starving and dehydrated, Ginny and her pups had come to the shelter after being found locked inside a closet in an abandoned apartment.

Soon after adopting Ginny, Gonzalez noticed that whenever he and Ginny were out for a walk, Ginny would pull on her leash at the sight of a homeless cat. The cat that actually started Ginny's cat-rescuing crusade was a long-haired golden kitten found in a vacant lot. Seeing Ginny's intense interest in this homeless kitten, Gonzalez began carrying cat food with him on their nightly walks together, and would feed strays whenever they found one. It was shortly after that first encounter that Gonzalez realized Ginny's unusual gift of being able to sense when animals (particularly cats) were in trouble.

A recent example of Ginny's special talent occurred as she waited in the car while Gonzalez fed some of the 120 stray cats they visit twice daily at one of eight "feeding stations." After Ginny suddenly began barking, Gonzalez let her out of the car. She ran over to a dumpster and began to whine. Gonzalez rummaged through the bin and discovered a box, completely taped shut, containing two black kittens. Sure enough, Ginny's sixth sense had come through again!

During their seven years together, Gonzalez and Ginny have rescued and placed into good homes more than 175 cats. Among the fifteen cats now living with Gonzalez and Ginny are Madame, Ginny's first adoption, who is completely deaf; one-eyed Revlon; Betty Boop, who has no hind feet; and a partially paralyzed kitten named Topsy, whom Ginny found in an abandoned building.

Although Gonzalez rescued Ginny from the shelter, it is really she who saved him. Through his feisty canine companion, Gonzalez learned to overcome his own disability, and is infused with a renewed zest for life. Their shared experiences inspired him to write two books, *The Dog Who Rescues Cats* and *The Blessing of the Animals*.

"I really do believe that Ginny is an angel," he says. "I believe completely that God sent Ginny down to earth to rescue cats who would have otherwise died, and to rescue me. Without her intervention, I would have remained a bitter, useless man."

The Buckshire Twelve

LAURA A. MORETTI

"My only hope," said chimpanzee scientist Jane Goodall more than a decade ago, "is that one day all chimps in research facilities will be retired and no more chimpanzees ever used again." Today, approximately 2,000 chimps dream of such a time, many of them languishing in solitary confinement, housed for their entire lifetimes in biomedical research facilities around the country from which they will never escape. But occasionally, a few find their way into the open arms of their defenders.

Such is the story of a dozen chimps who were retired by the Buckshire Corporation in Pennsylvania in 1996. Known by the activists overseeing their release as "The Buckshire Twelve," the chimps—most of whom were originally displays in roadside circuses and zoos—left their barren and solitary five-by-five-by-seven-foot steel cages for a spacious home at the Primarily Primates refuge in San Antonio, Texas.

"Elsie, the forty-two-year-old grandmother of the bunch," says Stephen Rene Tello, corporate secretary for Primarily Primates, "was the first to walk onto our soil." He recalls that the chimp immediately began to stretch her legs and stroll about her new enclosure. Even her attached private "bedroom" was larger than her lab cage. In 1981, Elsie had been purchased from an amusement park by a laboratory; she hadn't tasted freedom or felt the sunshine in fifteen years.

Because it is now illegal to capture chimpanzees in the wild, the animals are being bred in captivity. Most of them are being used in toxicology, AIDS, and hepatitis research, making it impossible for them to be retired with other chimps. The Buckshire chimps, however, had been used in various vaccine testing, enabling them to either be granted retirement or transferred into invasive research (like AIDS).

That's exactly where they were headed when Primarily Primates' directors Wally Swett and Tello came into the picture. The sanctuary launched a massive fundraising campaign designed to help build a twenty-by-thirty-foot enclosure, and to care for the animals once they arrived. "There were originally eight chimps," recalls Swett, "and we had only one enclosure in development." Then the Buckshire Corporation did the unpredictable thing: it offered the sanctuary another four chimpanzees.

The Jacob Bleibtreu Foundation of New York couldn't deny them. It granted the funding of a second enclosure in its entirety. Thanks to the generosity of the foundation, as well as financial gifts from such organizations as the National Anti-Vivisection Society, the Massachusetts SPCA, and Psychologists for the Ethical Treatment of Animals (among others), Tello was able to exclaim in April 1996, "They're here!" All twelve of them—Elsie, Siri, Wanda, Beauregard, Buffy, Marty, Oliver, Raisin, Cassie, Carmen, Abednago, and April—arrived safely. They adjusted rapidly and well to their new lives, shattering the research community's myth that such animals cannot be rehabilitated.

"This transfer represents the first and best documented research chimpanzee retirement effort in history," says Tello. "Retirement for such animals is possible."

But the effort is far from over. "We have a chance to retire another group of chimps," says Swett. "If we can raise the money to build another enclosure as an addition to the chimp complex, we can prevent more chimps from being transferred into invasive research." Adds Tello, "As we enter our second decade, Primarily Primates has become a place of promise for the animals we have sworn to protect, save, defend, and nurture."

Jane Goodall may very well see her dream come true after all.

❧

The Heart of Harbinger

KIT PARAVENTI

Harbinger was an affectionate three-year-old gelding sired by the renowned Thoroughbred racing stud Flying Paster. Owned by the Ridder family of Knight-Ridder news service fame, Harbinger lived a life unlike that of most race horses. His was a privileged world of knee-deep straw bedding and feed bins brimming with quality hay and grain. Heart-pounding morning workouts were followed by leisurely rubdowns. Harbinger loved people.

And with all the vitality of a young, healthy horse, Harbinger loved to run.

In his first race at California's Hollywood Park, Harbinger's running was stopped. He had swept over the turf with huge, ground-swallowing strides, a strong third in the final furlong. Jockey Chris McCarron held the colt's most daunting burst of speed in check until the moment came to challenge the leaders. Then, as Harbinger surged forward, a fourth horse bumped him, throwing him off balance. The colt stumbled, then continued. Unknown even to McCarron, Harbinger finished the race in sixth place on a shattered front leg. He had that much heart.

After a veterinary evaluation, Harbinger was passed on to one of those trainer/horse traders who hang around tracks and quietly dispose of used-up horses. Within weeks, Harbinger was huddled beside an emaciated old gelding named Grandpa in a stock pen at a killer buyer's feedlot.

His broken leg was now a swollen, fly-infested mass of raw flesh, and he had lost much of his body weight. With a hundred or so other horses in other corrals, Harbinger and Grandpa awaited the two-tier cattle truck that would transport them to a Texas slaughterhouse. In the back pen together, Harbinger and Grandpa had bonded with the desperate camaraderie of the doomed.

"He was in tremendous pain," recalls Cathleen Doyle, founder of the California Equine Council. "There's no question he should have either been immediately shipped to the clinic or euthanized following his accident."

But as Doyle and a small group of horse rescuers stood outside his enclosure on a Sunday afternoon, Harbinger lurched to a standing position, limped painfully to the fence, and thrust his muzzle into the chest of one of his visitors, closing his eyes. He still loved people.

"What am I getting myself into?" thought Doyle.

"You're taking home a dead horse," a wrangler warned when Doyle returned with a horse trailer the following day. As his only companion was haltered and coaxed, step by agonizing step, into the trailer, Grandpa raced the length of the pen bugling his distress and shaking the pipe corral poles with overgrown cracked hoofs, his bony sides heaving. Knowing they couldn't leave Grandpa behind, two of the rescuers came back the next day and saved him, too.

As for Harbinger, "He has about a one-in-a-thousand chance of surviving," said the veterinarian who finally agreed to perform rehabilitative surgery on the injured horse. But there was something about the colt's spirit, some invincible joy the agonizing pain couldn't mute. Miraculously, Harbinger survived the operation.

His problems were far from over. Down much of the time, he foundered on his unbroken right leg and endured the pain of a crumbling hoof. His wounds always bordering on infection, Harbinger required long hours of medicating, cleaning, and wrapping each day. Doyle's back became inflamed by the physical demands of the treatments. "I'd say, 'I can't do it, not tonight,'" she remembers. "But eventually it came down to my inconvenience versus his life."

After nine months and $10,000 in medical bills (which Doyle raised from several contacts), Harbinger eluded doom for the second time in his life. He survived.

Life is good again, and there are new friends. Like many other horses, Harbinger has adopted a companion animal: a tough-looking wild rabbit who wandered into his stall one day, tattered by predators. When Doyle throws in the morning's flake of hay each day, Mister Rabbit quickly leaps on top of it. Just as quickly, Harbinger goes to the hay, grabs a corner, and flips the rabbit away. With Harbinger's mouth full, the rabbit defiantly hops back on the hay and the game begins again.

After breakfast, Harbinger moves across the outdoor paddock with increasing anticipation, picking up speed until he breaks into a clumsy but enthusiastic run.

He has that much heart.

Rusti's Angel
PETER HNATH AND SHERRYL VOLPONE

When we first saw Rusti it was like finding a forgotten prisoner of war. This eighteen-year-old, 270-pound, mixed-breed orangutan was trapped in a ten-by-twelve-foot cinderblock cell hidden in a cramped corner of a roadside zoo in Scotch Plains, New Jersey. Abandoned by his mother and hand-raised by humans at Seattle's Woodland Park Zoo, Rusti had been shuttled between various sites before ending up in New Jersey among 120 other animals at the 5.8-acre zoo. He had spent nearly a decade in solitary confinement, with only a tree stump bench to sit on. With his fur matted with wood shavings and feces, Rusti would sit on the bench for hours to avoid walking in his own excrement.

His only contact with the world came from two small Plexiglas windows that were so scratched that only limited amounts of light entered the cage. Rusti could hear no outside sounds, feel no wind, and smell no fresh air. We could not forget the image of his loneliness and decided to wage a war in order to save his life.

Further investigation revealed that this zoo had a long history of Animal Welfare Act violations. Government inspection reports documented continuous violations such as contaminated food and water, outdated medicines, unbalanced diets, fly infestations, and poor sanitation.

A year of protests, letter-writing campaigns, and court battles ended with the news that the New Jersey Division of Fish and Game would not renew any of the zoo's permits. The animals would have to be relocated to approved facilities. Some of the best zoos and sanctuaries stepped in to offer permanent homes for all of the animals except Rusti. Apparently not many places are set up to house a primate as large as an orangutan.

We did not know it at the time, but Rusti had a guardian angel. Her name is Birute Galdikas, president of the Orangutan Foundation International (OFI), an organization we discovered after contacting several for assistance. OFI had never rescued a captive orangutan and did not have a home for Rusti. That did not stop Galdikas, who made a two-day journey all the way from Indonesia to see for herself. "I had no choice," she said. "I raced to the zoo, where I found him in a tiny, dark cage half underground. Just looking at him broke my heart." As a result, Rusti was going to be personally escorted to the Los Angeles Zoo by the foremost orangutan expert in the world.

In Los Angeles he was quarantined for thirty days, receiving a complete physical and grooming. After getting a clean bill of health he was moved to his temporary home at the Honolulu Zoo, where he is considered a V.I.P. (Very Important Primate). Rusti will remain there until OFI completes its twenty-two-acre orangutan sanctuary in Hilo, Hawaii. He will be the first resident of the only sanctuary in the world for abused and abandoned orangutans.

Rusti now has a large outside area with lots of room to climb, and an air-conditioned inside enclosure where he enjoys watching videos on his personal TV/VCR (his favorite movies include *Gorillas in the Mist* and *Aladdin*). When the sanctuary is completed, Rusti will be taught sign language by Gary Shapiro, Ph.D., of OFI and will even have his own computer. And although he may never be able to live the life of a normal, wild orangutan, this prisoner of war is a prisoner no more.

Editor's note: Although in 2000 the state of Hawaii failed to appropriate partial funding for the orangutan sanctuary, OFI continues its fundraising in earnest.

Butch and Sundance:
The Last Stand

Kit Paraventi

Like the United States, Britain is a culture in which the slaughter of animals is a routine, even mundane, daily occurrence. Although it lacks the visibility of the local constabulary, pub, or rugby league, slaughter saturates the fabric of British life. It is as pervasive as the early morning aroma of bacon sarnies or the sight of dead ducks hanging in the window of the neighborhood butcher shop. Slaughter is everywhere; so much so, in fact, that it has become invisible.

Enter the "Tamworth Two," a feisty, scrappy pair of ginger-colored Tamworth boars selected by destiny to put faces and names to the fifteen million anonymous pigs slaughtered each year in the United Kingdom. Butch and Sundance, as they became known, were scheduled for "processing" at the Newman Slaughterhouse in Malmesbury, Wiltshire, when they somehow slipped away from stock workers on January 11, 1998. The scrambling of cloven hoofs over the quiet streets of the picturesque town attracted little attention at first. It was a matter for the local constabulary and Newman workers to coordinate and expedite, returning the pigs to their appointed doom with as little fuss as possible.

But when the pair was finally cornered at the brink of the River Avon, they did something that began a swell of press coverage and public applause. Together, they plunged into the river and swam, snouts held high, to the opposite shore.

Like their outlaw namesakes, Butch Cassidy and The Sundance Kid, the two led their pursuers on a merry and very publicized chase. For five days they dodged, sped, ducked, and confounded fate at every turn. Sympathies began to mount with each reported near-capture. Their plucky determination was the stuff of legends. "I would describe these pigs as extremely cunning and devious," said Wiltshire Police Constable Roger Bull after yet another unsuccessful run-in with the two.

Media coverage of the drama ignited the underlying human tendency to root for underdogs—or in this case, underpigs. The sluggish public sense of sympathy began to awaken. In response to rising demands and pleas that the pigs' lives be spared, their "owner," city street sweeper Arnoldo Dijulio, was terse and to the point. "They were bred for slaughter," he said, adding that he was "unprepared to discuss their future." But as offers of money and homes began to flood in from around the world, public scrutiny began to chip away at official indifference. Attempts at capture, which first included entrapment with barbed-wire barriers, gave way to a self-conscious concern by officials for the pigs' welfare. A few police constables were openly supportive. "Everyone is rooting for the pigs," said Pc Phil Snow of Wiltshire.

Butch and Sundance made their last stand in a two-acre garden next to the home of Harold and Mary Clarke of Tetbury. A deluge of well-wishers, curiosity-seekers, schoolchildren, animal rights advocates, and national and international media representatives descended on the quiet neighborhood. The porcine pair was captured. In a universally approved gesture, the *Daily Mail*, a London newspaper, announced that it had rescued the pigs after Dijulio finally agreed to let the paper buy them. Butch and Sundance were reportedly relocated to an animal sanctuary near Chippenham, but the *Daily Mail* is keeping the exact location a secret. "We're trying to protect the sanctuary from throngs of visitors," a spokesperson told *The Animals' Agenda*, "but the pair are doing quite well and will soon be making a public appearance." Impending slaughter, it seems, will never again hang over the heads of the notorious two. "All the media interest has saved them," said Mary Clarke following the capture. "So, that's good."

Now that the media madness and collective compassion has ebbed, has anything really changed? Daily calls to the Vegetarian Society of the U.K. (VSUK), which had tripled to 150 during the peak of the pig crisis, are beginning to dwindle. The agricultural interests remain unimpressed with the hoopla. "People predicted [a decrease in pork consumption] would happen with the release of the movie *Babe*," noted Anne-Marie Farmer of the British Pig Association. "But there was no fall at all. In fact, consumption went up slightly."

However, countered VSUK spokesperson Steve Connor, "Things like the Butch and Sundance escape do have an impact, but the effect is very gradual." Still, he added, "Many people now just don't feel able to face their bacon sarnies in the morning."

So, that's good.

Death Row Pardon

KIT PARAVENTI

❜❜Oregon can be the cruelest place on earth if you have four legs and wag your tail." The words, intoned by *Hard Copy* correspondent Doug Bruckner, introduced the show's fifteen million viewers to the story of Nadas, a dog slated for death by a longstanding Oregon law. As the show aired, Eric Mindel, the executive director of Last Chance for Animals (LCA), was poised over a fax machine, waiting for the ensuing storm of public disapproval to peak. In his hands was a last-ditch proposal to the Jackson County Commission outlining conditions for Nadas' pardon. In the meantime, Nadas, a friendly tricolored collie/malamute mix, waited in a concrete holding pen designated for the dangerous and doomed.

Nadas' odyssey began sixteen months earlier when his guardian, eighteen-year-old Sean Roach, chained him in the yard, roughed up his ears in a familiar farewell ritual, then headed for work at the family-owned storage company he ran with his mother. At some point, Nadas slipped out of the yard for a short but fateful romp through some adjacent properties in the rural neighborhood just south of Medford. Roach returned that afternoon to find Nadas safely back in the yard, but the damage had been done.

A thirteen-year-old neighbor claimed she'd seen Nadas chasing her family's horse. Despite Roach's protests that his dog had never displayed aggression or interest in livestock, a judge condemned Nadas to die, citing a law designed to protect "food" animals from domestic dogs. The statute is responsible for the deaths of hundreds of dogs annually.

Roach and his mother, Sharon, embarked on a desperate and unprecedented crusade to save Nadas' life. They linked with attorney Robert (Reb) Babcock and his wife, Gail O'Connell-Babcock, Ph.D., a dynamic duo in statewide animal protection issues. Babcock, who represented the Roaches free of charge, led the ensuing series of legal and promotional skirmishes. Nadas' main adversaries emerged as the predominantly livestock industry-supported county commission and an indifferent court system. Unfortunately, appeals did little more than stall the death sentence.

In 1997, Mindel spotted the story on the Internet. As Babcock's last bid for mercy and reason was rejected by the state's judicial system, LCA joined with Bob Schlesinger of ArkOnline, Roger Troen of Cascade Defenders of Animals, and other activists to bring the matter to the court of public opinion. A *National Enquirer* article was the first in a furious volley of bad press to batter the state of Oregon.

The coverage triggered a counter-offensive designed to vilify Nadas and Roach. The spelling of "Nadas" (taken from a champion skateboarder) was altered by county officials. In press statements, they misspelled the name as "Natas," claiming that it spelled "Satan" backwards. A barrage of what Mindel calls "trash articles" cropped up in the local press, alleging that Roach was guilty of everything from dereliction to devil worship. "It's hard to believe how many lies they were willing to make up," he recalls.

A week before Nadas' February 17 execution date, a *Hard Copy* story brought more than 500,000 responses to the show's web site and phone lines. Mindel, who had hoped to capitalize on the timing to pressure the commission into considering his proposal, hadn't anticipated that the storm of outrage would end up crashing the Jackson

County administration's phone and fax systems. Unable to transmit the document, Mindel and LCA founder Chris DeRose began a desperate race, first to find a way to get the proposal to the commission, then to negotiate its terms.

It was not until the second in a series of Hard Copy stories aired that county commissioners relented. Although Los Angeles Times TV columnist Howard Rosenberg derided the stringent conditions imposed on the pardon as "surreal," Nadas would live: he would be shipped to Best Friends Sanctuary in Utah, remaining there for the rest of his days without the possibility of adoption. In exchange for his dog's life, Roach agreed not to sue the county or its representatives for any of a variety of causes, ranging from illegal search and seizure to defamation of character.

Meanwhile, Babcock and O'Connell-Babcock are spearheading Stop Killing Our Dogs, a voter initiative campaign to amend Oregon's dog-killing statute. They're calling on state groups and voters to assist them.

The final Hard Copy episode about the case featured the poignant reunion of Roach and Nadas at the Best Friends Sanctuary a few days after the dog's arrival. Cowed by sixteen months of confinement, Nadas greeted him with shy hesitancy. He sniffed Roach's hand, then ducked away. Approaching again, he paused, sudden recognition lighting his eyes. The scene gave way to yelping, wagging, kissing doggy ecstasy as Nadas threw himself into the arms of the man he loved.

Mindel reflected on the sweetness of the hard-won victory. "LCA has been made out to be the hero in this case, mostly because of our Hard Copy involvement," he said. "But Nadas would have been killed long ago without the countless activists in Oregon. They saved Nadas, and now they're changing the law."

Editor's note: The state of Oregon passed a law in 1999 that requires all counties to hold hearings on dog-chase cases, and establishes a graduated penalty system that shifts the focus to the dog guardian rather than the dog.

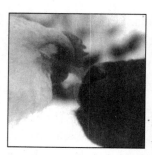

Lilly
MATT KELLY

S olitude. Captivity. Fear. Hunger. Pain. And for twenty-five cents, ridicule and domination. These are the feelings a chicken named Lilly had experienced for most of her time on earth. The life of a chicken inside an arcade machine, all for the amusement of unfeeling humans. Amazingly, this real-life nightmare did not break her spirit.

Eight Mott Street is not a notable address in New York City's Chinatown, but it was Lilly's home for years. Inside a dingy tic-tac-toe machine, not knowing day from night, week from month, Lilly lived. She was fed only when someone felt the urge to spend a quarter to be entertained by a "dumb" chicken trying to scratch out tic-tac-toe. The arcade had been a target of animal rights activists for more than twenty years, to no avail.

After hearing about the "Chinatown Rooster," as Lilly was first called, I really wanted to rescue her. My wife, Mary, and I have a bit of land in Massachusetts where we have made a bird sanctuary. Sure, we had room for one more deserving soul! I contacted a friend, T.W., to check out the situation. She has been an animal lover, rescuer, and activist since before I was born. She was shocked at the filthy condition in which Lilly was kept, and how the poor bird was being forced to play the stupid game before a group of gaping people in order to get food. It moved T.W. to tears.

T.W. found the manager, Mr. Samuel, in his booth, making change for customers. T.W. gives a very good appearance as a sweet old lady, conservatively dressed and well educated. The noise in the arcade was so loud that they could barely communicate. T.W. begged Mr. Samuel for Lilly (the name T.W. had given the hen). She told him of a beautiful home with other chickens where this tortured bird could live with peace, respect, and companionship. Mr. Samuel asked her to come back in a month, but she pleaded that she had a ride for the bird in a few days. He told her to come back in a week. She remained polite, but very firm; she assured him the bird would not be abused, eaten, or harmed in any way. He then said he needed a moment to pray on it.

After a few minutes of silence, Mr. Samuel said, "Take the chicken!" He explained that he did this because it was the first time anyone had treated him like a human being in regards to the chicken. He said he had been picketed, screamed and cursed at, and threatened with fire and destruction and all manner of violence. No one had ever asked nicely. He had actually felt bad for the chicken for a long time, and felt guilty about the whole situation.

Lilly rode home with T.W. that night in a taxi. Lilly seemed thrilled to walk on carpet; it was the first time she didn't have wire under her feet. Lilly also got a much-needed bath. When given food, Lilly still pecked at the walls before eating, as she was used to, thinking this was where her food was supposed to come from.

When another friend rented a car just to drive Lilly and another rescued bird to us, we were ecstatic. Lilly is a white hen with a big floppy comb who looks to be around ten years old. She loves attention, and to be stroked and petted. She seemed fascinated with the other rescued birds. She must have picked up and tasted 100 different pieces of hay! We placed her in a pen with our most mellow birds. It was immediately apparent that the other birds (even the two roosters) were going to give her the top spot of the pecking order right off. It might have been because she had the tallest stature, or has all of her beak intact, or maybe because she had been freshly bathed and was a dazzling white. Not a feather was ruffled on anyone, a true "coop" de grace. What a gentle soul she is!

Back at the arcade, Mr. Samuel keeps framed pictures of Lilly in her new home posted in his change booth. He is very happy about Lilly. We had heard from another animal lover in the city that the tic-tac-toe machine was seen smashed in a garbage pile. We commend Mr. Samuel for this.

Nowadays, Lilly spends her time doing what she loves: dustbathing, sunning herself, chasing bugs, and scratching in the dirt.

She does what chickens were meant to do, and is surrounded by comrades. She will live out her life in our little poultry community with as much peace and love as we can give her.

Editor's note: Sadly, Lilly died in 1999. See the profile on Matt and Mary Kelly in Section Three.

Lobsters are prepared for release (above) while Lorraine Nicotera helps one acclimate to a new environment (right)

Homeward Bound
KIRSTEN ROSENBERG

For the five lobsters imprisoned in a tank in a Cambridge, Massachusetts, supermarket, August 8, 1998 was the day their lives took a turn for the better, thanks to members of the Boston Resource for Animals, Vegetarians, and the Environment (BRAVE) who rescued the creatures and returned them to the wild.

Although the activists had hoped to convince the Bread and Circus market to freely surrender the lobsters in a gesture of good will (and good public relations, since the chain has come under fire from animal advocates for its recent acquisition of lobster tanks), the price to be paid for freedom was a non-negotiable $90. "We did take seriously the fact that by buying the lobsters we were supporting, in a small way, the lobster industry, and not all of us were totally comfortable with that," explained BRAVE member Jane Wamback. Hopefully, they will be able to get lobsters donated in the future, said Richard Griffin, the group's founder, and make this event the start of a tradition.

Yet this mission of mercy was not executed in haste. The group had planned well in advance, even calling in a renowned and experienced lobster liberator to oversee the operation. Ophelia Esereth, a New Hampshire activist who had done "hundreds of lobster liberations," according to Griffin, led a workshop for the would-be crustacean crusaders, covering such topics as how to transport the lobsters and what kind of ocean habitat to release them in.

Once the lobsters were sprung from their grocery store gloom, the rescue team—Esereth and seven members of BRAVE—carefully packed the shellfish in coolers according to plan: first "blue ice" packs were placed on the bottom, followed by wet newspapers, then the lobsters were placed on top covered by more wet newspaper. After an hour-and-a-half drive, the lobsters and their support crew arrived at the release sight, a semi-secluded beach in New Hampshire. Although the lobsters seemed "lively and ready to go," said Griffin, they were first placed in shallow water so they could adjust to their new environment and the activists could remove the rubber bands binding their claws. Now, free from bondage, the crustaceans were led (or rather, gently carried) to the promised water, to freedom, to their home in the Atlantic.

Because it was important for the lobsters to be released among seaweed and rocks (where they would naturally reside), the liberators ventured far out on slippery rocks before letting the lobsters slip from their hands into the sea. "Stay away from traps, live a long life, be happy," were Griffin's parting words to his nameless charges. (Two of the five lobsters were large enough so that they could not legally be kept if caught.)

Not surprisingly, the liberated lobsters were not the only ones to benefit from this experience. "Normally, those of us who are sensitive to the plight of lobsters tend to avoid lobster tanks in supermarkets. But on lobster liberation day we were free to get a close look at these marvelous creatures without the discomfort we usually feel," Wamback shared. For Griffin, taking part in this action allowed him to feel a sense of connection to "these wonderful animals."

"It was the highlight of my summer," he added.

Saving Sasha
Pat Derby

The air was cold and the landscape bleak as Ed Stewart and Performing Animal Welfare Society (PAWS) volunteers came to Hiles, Wisconsin, on September 15, 1998 to rescue Sasha, a fourteen-year-old black bear known as "The Gas Station Bear." After many years of confinement and mistreatment, Sasha was finally going to a safe and permanent home at the PAWS sanctuary in northern California.

The dream of this move had become a reality thanks to years of hard work by Wisconsin's Alliance for Animals and by Renee Ladd and Dixie Olsen, dedicated activists from Hiles who launched the effort, raised public concern, and got media attention for Sasha's plight. After enough public pressure was brought to bear, Sasha's "owner," Rick Munz, ultimately allowed the Alliance to buy her freedom for an undisclosed sum. As part of the deal, Munz signed a legally binding statement that he would never replace her.

Sasha had spent all her life in a ten-by-twenty-foot cement enclosure at Munz's Northern Outpost, a gas station/convenience store that served as a truck stop, beer store, and provisioner for local hunters. She was purchased as a cub from Weber's Wildlife Park, a local breeding facility that also breeds coyotes, raccoons, and other animals. Sasha's pen was located just 100 feet from the highway and a mere forty feet from where rattling tractor-trailer rigs pulled in for gas. Sasha clearly did not like trucks; she paced more rapidly each time one thundered by.

Sasha was fed low-grade dog food, table scraps, and pastry. Visitors could supplement her diet by feeding her Kool-Aid and M&Ms from dispensers outside her dirty pen. According to Tina Kaske of Alliance for Animals, "I would go and visit her and she would just moan. I've never heard a bear make a sound like that."

Stewart and the PAWS volunteers were accompanied by a driver and a horse trailer, a last-minute substitution for the special truck that was supposed to be waiting at the Minneapolis airport but was not. In the trailer was a state-of-the-art, 1,000-pound aluminum enclosure that would house and protect Sasha during her trip to her new home. Stewart and his crew laboriously hauled the crate up to the cage and began the long process of loading Sasha into her traveling quarters. Says Stewart, "Sasha was one of the most cautious animals I've ever seen. Walking into the traveling crate represented a real risk to her." Stewart got one of the local people whom Sasha knew and asked her to stand on the far side of the new enclosure to call Sasha and offer her treats. Several hours passed before Sasha began to trust the procedure. Onlookers held their breath as she put one foot, then another, into new enclosure.

Suddenly, a Jeep roared onto the scene, startling Sasha and the onlookers. To everyone's horror, a freshly killed bear was strapped across the tailgate. Several hunters jumped out of the vehicle, popped beer cans, and began stringing up the bear to tag and measure him. One look at the grisly scene was enough for Sasha—she withdrew into her pen and began an agitated pacing. The loading process would have to begin all over again.

It took several more hours to regain Sasha's trust. Gradually, she entered the crate and the trailer set off for the airport, where a Federal Express plane took her to California.

Sasha made her trip to PAWS easily and with little stress. Upon her arrival she was released into a spacious 3,500-square-foot grassy enclosure that includes hills, trees, flowers, and a swimming pool. She had never seen grass or landscaped ground in her life, and she reacted at first with fear and suspicion. For days she stayed near the enclosure's fence, fearing to move farther than a few feet in any direction. After all, those had been the dimensions of her life since the day she was born.

Says Stewart, "Everyone wants to rescue animals. But it is important to remember that these trips aren't easy for the animals.

They don't just walk into their new enclosures and live happily ever after. They have to overcome the fear and trauma of totally new conditions."

Sasha has started to relax at PAWS and each day she explores more of her enclosure. Her favorite foods are carrots, oranges, grapes, plums, and apples. She has not yet discovered her pool and, even when she does, it may take her a while to understand what it is for. Sasha will eventually be joined by Lenny, a brown bear and longtime sanctuary resident; he will provide just the kind of help Sasha needs to learn how to use her pool and climb the hills. (Lenny is neutered—there is no breeding at the sanctuary.)

Thanks to the hard work of animal advocates all over the country, Sasha's nightmare is finally over. She can now enjoy the peace and dignity she has always deserved. PAWS's staff will be with her every day to help her walk—one step at a time—into her new life.

Editor's note: Sasha is thriving on a healthy diet in her new home, which she shares with an orphaned black bear named Cindy.

No Little Piggies Went to Market

LORRI BAUSTON

After a showdown between animal rights supporters and members of the pork industry, 167 abandoned pigs have found permanent sanctuary from slaughter.

The pigs were being transported from a factory farm in North Carolina (the country's largest pork-producing state) to a Pennsylvania slaughterhouse. En route, on October 1, 1998, the driver abandoned the triple-decker trailer on a Washington, D.C., street, leaving the animals in the hot sun without water or basic care. Local residents notified the police and the Washington Humane Society, which seized the trailer. Shortly after midnight the pigs were towed an hour away to the Poplar Spring Animal Sanctuary in suburban Maryland.

Animal activists worked tirelessly throughout the night to remove the terrified pigs from the trailer. Most of the animals were too frightened to move, trembled uncontrollably, and had trouble walking. One volunteer recalled, "I'll never forget when I first saw the pigs in the truck, because I have never seen fear in an animal's eyes the way I did in those pigs. But once they were off the truck, they were no longer afraid of us...it was an amazing transformation."

The next day, agents from the Hanor pork company and their legal counsel arrived at Poplar Spring with local police to retrieve the pigs. Hanor's representatives were asked to provide a cash payment of more than $10,000 to cover the costs associated with caring for the animals. In lieu of making the payment, Hanor agreed to sign the pigs over to the sanctuary, which was represented by attorney Laura Nelson of the Animal Legal Defense Fund.

Authorities decided not to bring criminal charges against the Hanor Company for abandoning the pigs, although the truck driver may face misdemeanor animal cruelty charges. Hanor's biggest penalty was the loss of the approximately $14,000 market value of the pigs.

The pigs—who had spent their entire lives confined in small indoor pens, unable to walk or even lie down comfortably—are now roaming greener pastures. For the first time they are free to romp and root, play with other pigs, and sleep in comfortable straw beds. No longer afraid of people, the pigs now roll over for belly rubs at the touch of a hand, and look so happy that some seem to actually be smiling.

Once they have fully recovered, more than half of the pigs will be transported to PIGS, a sanctuary, in West Virginia and to Farm Sanctuary's New York facility. The three sanctuaries are coordinating a massive adoption project to provide lifelong care for all of the rescued pigs, and are seeking homes and funding to complete the project.

Editor's note: After a brief convalescence, 103 of the pigs went to the PIGS sanctuary, forty went to Farm Sanctuary, and two were adopted by attorney Laura Nelson. The rest (except for one injured male who was euthanized) are living happily at Poplar Spring, and now weigh 500–600 pounds each.

Belka's Longshot
Kirsten Rosenberg

What are the odds a greyhound will make it out of the U.S. dog-racing industry alive? Not good, given that more than 20,000 healthy greyhounds are killed each year for simply not running fast enough. And what if that greyhound races at Greenetrack, one of the country's worst tracks, where an average of 150 dogs die each month and which also happens to be the largest supplier of live greyhounds to research institutions? Her chances of avoiding a bullet to the head, being bludgeoned to death, electrocuted, or facing the vivisector's scalpel are just about nil.

But Belka beat the odds.

Ever since Sam Jaffe saw a TV program about the plight of greyhounds, he and wife Miyung Kim knew they wanted to share their lives with one. But it wasn't until the couple bought their first house a few years later that they were able to have a dog in addition to their three cats. So the day after they moved in, Jaffe wasted no time sending an application to the National Greyhound Adoption Program (NGAP) in Philadelphia. And that's how they came to meet Belka.

The two-and-a-half-year-old brindle-colored female was one of 200 racers rescued in September 1998 from Greenetrack in Eutaw, Alabama's second poorest county. Dubbed the "killing field" by many, the track also has the dubious distinction of having a serious bacterial disease named after it (Greenetrack Disease, also known as Alabama Rot).

When an attempt to reinstate live racing proved to be a financial failure, track officials closed the season early, and several individuals and organizations from around the country—including NGAP, the Greyhound Protection League, the American Society for the Prevention of Cruelty to Animals, The Ark Trust, Inc., and PetsMart Charities, Inc.—mobilized to save the more than 350 dogs kenneled there. (Sadly, activists were unable to save 160 of the dogs from being shipped to other low-end race venues.)

By the time Kim and Jaffe met Belka at NGAP in November, a missing front toe (amputated because of infection) and a healing abscess on her hip were the only physical signs of her ordeal. In addition to her injuries, Belka had epilepsy. But that didn't faze Kim and Jaffe; they wanted to adopt a dog who might otherwise have trouble finding a home. In fact, that day they returned home with two "special needs" dogs: Belka and sweet but high-strung Leo, another former racer who was returned to NGAP after a previous adoption didn't work out.

Despite being abused by the racing industry, Belka, like so many greyhounds, remained friendly and trusting. Yet she still had to adjust to her new lifestyle. At mealtimes, Belka would bolt down her ample ration and then root around almost frantically looking for more. It was clear to Kim that the dog was used to never getting enough to eat at the track. Belka also took a long time to become housetrained. But perhaps most troubling of all was that Belka never wagged her tail.

Happily, times have changed. The dogs' daily routine goes like this: eat, sleep, play, sleep, play, eat, sleep. Fortunately, Jaffe works at home and can let the dogs out into the back yard to chase and wrestle each other as often as they please. Perpetually playful, Belka loves to toss her rope toy into the air and then catch it—tail now wagging all the while.

Saving Trudy

CAROL MCKENNA

Trudy the chimpanzee was wearing a diaper and blue romper when primate rescuers Jim and Alison Cronin arrived to collect her from the home of British circus trainer Mary Chipperfield. The two-year-old was so lethargic she was like a rag doll, and had suffered disfiguring injuries. "The tips of two fingers on her left hand were missing," said Jim, "and the tip of a toe from her right foot. She also had a lump on her head."

The Cronins were on an emergency rescue mission for the police, who had decided to confiscate Trudy after seeing evidence obtained by Animal Defenders during an eighteen-month undercover investigation which began in 1996. The Cronins were asked to care for Trudy at their forty-acre Monkey World sanctuary in Wareham, Dorset, England. This was the start of a court case that would outrage and mobilize the British public. It would also bring about the downfall of Mary Chipperfield, a member of the 300-year-old Chipperfield Circus dynasty.

On the drive to Monkey World on April 22, 1998, Trudy didn't make a sound and never moved. Jim recalled, "She was typical of the chimps we've rescued from beach photographers who had been beaten into submission. Chimps work out that if you do nothing you're not noticed. It's like children who've been beaten."

Chipperfield's husband, Roger Cawley, told the Cronins that Trudy was a like a member of the family. But the undercover video of events at the circus's winter quarters showed a different story. It led to Chipperfield being convicted of twelve counts of cruelty against Trudy as a result of three beatings in five days, and to Cawley being convicted at the same time for cruelty toward an elephant.

At the Chipperfield compound, Trudy was kept isolated from other chimps and made to sleep in a dog carrier inside a dark, unheated barn. She spent up to fourteen hours a day in the crate and was fed garbage scraps. Her only comfort was an orange ball with a smiling face.

Watching the tape, the court heard and saw Chipperfield beating the eighteen-month-old chimp with a riding crop when she wouldn't go to bed. Chipperfield also kicked Trudy in the back up to fifteen times while holding her by the arm. At one point, Chipperfield took away the orange ball, saying "You can bloody cry." As the video fades away, Trudy sobs.

World-renowned chimpanzee expert Jane Goodall said in court that Trudy was "vocalizing fear and a kind of despair" as Chipperfield chased and beat her. Goodall said Trudy was "dealt with in a harsh, totally inappropriate, and cruel fashion," and asked how Trudy could be expected to "learn anything about chimp behavior in a barren, sterile, inappropriate, and cruel environment?"

And indeed, according to the Cronins, Trudy was "the shell of a chimpanzee" upon her arrival at Monkey World. Unable to relate to her own kind or even play like a normal primate, she would gather a ball of straw around her and rock for hours staring into space.

Alison kept a diary about Trudy's rehabilitation. For the first ten days Trudy was put in a room on her own with chimps occasionally visiting her. She was introduced to Sally, a mother to eleven adopted chimps. "She clung to us and looked at Sally as if she were from Mars," Allison recalled. "She was scared to death. Sally held out her arms and tried to cuddle her—to no avail." After Sally there were other playmates, and Trudy slowly responded. The turning point came when she was introduced to Peggy, who is now Trudy's surrogate mother. Trudy adores her, and travels around on her back.

By the time the court hearings started in January 1999, Trudy had become a fully integrated member of a troop of twelve chimps. The cruelty convictions came on Trudy's third birthday. But in a horrifying turn of events, it was announced that Mary Chipperfield planned to fight to have Trudy returned to her.

The Cronins launched a "Trudy Defense Fund" and the media led an outcry. Letters were received from as far afield as Australia. Jim argued, "It would be a terrible thing to rip her away from here given that she has been adopted by a female and has brothers and sisters now. If they did try to rip her away, her new chimpanzee family would defend her."

In April, when Chipperfield was finally sentenced with a fine of $12,225 for cruelty to Trudy (and ordered to pay an additional $19,951 for court costs), she announced through a statement by her attorney that "[t]he monkey will stay with its new owners...they can keep the monkey."

Animal Defenders continues to campaign for a ban on animal circuses, and for legislation to protect all performing animals. Director Jan Creamer said, "Mary Chipperfield's conviction is representative of a culture of violence that exists across the board for circus and performing animals, simply because legislation does not protect them. Acts of abuse and neglect against these animals will continue until legal loopholes are addressed."

Trudy, at least, is safe at Monkey World. She has a mother, brothers, sisters, aunts, and uncles just like she would in the wild. Said Jim, "She has been given the right to be a chimp again and to be with her own kind."

Miracles and Joy

CAROL BUCKLEY

Shirley, an Asian elephant who has spent most of her fifty-two years performing in front of audiences all over the world, recently was retired to The Elephant Sanctuary, a natural habitat pachyderm refuge in Hohenwald, Tennessee.

Shirley has a beleaguered past. At age five she was captured from the wilds of Asia and purchased by the Kelly-Miller Circus. In 1958, while the circus was traveling through Cuba, Fidel Castro seized power and the entire circus was held captive by Castro's forces for several weeks before being set free. A few years later, her circus ship was docked in Nova Scotia when a fire broke out in the engine room. The ship sank and two animals were killed, but luckily Shirley was rescued without harm.

In 1977, at age thirty, Shirley's circus career finally came to an end after another elephant attacked her. The incident left Shirley's right leg shorter than all the others, causing everyday life to be somewhat difficult. It was after this that the Louisiana Purchase Gardens and Zoo in Monroe, Louisiana, kindly took in the injured elephant despite the possibility that patrons might assume her condition was caused by negligence on the part of the zoo.

Captive female elephants usually are kept in groups, but for safety concerns related to her injury, Shirley was kept apart and had lived alone for the past twenty-two years. Then, after the zoo curator saw a piece about The Elephant Sanctuary on television, he contacted us. I explained to him that while elephants confined in small spaces can become aggressive out of frustration, those that have access to open expanses are able to avoid confrontation and live together peacefully. Having assured him that Shirley would not be at risk living among the sanctuary's other three elephants, the decision was made.

On July 6, 1999, Shirley's friends from the zoo helped welcome her to the sanctuary. Also on hand were local media and a crew from Argo Films, which is filming a documentary about the sanctuary for National Geographic. As the specially equipped elephant transport truck slowly turned into the grounds, all eyes were riveted and hearts thumped as we waited for our new girl to arrive. The truck backed up to the door of the new barn, the back door of the truck was opened, and a soft ramp of hay was created so that Shirley could exit gently. But she didn't move! She wasn't sure she wanted to go anywhere else. Finally Shirley backed out safely, and the last chain she will ever wear was removed from her leg.

Shirley was placed in the barn where she was greeted with a basket of goodies and a cooling shower. Her loving caretaker at the zoo,

Solomon James, Jr., accompanied Shirley to her new home. Solomon was very impressed with the facility and expressed joy that Shirley would be able to spend her remaining years in such a wonderful environment.

After Shirley rested for a few hours, Tarra, the sanctuary's first resident and "First Lady," was allowed to visit. Shirley and Tarra liked each other right from the start! Everyone watched in joy and amazement as the two intertwined trunks and made "purring" noises at each other. Shirley very deliberately showed Tarra the injuries she had sustained at the circus, and Tarra sympathetically inspected each one.

Much later in the evening, after the gate was opened, another elephant, Jenny, came into the barn. Jenny and Shirley were both at the same circus when Jenny was a calf and Shirley was thirty years old, and were separated for twenty-two years. There was an immediate urgency in Jenny's behavior. Divided by two stalls, she desperately wanted to get close to Shirley and became agitated. She began banging on the gate, and the two roared in unison. The interaction was dramatic, to say the least, with both elephants trying to climb in with each other and frantically touching each other through the bars.

We opened the gate and let them in together, and they became immediately inseparable. On their first day together they moved side by side, and when Jenny lay down, Shirley straddled her in the most protective manner and shaded her body from the sun and harm. Their relationship is intense, and resembles that of mother and daughter.

Since their reunion, Shirley and Jenny are virtually never apart: swimming together, napping head to tail, and continually touching, caressing, and vocalizing to each other. Tarra and the sanctuary's fourth refugee, Barbara, are included in the outpouring of affection and share in the happy reunion. They are transformed and have affected all of us in the most profound way. It is a miracle and joy to behold.

Cassie and Michelle's Comeback

KIRSTEN ROSENBERG

As Jamie Cohen followed the lab technician down the corridor of a Maryland animal research facility that day in May 1999, she didn't know what to expect. They passed several windowless rooms before entering a sterile room containing a cabinetlike structure on wheels with ten or so metal drawers. Each of the drawers housed two to three guinea pigs. Inside the ventilated compartments the bedding material was clean, but that was all there was—no toys to toss, no treats to enjoy, no straw to snuggle in. There were just scared animals: pregnant females, mothers with young, and stud males all being used in a project to analyze the protein and fat content of breast milk. They were all ultimately expendable, as any test tube would be.

Except these little pigs were different—different in that they were lucky. A caring lab worker, wanting to save the animals from death by carbon monoxide once they were no longer needed, contacted a local humane society, which referred the call to Judi Lainer of the Virginia-based Metropolitan Guinea Pig Rescue. With so many guinea pigs needing homes, Judi quickly notified a local network of animal rescuers. Jamie heeded the call, and the two traveled to the lab. As they entered the room, Jamie, a staunch animal rights activist, felt the quiet, nervous excitement of being "behind closed [laboratory] doors" for the first time. They had ten animal carriers between them and couldn't help "oohing and aahing at every precious little pig we picked up," recalls Jamie. They left with all thirty guinea pigs that day.

Jamie agreed to take four back to her Baltimore home to temporarily foster and have neutered, ending up with two girls and two boys. They had no names, only numbers in their ears, so she christened them Cassie, Michelle, John, and (you guessed it) Denny. And what could be more appropriate than naming them after The Mamas and the Papas? After all, that's what they were bred to be in the lab.

But the good times had yet to roll.

Two nights after her arrival, a very pregnant Cassie lay in her cozy hay-filled box, panting and clearly in distress. "I knew she didn't feel well because she let me pet her," said Jamie, who soon discovered that Cassie had just given birth to six dead babies. Alarmed, she rushed the animal to the emergency vet clinic where Cassie was treated for complications and sent home the next day to recover. It was during Cassie's convalescence that Jamie was able to make friends with the unsocialized, terrified creature. "She let me pet her because it was the path of least resistance," laughs Jamie.

Over the course of the next two weeks, Jamie noticed that Michelle's stomach was growing. Sure enough, an ultrasound revealed two live babies. Several days later, seven babies were born, but only two were alive. Yet Michelle showed no interest in her young, even stepping on them. They died within an hour; Jamie believes the mother must have instinctively known the newborns were doomed.

Although the male half of the quartet (now neutered) was transferred back to Judi while they waited to be adopted, the guinea pig midwife found that she couldn't part with the girls. So they joined the rest of Jamie's family, a lively mix of five guinea pigs, three rabbits, a dog, and a cockatiel.

Even though the new members assimilated well into the group, Jamie was still concerned the shy girls might never happily accept the human touch. And who could blame them, after life in the lab? But her fears dissipated as Cassie and Michelle gradually allowed her to reach down and touch their heads. In time, the two were able to forgive, if not forget, the harm done to them at the hands of humans.

Then life in the Cohen household really started groovin'. Although it took weeks for them to develop a taste for greens after having subsisted on lab pellets, "now they eat everything: corn on the cob, romaine lettuce, watermelon, oranges, oats, and they love bananas," reports Jamie. In the morning, it's oats and bananas for breakfast, and in the evening it's fresh veggies for dinner, eaten smorgasbord-style with the rest of the guinea pig gang.

After veterinary care to clear up a skin mite infestation, remove the corroded metal ID tags from their ears, and spay them, plus daily doses of vitamin C, the girls really blossomed. Their coats, much of which had fallen out due to the stress of their traumatic pregnancies, grew back thick and luxuriant. Now they happily putter about the living room, their nails lightly click-clacking on the wood floor as they go about their business, talking with the other pigs, munching leftovers, snoozing. Then there's always the couch, with its firm pillows that Cassie, being the more outgoing of the two, loves to climb and Michelle likes to hide behind.

And can they sing! Every morning when Jamie pours her cornflakes and soy milk into the bowl, Michelle, anticipating breakfast, will start in loudly, leading the others in a rousing chorus: *wheep, wheep, wheeeep!*

"California Dreamin' " it's not, but the pair have certainly made a comeback.

⟿

Purrfect Outcome for Hillgrove Cats

CAROL MCKENNA

"Sky and Freedom love to jump onto our knees for a cuddle," says Louise Koc. "They behave just like two young kittens even though they are two years old." Just a few months ago the two cats were confined in a group cage at Hillgrove Farm, the only establishment in the United Kingdom where cats were bred for experimentation. They didn't know freedom and hadn't seen the sky.

The Royal Society for the Prevention of Cruelty to Animals (RSPCA) rescued the cats from Hillgrove on the night of August 12,

1999, after owner Christopher Brown announced his retirement and asked for help placing the cats after failing to sell his business. In a twelve-hour operation, using a fleet of sixteen vans, the RSPCA vaccinated and microchipped 800 cats and kittens and moved them to a special holding center.

Brown's retirement came after thirty years of breeding cats for research and after an intense two-year campaign against his farm that included 350 arrests, twenty-one jail sentences, and a cost to local police of $4.8 million. He and his family received threats and were physically attacked on numerous occasions. The business had been lucrative. Kittens sold for $320–$480 and one-year-old cats for $640. Brown said after the closure, "They were gorgeous, lovely creatures. I will miss them terribly. It was always a pity they could not roam around the farm, but you see they had to be totally disease-free."

According to the government's Home Office, in 1998 more than 1,100 cats were subjected to experiments in U.K. laboratories. About half involved "fundamental" biological research; the rest were divided between veterinary research (such as the development of feline vaccines) and neurological experiments investigating the causes of Alzheimer's disease and motor neuron disease. In 1999, Animal Aid gave a Mad Science Award to a team of SmithKline Beecham researchers for experiments carried out on at least 100 cats supplied by Hillgrove. To test possible migraine drugs, anesthetized cats had tubes inserted into their blood vessels, holes cut in their skulls, and electrodes positioned in their brains so that an electrical current could be applied and various experimental drugs injected.

With Hillgrove out of business and no other U.K. supplier currently licensed to breed cats, there is concern about cats being imported to U.K. laboratories from countries where animal welfare standards may be much lower than those in Britain. However, 800 cats now have a bright future in loving homes rather than await a dark fate in a laboratory.

The RSPCA set up an emergency hotline seeking new homes for the Hillgrove cats, and the response was huge. RSPCA Chief

Veterinary Officer, Chris Laurence reports, "The cats are now at a holding center where they will be neutered. All of the cats from Hillgrove are healthy and used to human contact so they will be suitable for rehoming." As the cats were used to living in social groups, the charity decided that they would have to be adopted in pairs or to people who had cats already.

Louise was one of the 10,000 people who called the hotline. Sky and Freedom now live with her and husband, Tolga, on their narrow boat together with two rescue dogs—Inca, a chocolate Labrador cross, and Becky, a whippet cross—and Caffreys, a rat. Although they were timid at first when introduced to the domestic environment, the cats coped well and adapted. "Sky and Freedom are very playful," says Louise, "and get on well with our other animals, although Sky and Freedom certainly have the upper hand! Whilst they haven't ventured off the boat yet, they enjoy sunbathing on deck and are growing bolder every day."

A Lesson in Life
RACHELLE DETWEILER

A high school field trip turned into a life lesson for a group of students in October 1999 after a weekend visit to the Cox Creek organic farm near Guelph, Ontario. And in the process, about 250 rabbits, chickens, and pigs were saved from eventual slaughter.

"One of our concerns is that the kids would leave the program without utilizing the values they learned through us," said John McKillop, founder of the Bronte Creek Project, an alternative school in Toronto. He just wanted the students to learn the benefits of sustainable farming, and had teamed up with other area sch/ the Costa Rica 2000 program, an extracurricular enviro program sponsored by Earthtrek International. He didn't foresee that while visiting Mary Hopkins' farm to learn more about low-impact living before a spring ecological tour of Costa Rica, the students would take a vegan-focused educational session to heart and begin an animal rescue.

After seeing the farm's animals up close and listening to educational sessions about agriculture, the environment, and animals by Joseph Pace, a researcher active in animal rights causes, the teenagers and Hopkins all had a change of heart. The animals had sufficient space and adequate care on the farm, but each creature eventually would have been killed. At first, Hopkins—a former vegetarian—was leery about switching back to a plant-based diet and farming style and possibly going out of business. Fearing for the animals' lives, the students entered a partnership with Hopkins. The animals would be adopted and Hopkins would receive $2,500 to help her through the transition and repay some slaughterhouses that had already purchased some of the animals.

Six weeks after visiting the farm, the students had arranged for the release of all the animals. Four pigs now frolic at Hoofer's Haven near Thunder Bay, Ontario; the Fauna Foundation near Montreal is caring for the "broiler" chickens; Farm Sanctuary in upstate New York is tending to about 200 of the "laying" hens; and about ten rabbits were adopted by a kind man in Burlington, Ontario.

Even though the students did get some donations from such large animal rights groups as People for the Ethical Treatment of Animals and Animal Alliance that helped cover transportation and sanctuary expenses, they are still working to pay off about half of the money they owe Hopkins. The students are learning creative fundraising techniques and have even canvassed the bleachers at high school football games to get donations. "They're very idealistic," Hopkins said. "I was very pleased to see them do this. I was a former teacher and I think that their experience was invaluable."

Despite their success in saving these fortunate animals, the students realize that there is much to be done in order to help lessen animal suffering. "It was saddening when we moved the animals," said Jason Samilski, an eighteen-year-old who helped organize the mission. "I realized that this was just a small drop in the pail, because millions of animals are slaughtered each year."

Bray-ving a Battered Past
RACHELLE DETWEILER

From her vantage point, Susan Wagner could barely distinguish individual mules through the blur of animals rushed into a sale ring at the New Holland Sales Stables. What was clear were the three men who struck every mule forced into the arena. The Amish men goaded the creatures into place, faces against a wall and hindquarters pointing outward—a lineup in which lame or spry, healthy or sick mules all became indiscernible.

"I couldn't even see straight," recalls Wagner, president of Equine Advocates, when her eyes fell on an individual mule among the chaos. "I couldn't believe what they were doing to him." He was being prodded and beaten until his halter was imbedded at least one inch into his face, but Henry would be one of the lucky mules: he would find a safe home.

Since December 1999, Equine Advocates, a national nonprofit protection agency based in Flushing, New York, has bought fourteen mules at auctions in Lancaster County, Pennsylvania, and found them new homes throughout the Mid-Atlantic and the Pacific Northwest. Its campaign aims to heighten awareness that on some Amish farms, not just horses are used—and broken—like machines. Thousands of mules also are worked by some of the county's 19,000 Amish farmers and often befall the same fate of providing meat to European and Japanese food markets. The mules are bought by high-bidding "killer buyers" who work the auction circuit to supply the nation's four equine slaughterhouses. Five hundred mules moved through the New Holland Sales Stables that day in early March. Only seven narrowly missed being trucked to a slaughterhouse or worked to a premature death on another farm, but, of the whole bunch, Henry's the best at winning—and breaking—the hearts of everyone he meets.

Picking Henry (who is named for the late activist Henry Spira) was based more on a hunch than a thoughtful decision. In the confusion of the sale, Wagner said that she nabbed those mules with the least chance of survival. She picked an old mule on the end, another one with a gashed side, then a mule with a strained neck, and any other animal who seemed too dinged up to work. "I've been to many horse sales all over the country and many were worse than this one in terms of the conditions of the animals," Wagner says of the New Holland auction, where just three days later an emaciated Appaloosa horse was sold for just $5. "However, I have never since [seen] the type of cruelty and sadism in a sales ring as I witnessed in New Holland that day." Although the event had a festive air, with the animals' death march transformed into a social event, Wagner said that some Amish people were ashamed of how their culture perpetuates animal abuse. One such man befriended Wagner and helped bid part of the $30,000 that the organization raised for rescue efforts.

Today, the big-eyed and charismatic Henry isn't just munching sweets and frolicking at the North Fork Stables in Putnam Valley, New York; he stubbornly clings to his well-developed work ethic. This time his labors are for himself and other mules like him, and he's been helping people understand the terror mules face as they're moved through the auction ring. "People were weeping because he'd been so abused," Wagner recalls of one of Henry's first rounds of training during an Equine Advocates fundraiser. He was so skittish that he repeatedly tried to scramble over the roundpen, but within forty-five minutes, Bob Jeffery, a trainer who prefers to "get into horses' heads rather than use gadgets and tie downs," had calmed down Henry enough to rub the top of his head.

Henry still brays a bit nervously when he sees a shovel or when people approach him too quickly, but he's responsive and sedate during his daily routines, according to Carolyn Liverzani, who runs Henry's stable. He lets people touch his head, clip his feet, and comb his coat. He's also developing relationships with the other mule and the twenty-five horses who live at the stable. And as for the humans who have coaxed him toward a steady if not quite fully realized recovery, they say they notice a transformation after every hour spent with him. "You could see he wanted the treats in your hand, but as much as he wanted it, he just wouldn't come near," says Liverzani, who watches over Henry every day. "Emotional scars often are deeper than physical ones."

What the Cat Dragged Home
RACHELLE DETWEILER

Some say that cats have nine lives and swap one for each daredevil adventure. If that's the case, then Pyewacket—a tough tomcat from Maine—must have cashed in a few for this harrowing experience.

Pyewacket roamed the countryside near Fayette for about five years, living off handouts from eighty-nine-year-old Isabelle Moore, who says stray cats were always coming and going from the areas near her home. When the scruffy cat vanished, she thought he'd eventually come back, but when he did, she didn't expect him to bring along a heavy Conibear trap clamped tightly to his rear right leg.

He dragged himself and the trap up to the food bowl last Thanksgiving and began his winter of lugging around a one-pound metal trap that often left odd-shaped marks in the snow. Moore tried a few times to catch him, but kept failing until Ron Merrifield, a former Fayette animal control officer, set up a different type of trap for the cat: one that would help save his life. Pyewacket hobbled into the trap just two days after it was planted—about four months after the original trap latched onto his leg.

Even though many cats are killed or maimed each year by traps set for commercially valuable animals or those targeted as pests, Pyewacket's misfortune is astonishing to those people who repeatedly encounter such tales. "This cat was darn lucky and quite a survivor to last that long," says George Clements, the executive director of The Fur-Bearers, a Vancouver-based group that leads education campaigns on behalf of ensnared companion animals. "Many people don't know how to open the jaws of a Conibear trap, so people have their cats and dogs die in front of their eyes." Stumbling into an older trap intended for a smaller animal was one of the graces that saved some of Pyewacket's lives.

Soon after the cat arrived at the Kennebec Valley Humane Society (KVHS) in Augusta, a vet removed the trap from his leg, took x-rays, and treated his injuries. After expressing shock and concern about Pyewacket's condition, the staff began marveling that he survived so long in a trap, would keep all four legs, and didn't even have a single broken bone. "We were excited when he recovered so quickly," says KVHS Executive Director Deb Clark. "We thought we'd get a happy ending."

That positive outlook was tempered once the vets at Pine Tree Veterinary Hospital announced that Pyewacket tested positive for feline immunodeficiency virus (FIV), a contagious disease that he most likely caught while living in the wild. Finding an adoptive person for this heroic cat was more difficult than they had imagined. "This was a high-profile case," Clark says. "But not many people came out for Braveheart [Pyewacket's former name] like they do for dog stories. It shows how people think that cats are a dime a dozen."

The couple who "came out" for Pyewacket lived a bit farther away than would be expected; they cashed in frequent-flyer miles, bought a round-trip ticket from Seattle to Boston, and, after many phones calls and planning, Brian Zick flew across the country to pick up the once-wayward animal from the shelter workers who had driven the cat down from Maine. A coordinator for Washington's "Yes on Initiative 713" campaign to pass a state ballot measure banning cruel traps and poisons—for which Zick and Cath Fisher were among the top volunteer signature-gatherers—tipped the couple off about the cat's plight. The pair quickly agreed that jetting across the country was a small sacrifice to help an animal. "We initially wanted the cat, and I thought, 'No, I can't let this little guy slip away,' " Zick says about the spunky cat who can get wound up and dive-bomb ankles and arms to show his affection.

Soon Fisher was greeting the big, fluffy feline and Zick at the airport after their return flight from Boston. Once the couple got him home, Pyewacket, who was named after a scrappy street cat in a children's book of the same name, rapidly took a liking to the dogs and the other FIV-positive cats living in his new home outside Seattle. Now Pyewacket's leg is working fine and his adaptation to humans makes his adopters wonder if he was ever really a full-fledged feral. They say that he's just a guy who wants a little love since he has overcome his struggles, and that his story rarely fails to make others marvel.

"Some people think we're a bit over the edge when we talk about Pyewacket," Fisher says. "But people who are really into animals get it; they think it's great."

Running Like a Wolf

RACHELLE DETWEILER

For two seven-year-old hybrid wolves who were deemed unprofitable, being plac tirement left them barely c sanity inside a cramped dog run. Although they we traveling with an East Coast circus menagerie, the pair endured almost two years of intense boredom locked inside a barren six-by-six-foot enclosure.

"They were so neurotic that they were not pacing back and forth, they were literally running back and forth," recalls Jane Garrison, who coordinates captive-animal releases on behalf of People for the Ethical Treatment of Animals (PETA) and organized the wolves' release in October 1999. Now the pair has room to roam in a densely wooded one-acre enclosure at the Texas-based Wildlife Rescue & Rehabilitation, Inc. (WRRI).

A bear, a coyote, and a lion affiliated with the same circus also gained their freedom and were placed in various sanctuaries or zoos throughout the country, but the circus owner—who requested anonymity—currently retains eight big cats for his acts.

"He easily could have sold these animals to another circus or a hunting ranch," Garrison says, "but I told him that if he wanted to do right by these animals, he would help them." And after a few months of cajoling, the owner took a kinder turn and relinquished some animals, even after he was forced by PETA to ditch his original plan to sell all the animals and equipment. Garrison refused to pay for the release of the animals, and instead incurred about $1,000 in costs for their care and transportation to a more hospitable environment. For now the wild canines are living alone in their new home, while another wolf rescued from a similar situation stays in an adjoining area. When both sides are ready for further contact, sanctuary workers will remove the fence that separates them.

Because wolf-dog hybrids can be shy around humans, wooded enclosures with ample roaming area are extremely important, says Jen Westlund, program specialist at the Minnesota-based International Wolf Center. In the wild, wolves can travel up to forty miles each day; these hybrids traveled for twenty-three hours from just outside Washington, D.C., to such a home. Although the anxious male tried to gnaw his way out of the travel carrier, he eventually settled down nd relaxed during the cross-country journey. Once the pair arrived at the sanctuary, their seemingly peaceful state turned to cries and whines of what could have been happiness when they saw the heavily wooded preserve.

"Animals are initially very cautious, and these were no exceptions, but they are also very intelligent, and these wolves quickly realized how much their situation had improved," says WRRI founder Lynn Cuny. The animals peered out of the carrier and soon took off through their new home, investigating everything with their noses. The female even stretched up against a low-hanging tree and scratched away that itch that had been building up for so long before she and her companion disappeared into the undergrowth.

3: Unsung Heroes ∼

Introduction ∼ KIM W. STALLWOOD

EVERYBODY KNOWS ONE: THE LADY DOWN THE STREET who takes in strays; the letter-writer whose name regularly appears in the paper; the sign-carrying protester seen at rally after rally; the man who speaks up when the rest of the room stays silent. These are the people who stir the pot so those at the bottom of society don't burn. Whether their efforts on behalf of animals are local or global, regaled or ridiculed, they are the role models who keep the animal protection movement rolling.

There have been many unsung heroes in my life who helped me along the path to animal liberation. I particularly remember one whom I suspect did not even know I existed. Her name was Kate Ward.

As a young boy growing up in England, I remember an elderly Kate pushing her wooden cart filled with dogs, with many more tied by string to the cart's sides, the wrong way down the one-way main street of Camberley, my hometown. Through my young, impressionable eyes she was a fascinating figure. I knew no one else like her. She put her dogs first and did not care what others thought about her.

Years later, as I try to understand why I have chosen to dedicate my life to animal liberation, I think back to Kate Ward. The example of her lifelong commitment to animals made an impression on me that took years to develop.

There is no doubt in my mind that the actions of these unsung heroes, as previously seen on the pages of *The Animals' Agenda*, are also having a considerable impact on countless numbers of people with whom they come into contact—directly or indirectly—every day. It is surely our responsibility to match their example in our everyday actions toward establishing a free and just world for all beings.

Tony and Vicki Moore
KIM W. STALLWOOD

Vicki Moore couldn't believe what she read in the British newspaper *Today*. In a forthcoming Spanish fiesta, a donkey was to be drugged and forced to consume alcohol before being led by a cheering crowd through the packed streets of Villanueva de la Vera, a village 150 miles west of Madrid. The climax of the religious holiday was the drowning of the donkey in the village's fountain.

Vicki and her husband, Tony, had always cared for animals, filling up their Lancashire home with rescued cats and dogs. They served on the board of the local chapter of the Royal Society for the Prevention of Cruelty to Animals. They made their living as performers in nightclubs throughout Britain. But the horrifying thought of another donkey drowning among a frenzied mob haunted them until they felt they had no alternative but to intervene. Vicki was to go to Villanueva de la Vera before the fiesta to persuade the people to spare the donkey. Tony would stay at home to coordinate any media interest.

In 1987, the Moores had no idea their protest would catapult them into the headlines of the British media. Nor did they know they and their small organization, Fight Against Animal Cruelty in Europe (FAACE), would become internationally recognized as the English people who exposed Spain's cruel blood fiestas.

Surprised by the media army that accompanied Vicki, the people of Villanueva de la Vera quickly agreed to protect the donkey during future fiestas. Although the Moores wanted no donkeys to be involved in the fiesta, the donkey is now surrounded by a circle of human "guardians" as she passes through the village, and is never killed.

For more than ten years, the Moores have made repeated visits to Spain armed with nothing more than a video camera. Their video documentation of blood fiestas—events that involve decapitating chickens, castrating bulls, and tossing goats from church towers—has been broadcast throughout Europe on television and appeared in countless newspaper and magazine articles.

The Moores' investigations revealed the blood fiestas were not part of Spain's century-old traditions but were a recent spin-off organized by the bullfighting industry. Spaniards consider bullfighting an art, and 37,000 animals are killed annually in both bullfights and blood fiestas.

In 1995 Vicki was gored by a bull while she was videotaping a blood fiesta in the village of Coria. Vicki suffered eleven serious wounds, including eight smashed ribs; she lost one kidney and nearly died. It has taken her more than a year to recover, but Vicki's conviction to end Spain's blood fiestas is limitless. She was once again in Spain last summer videotaping more of the violent events.

In October 1996, Vicki and Tony visited the United States to speak at activist meetings organized by *The Animals' Agenda* in Baltimore, Maryland, and, in conjunction with *Satya*, in New York City. In Raleigh, North Carolina, the Moores inspired the audience at the annual festival organized by the Culture and Animals Foundation with their heroic efforts to document animal suffering.

Vicki and Tony personify the very best qualities of what it is to be an advocate for animals. Both in their public presentations and in their private conversations, they display a quiet but intense dedication to ending blood fiestas. They are not interested in being movement leaders or in building international organizations. Theirs is a special partnership committed to acting as witnesses to the animals' suffering. Their altruism and dedication is paying off as the European media increasingly rely upon the Moores as an honest and accurate source of information. Moreover, the Moores could so easily lack respect for the Spanish people, but they do not feel any hostility toward them. "I just wish their attitudes toward animals would change," Vicki said.

Editor's note: Sadly, Vicki Moore died on February 6, 2000, of complications from her 1995 injury. She was forty-four years old.

❧

Ladies of the Night

KIRSTEN ROSENBERG

It's 3 a.m. on a December morning when a police car slowly pulls up behind a vehicle idling in a dark alley in one of Baltimore's roughest neighborhoods. A muffled police radio can be heard for an instant as the car doors open and slam shut, then the sound of glass crunching under the officers' boots as they approach the vehicle. The car's occupants squint into the glare of the flashlights trained on their faces; a moment passes, then, suddenly, recognition: "Oh," says one of the officers, "it's the 'Cat Ladies.' " With that, the officers leave.

The "cat ladies" are Dee Patras and Stefanie Clay of Alley Animals, a small group committed to rescuing and feeding Baltimore's homeless animals. Founded by Alice Arnold in 1984, the group dispatches two-member teams every other night, regardless of weather, to traverse more than 385 alleys and feed approximately 3,000 animals per night. Alley Animals tries to adopt as many animals as possible; those remaining on the street are provided with sustenance. On call twenty-four hours a day, Alley Animals deals mostly with cats but also tends to dogs and other animals.

Tonight Patras and Clay begin their run at 11 p.m. With a car filled with dozens of pounds of food, a couple of traps and carriers, and me crammed in the back seat, we begin a thirteen-hour, fifty-mile journey through what feels like another dimension: a seemingly neverending maze of inner-city alleyways. The feeding and trapping is done under cover of darkness so as not to attract the curiosity of cruel teenagers or the ire of unsympathetic residents.

Patras, a horse trainer by day, has been doing this three nights a week for more than five years. "Homeowners are my worst enemy out here," she says. Adds Clay, "They get angry because they think the food is drawing the rats; never mind all the garbage everywhere." Indeed, virtually all the alleys are filled with broken glass and trash.

Both women are well aware of the dangers they face, but most of the time they don't feel fearful. "You can't be afraid of the dark," says veteran Patras. In the course of her duties, she has been Maced once and had a gun pulled on her twice. Clay, who works in the permissions department for Johns Hopkins University Press, has yet to experience such an encounter since she began six months ago.

In the dark, the web of filthy alleyways, boarded-up homes, and ramshackle houses takes on an apocalyptic quality. To the uninitiated eye, one alley looks like the next, and the distribution of food seems random. Yet the women follow a prescribed route: they know every alley they visit, each with one or more designated "drop" spots.

They know their cats, too, even though they don't usually name them. "C'mon, there's my girl....Psst, hey, whaddya doin' out in the street? You comin'? Good boy." Patras greets the regulars as she drives the car down the alley while Clay, from the passenger seat, plunges a cooking pot into a bag of cat food and then gently lobs the food out of the window at the proper location. With each drop, Patras whoops "Ka! Ka!" in cowgirl-like fashion to let the cats know that food has arrived. Several stray dogs receive allotments, as well, in addition to neglected dogs chained outside in cold, concrete yards. At the sight of a lone cat trotting down the sidewalk, Clay tosses the animal a hot dog in an effort to coax her back up the relatively safer alley.

Whenever possible the women lure a hungry animal into a box trap or carrier. Before taking a female, they make sure she is "clean"— not nursing young. "We have to pick up the 'friendlies' because they'll never make it out here," says Patras. In the early morning light, she shows me the shallow grave of a cat and her kitten killed by "fight" dogs set loose on them for practice. Later, in another alley, a boy with a Rottweiler on a leash eyes us as we pass through. Patras stops the car and rolls down the window: "You're not planning on running your dog on those cats, are you?" The boy gives a slight shake of the head. "Don't let me catch you," she retorts as we drive off.

When asked how they are able to continue such physically demanding, emotionally devastating work, night after night, for little remuneration, both are silent, as if they hadn't given much thought to how they could continue, only that they must.

It is nearly noon the following day by the time we hit all the spots. Somewhat reluctantly, I hand over the tabby kitten asleep in a towel on my lap—one of the six cats rescued during the night. I feel relieved that we have finished, and guilty because I know that the work never ends. The knowledge that these ladies of the night will return again and again to take care of Baltimore's thousands of street animals is both comforting and disturbing.

No, I don't eat meat
Yes, I get enough protein
No, my shoes aren't leather
Yes, I have a life!

Bill Dyer
LAURA A. MORETTI

He's...different. Not in some strange sense, but in his energy. He's relentless. Unstoppable. But die-hard activist Bill Dyer says he's just "making up for lost time."

Having spent most of his life in the entertainment business producing scripts for such television programs as *Columbo* and *The Mac Davis* Show, and writing lyrics for such performers Mitzi Gaynor, Diana Ross, and John Denver, Dyer didn't give animals a second thought.

But then a show business friend invited him to a demonstration against pound seizure at the San Bernardino Animal Shelter. "I knew absolutely nothing about animal rights," he recalls. There he met Last Chance for Animals Director Chris DeRose, and his life was changed forever.

"I think finding a cause gives meaning to one's life," he says. Later he heard philosopher/activist Tom Regan speak about factory farming, and he became a vegetarian that night.

Just as he relentlessly pursued his show business dream, Dyer is stalking a utopia for animals. In his own Southern California neighborhood, he led the fight to stop the slaughter of wild fowl in the Venice canals. One hundred demonstrators joined him to keep officials from killing 500 ducks and geese who were suspected of carrying the fatal virus enteritis. "We lost," he admits. "And all those killed [birds] tested negative for the virus."

But lost battles don't deter Dyer.

Last year, he became the Southern California Regional Director of In Defense of Animals (IDA). Through IDA, he's taken on the Japanese Consulate for its capture of wild orcas, the Los Angeles Zoo for its treatment of captive elephants, a demonstration at the University of California at Los Angeles for World Week for Animals in Laboratories, a Fur-Free Friday event in Beverly Hills, the cessation of the Santa Cruz sheep slaughter, and a ballot initiative that would ban trapping in the state of California.

In his spare time, while still writing successful plays, he works diligently on an anti-killing proposal for the local Department of Animal Services. "More than sixty-nine percent of the animals entering city shelters are killed," he's learned. "As Ed Duvin has said, 'breeding equals killing,' and it's past time to give it the same stigma furs and vivisection and other animal rights issues have."

On his horizon is another dream, a new and special one: The Animals' Museum. "In June of last year," he says, "during the March for Animals, I visited the Holocaust Museum and was so terribly moved, not only by the subject matter but by the way it was done." He has already founded the nonprofit entity that will make the Southern California-based museum a reality. "It will be an enormous task," he says, "but I am prepared for it because I strongly believe it can make a difference."

He is making a difference; he's just too busy to realize it. "I wish I were smarter and less emotional," he confesses. "Sometimes I know I have lost it and even admit to being a 'crazed animal activist' because most of this has driven me crazy." He may have spent more time in show business, but the meaning in his life comes from his true calling.

"At Radio City Music Hall," he remembers fondly, "Diana Ross once thanked me in front of a full house. Years later, Chris DeRose thanked me from the stage of the Federal Building in Westwood. I love Miss Ross," he adds, "but it was Chris's words that meant more to me."

His energy and relentlessness make him the envy of many. And yet, despite how much he's done in a short time, he regrets the past. "I recently watched *The Animals' Film*. I didn't want to see it, but now I'm glad I did, for I realized in the sixteen years since that documentary was made, I hadn't done enough." He reflects on the March for Animals. "I'm older now and wish I had started younger in our cause. That's what moved me so much in Washington, D.C.: the young people all yelling, 'Vegan Power!' They will see a change in their lifetimes."

They'll see significant strides in their lifetimes partly because of the work Bill Dyer has already done for orcas and monkeys and dogs and seals and cats and ducks and elephants—and from the relentless, unstoppable work he has yet to do.

≈

Linda Hatfield
KIT PARAVENTI

Linda Hatfield recalls stumbling upon a four-day-old fawn while searching for mushrooms with a hiking partner. Subtly, her voice changes from the self-assured tones of a seasoned animal activist to the lilting notes of a children's storyteller.

"It was just inches from my boot," she says. "It was so perfect, so clean." The fawn, trained by her mother to sink statuelike into the camouflage of her surroundings, simply stared back at the two humans with guileless curiosity. Unlike her companion, Hatfield was not surprised to discover the creature. "I have a knack for spotting animals in the wild. They seem to make their presence known to me," she explains. Although close encounters with raccoons, deer, and other wildlife are not uncommon for her, the experiences reaffirm her lifelong affinity for wild animals and her commitment to helping them.

Hatfield is one of the prime movers of Minnesota-based Friends of Animals and Their Environment (FATE). Together with founder Howard Goldman, she's spearheaded a successful drive to halt the wholesale capture and slaughter of migrating Canada geese, blocked dove hunting in Minnesota numerous times, and been instrumental in carving inroads into the state's entrenched fur industry. Described as a "tireless lobbyist" by Mike Markarian of The Fund for Animals, Hatfield has fueled and propelled FATE into a formidable, feisty, grass-roots "Little Engine That Could."

Ironically, she's a hunter herself. Hunting mushrooms is her passion, and trekking up and down the creekbeds and lushly forested slopes of her home state elevates and fortifies her buoyant spirit. It was in the mid-1980s when Hatfield, a part-time bookkeeper and freelance artist, was drawn into the wildlife animal protection movement by the fur and leghold trapping issue. "It was unbelievable," she recalls of the overwhelmingly pro-fur media presence. "They were holding fur fashion shows featuring the wives of local sports heroes."

It was then that she first encountered FATE—and Goldman, who was to become her longtime friend and mentor. In Minnesota, where an estimated twenty-seven percent of the adult population hunts, raising consciousness can be a back-breaking job. For years, Hatfield has helped local communities humanely deal with "nuisance" deer complaints by working with city councils to offer residents nonlethal options for resolving conflicts. Despite the enviable list of achievements Hatfield and Goldman have accrued, there's always the next challenge. Most recently, state senator Bob Lessard, a hunting outfitter by trade, introduced legislation to grant hunting the same protections as freedoms of speech, assembly, and other Constitutional rights. "The legislation reflects a very ugly national trend," says Hatfield. "Alabama has already adopted a similar measure, and approximately nineteen other states are showing signs of interest."

Another hot issue involves the fate of three orphaned black bear cubs whose mother was shot by a farmer. The three have been sent to the Mayo Clinic, where researchers want to conduct studies to determine why bears are able to maintain muscle and bone stores during hibernation. "The answer is simple," says Hatfield. "They're bears. They were designed that way."

As a lobbyist, Hatfield is a familiar sight to Minnesota legislators. Her articulate style, courtesy, tact, intimate understanding of the legislative process, and solid knowledge of the issues has earned her the respect of friends and foes alike. She "knows her stuff," says one colleague.

A recent decision by a federal court signaled a landmark victory for FATE and ended the recurring nightmare of a fifteen-year annual roundup of migrating Canada geese. In 1996, the Minnesota Department of Natural Resources (DNR) opened the floodgates to carnage based on hotly contested nuisance complaints. As a result, nearly 1,900 adult geese were captured and killed, their goslings caged and relocated. FATE, together with The Humane Society of the United States and the Minnesota Humane Society, launched a successful lawsuit that alleged that the U.S. Fish and Wildlife Service wrongfully authorized the state DNR to sanction the slaughter. In August 1997, the pro-animal coalition won. But they are still fighting a battle involving 260 geese the DNR rounded up from the Minneapolis-St. Paul International Airport over the summer. Claiming the birds can't be released because of the threat they pose to aircraft, the DNR plans to relinquish them to the University of Minnesota for research on goose meat contaminants. The birds' defenders argue that the geese should be cared for until they can be released in the spring.

With victories in hand and more no doubt to come, Hatfield's fate seems linked to FATE. Together with her husband, Garret, Andy the dog, and Casey the cat, Hatfield lives, lobbies, and still stalks mushrooms in the Minneapolis area.

〜

Sue McCrosky

Jill Howard Church

Anyone who thinks General William Sherman was the most formidable force to march down the streets of Atlanta hasn't met Sue McCrosky. At first glance she's a petite white-haired Southern lady with a calm voice and kindly air. But get her talking about vivisection, and Yerkes Regional Primate Research Center in particular, and you can feel the fires rise even if her voice doesn't.

McCrosky has been tirelessly leading the charge against Yerkes for twelve years, ever since a local humane society volunteer told her about how millions of taxpayer dollars finance experiments ranging from drug-addiction and maternal deprivation studies on monkeys to HIV infection in chimpanzees.

"I did not want to believe that our government would use our money for useless and senseless cruelty," she says. After reading mountains of documents about Yerkes, she says she realized that "there was absolutely nothing going on for human benefit at Yerkes except personal profit for the researchers." It riles her to know that even those who shun meat, fur, and other forms of animal cruelty unwillingly help pay for vivisection through taxpayer-funded agencies.

McCrosky and her husband, Mike, printed flyers and took to the streets outside the stone gates of Emory University, where Yerkes is hidden in a wooded section of campus. In 1993 she started a local chapter of Last Chance for Animals, and in 1994 led the first-ever civil disobedience demonstration at Yerkes, where she was among six activists arrested for blocking the road to the lab. She has since formed the group Animal Abuse Watch, aimed solely at fighting Yerkes. A former administrative assistant for Panasonic, she now devotes all of her attention to animal rights.

Her commitment to direct action was put to the test in April 1997 when more than 100 activists from across the country marched at Yerkes on World Day for Laboratory Animals. They were met by a police barricade and officers in riot gear. The activists had planned to once again block the road in a peaceful protest, but when they tried to cross the barricade they were grabbed by police and doused with pepper spray.

"Never before have they wanted to silence us the way they wanted to silence us that day," McCrosky recalls. She and sixty-four others were arrested and taken to DeKalb County Jail, where many of the activists held a hunger strike until being released pending trial. The incident made headlines and led television news reports in Atlanta and across the country, drawing further attention to the plight of animals at Yerkes.

McCrosky was arrested again in May 1997 for picketing near the home of Yerkes director Thomas Insel. She refused to post bond— "Why should we pay the system to exercise our right to speak?" she demands—and was sentenced to forty-five days in jail. As a final gesture of protest, she launched a twenty-day hunger strike that left her dehydrated, weak, and unable to walk.

"I have a right to speak for the animals," she says in her calm but steadfast tone. "When you take me away from everyone I love—family, animals—I've got one voice left, and I'm just ornery enough to use it." Her condition was worsened by the fact that the jail withheld her blood pressure medication and kept her alone in a cold cell with a faulty toilet and green water in the sink. She was hospitalized for a day and then returned to her cell, still refusing to eat and drinking only water and watered-down Kool-Aid.

Another prominent activist, Jean Barnes, organized support rallies outside the jail, and McCrosky became a local icon for issues of both animal rights and free speech. Says Barnes, "I think Sue is an effective activist because she is genuine. She takes risks. She practices what she preaches, and people respect that and want to follow that kind of inspiration." Always humble, McCrosky calls her support team her "heroes" and her husband her "lifeline." Her family and friends finally posted her release bond when they became fearful for her life, and she left the jail on September 23 physically weakened but spiritually recharged.

"I have a microscopic taste of what a lab animal endures," she says. "I got out of my cell—they don't get out of theirs."

At her October 3 trial, a judge sentenced McCrosky to six months in jail for the Yerkes demonstration. She remains free on appeal but must stay 500 feet away from Emory property. She believes her harsh sentence is politically motivated by the influential university, and she refuses to back down.

"Silencing me is meaningless," she says. "We have activists all over Georgia now....We're united, we're strong, and we're speaking out for all animals."

Among McCrosky's closest comrades is activist Phyllis Bedford, who was arrested with McCrosky during a fur protest in 1994. Says Bedford, "It takes something special to hold your eyes open and break your heart over and over again and still have something left to fight back with. I'm not sure what that something special is, but I know Sue McCrosky has an abundance of it."

Rick Bogle
KIT PARAVENTI

There's a spark, a single pivotal incident among many that ignites the leap from quiet ethicist to crusading activist.

For middle school teacher Rick Bogle, the flashpoint came early last year when his classroom rule against stepping on spiders provoked a tornado of controversy in his Oregon school district. Within months, he'd been ostracized, vilified, and forced to abandon his job by former friends and neighbors. In response, Bogle promptly formed one of the most creative crusades ever to challenge the prevailing dogma of animal cruelty: the Ape Army.

Bogle's salt-and-pepper beard, Thoreau-like countenance, and blue tent were fixtures in a series of nine-day vigils held at the nation's seven regional primate research centers from May to December 1997. Led by Bogle, the Ape Army consisted of a collection of more than 100 toy monkeys, tentloads of human supporters, and demands for a presidential moratorium on primate-based biomedical research.

"Rick's always been a fighter," says his wife, Lynn Pauly, who is also a middle school teacher. Bogle and Pauly met in the Peace Corps in 1981. After a two-year stint in Liberia, the couple returned to Bogle's 120-acre plot of Oregon forest land. It was Pauly, and a surprising sense of kinship with the surrounding farming/ranching community, that inspired the former carpenter to pursue a teaching degree.

Staunch ethical vegetarians, Bogle and Pauly lived their beliefs quietly among the feed store and hunting lodge crowds that populate Ashland. Both were considered excellent teachers and neighbors, though a vague social unease hung over picnic and dinner invitations.

All that changed when a parent went ballistic over Bogle's "no-kill" spider policy. "He's giving my kid a one-sided education!" accused one local businessman.

Bogle, who had quietly watched his sixth-grade students systematically inundated with 4-H seminars and National Rifle Association-sponsored clinics, grimaces at the irony. The experience still stings. "Some of the people screaming the loudest for my resignation were friends I'd known for twenty years," he says.

Shortly before Bogle's forced leave of absence from his job, Sherri Speede, D.V.M., the Northwest regional coordinator for In Defense of Animals (IDA), had awakened him to the plights of research primates. "I was sickened to learn that each day, behind closed doors, monkeys are being mutilated, tortured, deprived of vital contact with one another, and driven insane," he recalls.

Bogle launched the Ape Army's first campaign in Beaverton, Oregon, continuing on to the six remaining federally funded primate facilities in Washington, Massachusetts, Wisconsin, Louisiana, California, and Georgia. Taking his place among the donated monkey figurines, Bogle and a steady influx of local and national recruits held vigils at each location that included speeches, demonstrations, nonviolence seminars, and gripping visual displays highlighting the horrors of primate research. More than forty animal rights groups participated in the vigils. At the New England facility, activists burned a straw effigy of the late behavioral researcher Harry Harlow. During the University of Wisconsin center protest, an airplane banner sponsored by IDA rippled through the sky above a packed stadium proclaiming, "U-W murders monkeys."

Highlights of the tour infuse Bogle's newsletter and Web site with his flair for poignant anecdotes. There was the elderly polio victim who took the long way to work so she could gently reprimand the demonstrators for opposing vivisection. But after a friendly discussion with Bogle and anesthesiologist/activist Ray Greek, the woman returned the following day with a small, stuffed gorilla: the symbol of her enlistment into the Ape Army.

Especially haunting for Bogle was the moment he first peered through the glass doors of the facility named for Harlow. A plaque commemorating Harlow's work sits beside photographs of baby monkeys, Harlow's earliest research subjects. Wrenched from their mothers at birth, the infants in the photos cling desperately to a series of increasingly sadistic surrogate "mothers," inanimate devices designed to pierce the infants with spikes or mechanically repel them with cruel force. The infant monkeys' eyes seemed to stare into Bogle's, pleading for relief from Harlow's legacy of horror still practiced in varying forms at the research centers.

With the close of the Ape Army's initial campaign and the finish of his year-long leave of absence, Bogle must now take stock of his activism and employment prospects. He would like to apply his considerable skills as an organizer and teacher to a position with an activist organization.

"I was told I couldn't encourage my kids to be kind," he says. "So I decided to encourage the whole damn nation to be kind."

Editor's note: Rick Bogle is currently employed with In Defense of Animals.

Hillary Morris
Kit Paraventi

66 The Internet is an amazing resource," Hillary Morris says absently, her eyes focused raptly on a computer monitor. The click of a mouse button, a staccato tone followed by a brief blast of white noise, and she's online. Within the framed display lies everything she or anyone else needs to seize destiny and help change the world. Poised for discovery, engagement, and battle, Morris begins to type.

Morris is part of a new breed of social activist, one that forges inroads in the universal meeting place known as cyberspace. With a home computer, whose monitor is often draped with one of seven cats, she keeps busy as an activist and a full-time graduate student, while finding time for her companion felines and her significant other.

Solidly grounded in the mechanics and politics of cyber-surfdom, Morris researches vivisectors, launches campaigns, boycotts, and demos, writes and distributes articles for several online publications, supervises vegetarian discussion groups, and makes and maintains countless one-on-one connections. "I spend a minimum of two hours a day on animal rights activism," she says. Yet Morris is no stranger to on-site activism either. Some of her actions include getting arrested in 1996 and 1997 during Fur-Free Friday protests at a Revillon fur store, and running onto the shooting fields to rescue pigeons at the notorious Labor Day shoot in Hegins, Pennsylvania.

Right now, the activist-at-large is following up on her most recent action: helping out at *Satya* magazine's "meatout" table in Grand Central Station the week before. It featured a video monitor displaying graphic slaughterhouse footage to hundreds of commuters, many of whom requested vegetarian literature. "I judged the day to be a success," she says, adding quickly that success is meted out in much smaller doses when dealing with issues as buried in cultural sensibility as meat-eating.

"Keep in mind that you're part of a much longer, more difficult, and ultimately depressing journey when trying to convert meat-eaters," she says. "When it comes to meat, it's a matter of simply showing people the truth, and hoping they'll realize how horrible eating dead animals truly is, if not that day, then one day down the line."

Her own commitment began early. At the age of twelve, she pleaded with her father to spare the life of an errant house mouse he'd scooped into a dustbin and then tossed into the toilet to drown. "I was crying, begging him to put her outside," she says. It was a landmark insight into the paradox that tinges the human-animal relationship. Her father had always embodied and inspired every tenet of compassion and fairness, and in her close-knit urban home, cats and dogs were loved and cherished as family members. "Yet," she says, "neither I nor my family made the connection between meat and pets."

The connection loomed large the following year when Morris read Frances Moore Lappé's landmark *Diet for a Small Planet*. Morris promptly announced her vegetarianism and set out to mend the many gaping holes in the fabric of human compassion. Drawn to the field of cultural anthropology while attending Yale University, she became fascinated by issues of social and environmental injustice, and began working with an El Salvadoran human rights group.

A brief stint as a financial analyst on Wall Street followed college, a period marked by initial forays into animal activism. As her involvement grew, she eventually could no longer reconcile working for a financial institution that funded animal-exploiting businesses while personally espousing a vegetarian lifestyle. "I had an epiphany," she recalls, "and realized that I wanted to live my ideals completely and fully."

Morris is currently pursuing a doctorate-aimed course of study in Traditional Chinese Medicine (TCM), although her future vegan-based practice might be less than traditional since TCM historically uses animal products. "I love the idea of introducing new ideas to people," she admits, "whether it's about their health or how they look at animals."

She praises her hometown of New York as "a great place to spread awareness" with protests occurring every weekend. Her ongoing efforts include the regular anti-fur demos at Macy's Herald Square store and a large campaign against a primate vivisector in New York City that is being coordinated by Morris and others. She recently went to her local medical library to order copies of the vivisector's published work, much of which details in cool clinical detail the horrible suffering of the experimental animals. "There's nothing like hanging [vivisectors] with a noose they made themselves," Hillary says wryly.

Of her tireless cyberspace treks as well as her offline activities on behalf of animals, Morris says, "It's really not hard, it just takes a bit of organization and desire. On the Net, you can easily access so much information on animal issues, certainly enough to launch a campaign against a local fur store or a national cosmetics company that tests on animals. There's really no need to wait for someone else to take the lead. Believe me, if you want to help animals, you can do it too!"

Steve Hindi
JILL HOWARD CHURCH

Steve Hindi could be called a riveting activist, and not just because he co-owns a rivet-manufacturing business in addition to running the Chicago Animal Rights Coalition (CHARC). The main reason he attracts attention is because he has transformed himself from an avid hunter and fisherman into an outspoken (and some say outrageous) animal rights proponent.

Hindi's about-face came about after he visited the infamous pigeon shoot in Hegins, Pennsylvania, in 1989. He went there as a hunter who felt his reputation and that of other so-called "ethical sportsmen" was being maligned by shooters felling captive birds at close range:

"gutless wonders," he calls them. But when he complained to the locals, they told him that he, as a hunter, was no different from them—and his objections were ignored.

So Hindi started talking to the animal rights protesters about ways to shut down the shoot. "They thought it was a little weird" to have a hunter in their midst, he says. "They probably thought I was a 'plant.' " But what ended up being planted were seeds of understanding in Hindi's mind. After spending time listening to the activists' arguments, he became less convinced that his pursuit of pheasants, ducks, and "game" fish was excusable. "Over the next year," he recalls, "I found myself less and less able to defend what I'd been doing for the past three decades." He returned to Hegins the following year and got arrested while protesting the pigeon shoot. He went home to Ohio determined to redirect his sights.

In 1993 he founded CHARC and decided to take a very direct approach to activism. Instead of picketing events or just describing cruelty to others, he espouses a version of the motto "Show me the money"—in his words, "Give me the proof." For Hindi, technology is the weapon of choice. CHARC specializes in filming animal abuse (secretly or not, in Illinois or elsewhere) and distributing footage to news outlets so that the world can see cruelty in its uncensored ugliness.

One exposé involved two Asian markets in Minnesota where conscious, struggling pigs and other animals were seen being crudely slaughtered in clear violation of the law. (The markets are now under investigation.) A previous campaign involved filming the rocket-netting and captive-bolt killing of deer in two Illinois counties, a practice that had been protested for more than two years by conventional means without success.

"But the day we released the footage, the rocket-netting stopped," Hindi says, making him wonder how many animals' lives could have been saved if the public had been shown the truth sooner. Which goes back to Hindi's view that humane groups should let actions against animals speak for themselves. "We need to stop telling people what we're upset about and start showing them," he says. Yet even when the documentation does make it onto news shows, Hindi says CHARC doesn't always get proper credit for being behind the lens. As a result, the group is now $25,000 in debt due to the high cost of high-tech surveillance.

Hindi's efforts to recruit activists and other animal groups in CHARC's campaigns often come across with all the subtlety of a rivet gun, and he acknowledges that "some people in the movement are put off by the way we do things." The group's emblem is a big shark whose gaping jaws are ready to bite.

CHARC uses mainstream methods as well, and helped get pigeon shoots and horse tripping outlawed in Illinois. In 1996, Hindi took activism to new heights, literally, when he flew an ultralight aircraft over the Woodstock Hunt Club in McHenry County, Illinois, using a siren and bullhorn to spook the animals and annoy the hunters. He was arrested for hunter harassment (as he has been at least a dozen times) and sentenced to five months in jail, a decision he's fighting while out on bond.

"I sometimes say I wish every animal activist was in the military, in business, or a hunter," he says. "They would maybe learn a little how to strategize against the opposition." He thinks the movement always needs to think one step ahead, as in any type of battle. "You always have to keep trying to come up with a new twist," he explains. "The same principles may apply, but tactics have to change."

He may have traded his guns for cameras, but he has kept his predatory nature. "I still very much feel like a hunter," he says, "it's just a different chase and a different prey now."

Editor's note: Hindi's group is now called Showing Animals Respect and Kindness (SHARK).

Coby and Hans Siegenthaller
KIT PARAVENTI

"The purpose of life is a life of purpose."
—Robert Byrne

For more than forty years, Coby and Hans Siegenthaller have opened their hearts and home to a wide spectrum of two- and four-legged visitors. Their guest registry would read like a *Who's Who* of the animal rights movement. Listed beside the names of well-known crusaders Howard Lyman and Michael Klaper, M.D., you'd find a host of wayfarers who frequent their annual vegan holiday feasts and monthly potluck dinners. The registry would also reflect, somehow, the nameless, voiceless guests: the injured barn owl discovered on a hike, the truckload of rescued dogs that arrived late one night without warning, and many others.

You might say the Siegenthallers were just brought up right.

In the dismal, desperate years of World War II, with Holland foundering beneath the bristling Nazi occupation, Coby's and Hans' parents opened their respective attics, closets, and storage spaces to a steady flow of Jewish fugitives. The visitors arrived and departed by night, their eyes hollow with fear and loss. It was a time when Jewish sympathizers often earned themselves a berth on the same trains that shuttled more than six million Jews to their doom.

"Of course we did it," says Hans, with characteristic dismissiveness. "If you're not going to be a true friend at a time like that, what would you be waiting for?" His mother, Wies Siegenthaller, was a firebrand vegetarian and social activist eventually imprisoned for wearing a Star of David as an act of protest against Nazi genocide.

Coby and Hans met in their native Amsterdam during those years of turmoil. Lifelong vegetarians, their compassion was fostered by mothers who were members of the Dutch Vegetarian Society. Both were also Theosophists—members of an early social and vegetarian movement. Coby, a vigorous, sweet-faced, seventy-something woman with sparkling eyes, recites its tenets with serene passion. Theosophists believed in love for all living things, devotion to the truth beyond all dogma, and commitment to a life of active altruism. Vegetarianism was an immutable extension of that belief system. Her mother, Marta Heinen, would often remind her three daughters, "We are in the world to help each other." The lilt of Coby's Dutch homeland makes the words dance with gentle musicality.

During the war, Coby and Hans were members of the White Guild, a group of young vegetarians. Photos of a radiant young gymnast and classically handsome young man with a mischievous smile are remnants of those early days of courtship against the backdrop of war. Hans proposed to her in a rowboat. "He was absolutely beautiful," she says. "And he was vegetarian!" After the arrival of their daughter, Noor, and son, Hugo, the pair brought their family to the United States in 1955. Hans quickly landed a job as a chemical engineer, while Coby continued the nursing career she had begun in Amsterdam. Their eyes and voices still dim when conversation turns to Hugo, who died in a car crash at the age of twenty-four.

A 1960s forerunner to today's Fur-Free Friday marked their entry into the dawning animal rights movement in Southern California. Since then, they've become a constant presence at hundreds of rallies and demos. Coby and Noor celebrated Mother's Day in 1997 by marching in an anti-veal demonstration outside an Encino restaurant. The Siegenthallers remain diligently involved in numerous spay/neuter clinics and animal rescue groups. Coby also spends much of her time ministering to sick and disabled homebound members of the human species. Her vegan cooking is a prized commodity at fundraising events hosted by scores of animal groups.

Although they are quick to deflect fanfare and are most likely to attend high-profile animal functions as background volunteers, the Siegenthallers did receive a Last Chance for Animals (LCA) Certificate of Appreciation at the group's annual dinner in December 1997. "They have the energy of teenagers," says LCA's Eric Mindel. "Through thick and thin, Coby and Hans are continually active and outspoken in their commitment to animal rights."

Another of their landmark achievements also occurred in 1997, when marine mammal champion Paul Watson languished in solitary confinement in a Dutch prison. Watson, the legendary captain of the Sea Shepherd, stood accused of ramming a Norwegian whaling vessel, and faced almost certain deportation to Norway. Watson's supporters, along with other environmental groups, dreaded the outcome of his impending trial. "It was commonly feared that Paul, who'd been a longtime thorn in the side of the whaling industry, would disappear into a Norwegian prison and never come out again," says Nathan LaBudde of the Earth Island Institute.

The Siegenthallers packed their bags for Holland, carrying with them a vital videotape as well as a suitcase full of pro-Watson literature and T-shirts. Watson's stateside supporters had entreated them to deliver the tape in time for the trial. Recorded during the incident that sparked Watson's accusers, it clearly showed that the whaling ships rammed the Sea Shepherd, not the reverse. Flabbergasted by the new evidence and cowed by a strong activist presence and an outpouring of support, the Dutch judges freed Watson.

Without ceremony, Coby and Hans returned home to continue their relentless, everyday commitment to healing their world. "This is what we do," says Coby simply. "This is the rest of our lives."

Ed Blotzer
REBECCA TAKSEL

The newsletters keep coming, packets full of hand-typed sheets, photocopies of clippings, brochures on animal care, articles gathered from every imaginable humane organization. Even the envelopes are crowded: The return address reads, "Chief SPCA Police Officer, Animal Care and Welfare/S.P.C.A., P.O. Box 8257, Pittsburgh, PA 15218-0257," followed by the message, "For those who cannot speak for themselves but depend on honorable men and women for kindness, mercy, and justice." A quote from St. Francis is emblazoned next to the address label. It's another mailing from Ed Blotzer.

Animal advocates who've been getting the mailings for some time notice a difference these days. Although the envelopes are still overflowing with action alerts and informational bits, the enclosed typed sheets no longer list strings of citations and/or convictions for animal cruelty or neglect. Nevertheless, in the more than twenty years that Ed has been involved, he has had an eighty-five percent conviction rate for the cases he's prosecuted. But now that he's seventy-four years old and battling debilitating illnesses, he has had to curtail the punishing schedule of investigations and court appearances he kept up daily as an unpaid volunteer humane officer since 1970, when he founded the independent Animal Care and Welfare/SPCA.

Not that Ed is idle. The newsletters report his activities:
(1) Sending more than 500 letters to members of the judiciary and police about research on the connections between animal abuse and violence to humans.
(2) Advising a town council near Pittsburgh about the Pennsylvania animal protection and control laws. It's a poor steel town, one that needs to revise its statutes to deal with the pit bulls and dog-fighting rings. Blotzer is the premier expert on local and state humane law.
(3) Offering free brochures about the summer care of dogs. He'll send them to any address where a dog is suffering from neglect, as a first step in educating the dog's human caretaker.

Another of Ed's great points, one he's taught to the younger humane officers: Try to educate before you prosecute. "Most cases [of neglect] are caused by people who don't think, don't have the knowledge of care," he writes.

These days Ed is not as unsung a hero as he was in the years following the founding of Animal Care and Welfare. In recent years, he has been recognized by the Allegheny Bar Association, the state legislature, the media, and even by the Journal of the Brotherhood of Locomotive Engineers (he served forty years as an engineer on the Union Railroad).

Back in the 1970s it was just Ed handling animal abuse cases in the Pittsburgh area. "Call Blotzer!" the police dispatchers told anyone who had a concern. It's still the case that none of the municipalities in the counties in Ed's purview have a humane officer on their police payroll, and none of them are eager to enforce the animal protection provisions in the Pennsylvania Crime Code. Humane organizations pay the new SPCA officers, who are entitled to wear police uniforms. Because of Ed's training, the humane officers receive some measure of respect. Because of Ed, they wear the uniform with courage. Humane Officer Kathy Hecker, Ed's protégé in Allegheny County, is on a first-name basis with people in and around the dog-fighting rings.

Anyone involved in animal protection during the past three decades in Pittsburgh will attest to Ed's expertise. Animal rescuer Paulette Flaherty met Ed in 1980 at Mobilization for Animals meetings. "Ed took a tremendously strong stand on issues of animal abuse when it was not fashionable at all," she remembers. Her friend DeDe Anderson was inspired by Ed, too, and with a few other women they braved the indifference and ridicule of semi-rural Westmoreland County to build Adopt-A-Pet, a rescue, placement, and spay/neuter group that has grown steadily over the past twenty-five years. "Ed never refused his help. We could call him in the middle of the night, and, believe me, there were times when we did," Paulette says.

In 1996, Ed lost his partner in crime-fighting and humane action when his wife, Catherine, succumbed after a courageous battle against cancer. Married more than fifty years, the two were the "mom and pop" of the local animal protection community.

But he pushes on. His latest newsletter includes an item about a horrendous abuse case in Latrobe, where two teenage boys tortured and killed a dog. Humane Officer Elaine Gower of Action for Animals is working on the case. Ed was called in for help, and they are getting the seventeen-year-olds tried as adults. This time, Ed says, the local people are supporting the investigation. They're starting to get the idea that the human community cannot tolerate the abuse of animals. "It's a little different now, it's better," he says. To the extent that it's true, it is largely because Ed Blotzer was there.

Sherry DeBoer
Kit Paraventi

66 This initiative shows how the ballot process can be abused by the idle rich. A wealthy heiress wants to foist her pet project...on the rest of California. Get a life."

The words sizzled from the California ballot materials booklet like a freshly inflicted brand, a distinctly personal scorcher tucked amid pages of careful rhetoric. For more than twenty-two million state voters, it was the first round in a blustering Libertarian party rebuttal against Proposition 6, the initiative to criminalize the slaughter of California's horses.

Upon reading it, Sherry DeBoer—the target of the remark—smiled, rolled her eyes, and groaned like the victim of a bad pun at the office picnic. "Oh, come on," she laughed. "If they were going to take a shot at me, you'd think they'd have done better than that!"

The outspoken former actress has always been an enigma to her opponents. The veteran California volunteer lobbyist is a disarming meld of toughness and sensitivity. She lists "Gladiator" as her occupation and "God" as her employer on campaign contribution cards. She believes in faith, miracles, uncompromising legislation, and a well-maintained reserve of key political friendships. Hailed by California State Senator Bill Lockyer as "an incredibly effective legislative force," she has dedicated herself to making miracles come true for animals.

DeBoer founded the Animal Health and Safety Association in 1990, a coalition dedicated to humane legislative reform on the state level. She successfully lobbied for one bill to establish humane standards for puppies and kittens in "pet" stores, and another to criminalize the marketing of stolen animals for any commercial purpose, including research. She helped reverse a centuries-old law that allowed horses less than two years old to be raced in California, and founded Political Animals, which has grown into the largest political action committee for animal advocacy in the state.

The Save the Horses California voter initiative, co-sponsored by DeBoer, California Equine Council founder Cathleen Doyle, and philanthropist Sidne J. Long, marked the first attempt in U.S. history to ban the slaughter of horses for human consumption. By soliciting support from a diverse group of politicians, celebrities, and organizations, the initiative's sponsors hoped to create a blueprint for successful initiatives in other states.

Born in Hawaii, DeBoer acquired rank and privilege as an heiress to the Long's Drugstore fortune. As she grew into adulthood, she found herself lured farther and farther from the social whirlwind. "I had nothing to show from years of dating and pretty dressing," she says. She recalled a favorite adage of her stepfather, Joe Long, who said, "The real joy is in the giving, not the getting." In 1989, reeling from a failed marriage, she decided to take an entire year and do nothing but give.

Helping animals was an obvious choice. Hers was a family that cherished and nurtured its animals and never hesitated to rescue a few more when the opportunity arose. Her involvement in animal rescue in California had already led to a stint as a nurse in a wildlife hospital. But she longed to strike deeper and to uproot cruelty at its social and legal roots. She resolved to take California's political citadel by storm.

DeBoer soon realized that her voter's-eye view of the legislative process had not prepared her for the complexities of law-making. She enrolled in the state humane and police academies, and was certified as a state humane officer in 1990. She hired private trainers to school her in the rudiments of lobbying and intraparty politics. Watching the incessant parade of new laws convinced her that the California legislature was not the age-old immovable rock that had always stymied animal advocates, but was supple clay that could be molded into miracles.

"Like other animal rights people, I entered that arena with the assumption that moral correctness has power," she says. She soon learned that the guiding compass of legislators is, by necessity, their own re-election. "Simply put," she says, "legislators are powerless to help you if it will result in their defeat at the polls."

She discovered that the currency of the state capitol is campaign assistance: key facts that friendly legislators could parlay into endorsements, votes, campaign contributions, and favorable PR. The lesson was driven home one day during final deliberations on her "pet shop" reform bill. A staffer she'd befriended passed along the results of a freshly compiled government study that documented horrendous store conditions. With the study in hand, she was able to swing the final votes needed to get the bill passed.

"The legislature is no place for amateurs, no matter how enthusiastic or well-intentioned," DeBoer says. "If you want to help the animals, take your job seriously. Do the research, learn the ropes, hire professional lobbyists, and find a way to be of service to your friends and a problem to their opponents. Otherwise, you're just not doing it right."

Editor's note: In November 1998, California voters approved Proposition 6, banning the commercial sale of horses for human consumption.

Buffalo Nations
KIT PARAVENTI

At first glance, you'd think you'd stumbled into a Jack London fantasy—this group of hardy, flannel-shirted mountaineer types bunked in a remote log cabin in the subzero chill of a Montana winter. It's a place where words are punctuated by curls of frosty vapor, where your eyelashes ice over as you step outside to begin your 5:30 a.m. daily patrol. It's a place where the water pipes may or may not freeze before morning, and you don't want to sleep too far from your snowshoes.

Here lies what may be the last hope for the buffalo.

"The buffalo's character and identity are interchangeable with the land," says documentary filmmaker turned activist Michael Mease. Even when the magnificent Great Plains buffalo (more accurately known as bison) numbered more than sixty million in the 18th century, the gentle nomadic giants never stressed or overgrazed the plains. "Their hooves seemed to magically till the soil and replant the grass," Mease says. The Native American plains tribes, who had long revered the mystical power of the bison, saw its craggy image etched into the surrounding mountain horizons by the hand of the Great Spirit.

It was in 1996 that a questionable "disease management" program by Montana's Department of Livestock (DOL) led to the unprecedented butchery of 1,084 Yellowstone National Park bison by state officials. For Mease, who had been documenting the herd for several years, the event triggered a transition from observer to activist. "Once the buffalo entered my life, there was no way I could turn my back on them," he says.

Together with Lakota tribe member Rosalie Little Thunder, Mease founded Buffalo Nations, a coalition of Native American traditionalists and grassroots activists of all races. Its log cabin headquarters lies sixteen miles northwest of West Yellowstone in the remote foothills of the surrounding mountain ranges. Sustained by donated food and cold-weather gear, the all-volunteer group has set out to stymie a systematic DOL campaign to reduce Yellowstone's nomadic buffalo herd.

The DOL's recent tactics include baiting, "hazing" (chasing bison via snowmobiles and horses), shooting them outright, or herding them into so-called "capture facilities" (livestock holding pens) where the animals await transport to slaughterhouses. In response, Buffalo Nations volunteers monitor the movement of herds, shepherd groups of buffalo to safe areas when necessary, encourage landowners to post "Bison Safe Zone" signs on their properties, and devise legal and press strategies to ignite public support. Corey Mascio, a seventeen-year-old activist from New Hampshire, was arrested after placing himself in front of DOL guns in an unsuccessful attempt January 1998 to save a group of six targeted mothers and calves.

The Buffalo Nations log cabin has become a way station for a hodgepodge of activists. "I came down for a few days, then just kept on coming," says Jennifer Nitz, one of the members who now forms the core group. Nitz, an emergency medical technician and vegan, was prompted to make her first pilgrimage when a friend handed her a news article in January 1998.

For Texan Scott Brocker, the invitation came in the form of a request by Karen, his Native American fiancé, that they spend their two-week honeymoon in a not-so-usual hideaway. Lucas Salter, a vacationing Australian marketing student, was handed a Buffalo Nations pamphlet while on a northern Montana skiing trip. "It's incredibly fulfilling and exciting," he says of the experience. "And it's good to come from 9,000 miles away and be made to feel this welcome."

The DOL's buffalo reduction program ostensibly seeks to contain brucellosis, a relatively benign bacterial infectious disease that sometimes causes miscarriages of first-born calves. Though large numbers of bison test positive for brucellosis, less than one-half of one percent are potentially infectious, and then only to other bison. There has never been a single documented case of bison transmitting brucellosis to domestic cattle. Still, state officials claim buffalo brucellosis represents a threat to cattle herds.

"Ridiculous," counters wildlife biologist Virginia Ravndal. "Yellowstone bison have lived healthfully with the disease for eighty years and have never given it to a single cow." Moreover, though ranchers claim that Montana's federal "brucellosis-free" status is in jeopardy, the U.S. agency that grants the designation evaluates only the health status of domestic livestock herds, not wildlife. Ravndal characterizes the brucellosis issue as a thinly veiled ruse by DOL policy-makers in collusion with cattle barons, whose chief aim is to protect their enduring windfall of federally subsidized grazing land from competition by wildlife.

Battle lines were drawn when the DOL successfully obtained permission from the U.S. Forest Service to operate a federally funded bison capture facility in the Gallatin National Forest—a haven for wintering Yellowstone bison. Mease issued an urgent call for additional volunteers to help fortify the group's remote outpost, a beautiful twenty-foot teepee a few hundred yards from the planned location. There, the first truckload of pre-assembled corrals was expected to arrive.

In the prophetic words of volunteer Jim Coefield, "There will be many a cold night with a warm fire, and hot drinks and warm food as friends of the buffalo sit in the dark, waiting for the first light of dawn. Be strong, buffalo warriors!"

Editor's note: Buffalo Nations is now the Buffalo Field Campaign.

≈

Sean Day
KIT PARAVENTI

In May 1997, a tenacious cluster of chanting, sign-carrying animal rights activists gathered outside Miller's Furs in Washington, D.C. A clash erupted, with store owners, customers, and police on one side and the activists on the other. When the dust settled, five members of the grassroots group Compassion Over Killing (COK) stood handcuffed, arrested for allegedly assaulting a customer and a store employee.

There had indeed been an assault, but it was perpetrated by the employee against one of the activists. It's a familiar scenario in the animal rights movement, a hopelessly biased "they say, we deny" nightmare for small groups to whom expensive criminal defense fees or citations represent probable financial collapse. Testimony of police and other prosecution witnesses is typically given rubber-stamp approval by judges who set out to "make an example" of troublesome, activist defendants.

But the Miller's Furs incident was destined to defy tradition. To begin with, a hand-held video camera hoisted by one of the activists provided an irrefutable record of the entire encounter. Next, Sean Day, a crusading animal rights attorney, happened to be one of those arrested. Together with attorneys Dion Sullivan and Phil Hirschkop, Day used the videotape, which vividly showed the store employee's attack and that the customer had not been assaulted, to persuade prosecutors to drop the phoney charges.

"It happens all the time," says Day, with characteristic drawling candor. "False arrests, ridiculous charges that are designed to discourage peaceful protest." Typically, the dismissal would have triggered celebration among the activists. But, for Day, the battle was far from over; he lost little time in bringing the fur store, the employee, the customer, and the police department up on civil charges of false arrest and malicious prosecution. The suit is one of four he has launched that threaten to derail the ongoing, traditionally harsh, and often unconstitutional treatment of animal activists by police and the courts.

Day recalls the personal awakening that led him into the animal rights milieu. In 1990, as an undergrad business student at the University of Virginia, he was stunned by a display of graphic photos placed near the campus cafeteria by a student animal rights group.

Day—who was wearing a leather jacket and heading to the cafeteria for a hamburger at the time—was horrified by the images of animal slaughter and factory farming, and became a vegetarian instantly.

He first began hands-on animal rescue during a two-year postgraduate stint in Los Angeles where he began trapping feral cats for spaying and neutering. In 1992, after returning east to pursue a law degree at the State University of New York at Buffalo, Day co-founded Students of Law for Animal Rights. The group halted the poisoning of "nuisance" birds by campus officials, and spread an anti-vivisection, vegetarian message via its newsletter.

It was in early 1997 that COK co-founder Paul Shapiro found a portentous fax message in his office machine. "I'm a vegan animal rights attorney," it read, "and I'd like to help...." Since then, Day has become a near constant presence at the group's actions. Armed with a camera and a notebook packed with relevant police orders and statutes (which he readily recites to officers), he orchestrates the videotaping at each action, serves as a defense lawyer on the spot, and defuses potential physical and legal calamities. When handcuffs emerge, he's ready for the ride to jail, arraignments, bail hearings, and whatever other legal hurdles await his clients.

"He's an amazingly skilled, savvy lawyer," marvels Shapiro, "and he's never charged a penny for his services."

Day's advice to groups that risk police confrontation? "Keep your cool, have a lawyer present if possible, and keep those cameras rolling." As demonstrated by the Miller's Furs incident, civil suits are a major deterrent to civil rights violations, he says.

Since opening his own practice in 1997, Day's caseload consists mostly of family law, criminal defense, and personal injury, with a huge portion of his time dedicated to his pro bono animal rights colleagues. From his one-man office in Maryland, he's amassed an impressive record of legal victories. Still, his fledgling career has been a struggle when it comes to "pay[ing] the bills." But he intends to keep doing what he does for the animals and those who risk their freedom to defend them.

"D.C. is a much safer place to be an animal activist because of Sean Day," says Shapiro.

Amanda Walker-Serrano

LYNN MANHEIM

The drama is set in a location where pickup trucks rattle with gun racks and newspapers advertise cow-pie bingo. A cornfield lies down a winding, hilly country road from the new brick elementary school in this one-street town. This is Factoryville, Pennsylvania, only eighty miles from the notorious hamlet of Hegins and its annual pigeon shoot.

The lead player is Amanda Walker-Serrano, an eight-year-old third-grader with a brother, Adam, seven, and baby sister, Amelia. Their parents are Lisa Walker and Michael Serrano. Amanda is a dignified girl with a kind, intelligent face. Never without a book, she reads serenely at her mother's side during stultifying school board and city council meetings.

The scene opens in early February 1999 at Lackawanna Trail Elementary School. Amanda, upset that a class trip to the circus is planned for early April, has decided to do something to stop it. Accustomed to seeing animal rights literature at home, she has seized upon the idea of doing a petition. On a blank page she hand-letters, "We 3rd grade kids don't want to go to the circus because they hurt animals. We want a better feild [sic] trip."

During recess on February 4, Amanda sits on a bench while thirty-three classmates line up to sign her petition. She is elated. But the next day, only three children have time to add their names before a teacher says Amanda cannot have the petition at school and orders her to put it away.

Scolded for the very first time and denied permission to call Lisa, Amanda cries all afternoon. When she runs from the school bus into her mother's arms, puffy-faced and barely able to speak through her sobs, Lisa declares war.

Met with indifference from school principal Nancy Simon, Lisa fights for the opportunity to address an upcoming school board meeting about circus dangers, freedom of speech, and animal cruelty. On February 22, she asks the board to inform parents of circus dangers and to let Amanda circulate her petition. That night Amanda makes her TV news debut saying, "I was just trying to say to the other kids that the circus hurts animals....It makes me think...that I'm doing the wrong thing, but I know I'm doing the right thing, but they just made me feel that way."

The school strikes back the very next day by handing out parental permission slips for the circus field trip a full month ahead of schedule.

By February 26, a scathing editorial appears in the *Scranton Tribune*. It begins, "Here in America, the international guardian of democracy, the last thing on earth we would want our public schools to do is encourage children to think for themselves and embrace democratic principles." It ridicules school board President Donald Leonard for worrying more about his district "[taking] a really bad hit on this in the media" than about the abridgement of a young citizen's free speech. It concludes, "Whether circus animals are poorly treated is a matter of intense debate around the country. One would think that an educational institution would find ways to examine such an issue raised by a student instead of, in effect, telling her to shut up."

An editorial cartoon shows a resolute little girl standing on a circus platform holding a paper that says "1st Amendment" in one hand and one that says "Circus Petition" in the other. A mustachioed ringmaster, gun in holster, bullwhip in hand, wields a chair to protect himself from the child. The letters on his jacket read "Lacka. Trail Elem."

Other media are not so friendly. Local radio talk show hosts and their callers accuse Lisa of publicity-seeking and child abuse. She contacts a former U.S. Department of Agriculture veterinarian and two former elephant trainers, who phone in with first-hand stories of deranged circus animals and the routine, vicious beatings that make them that way.

Predictably, given the local mindset, the third-graders turn against Amanda. She is devastated, but more determined than ever to deliver her message. In school on Tuesday after protesting two circus shows with her family on Monday, she primes the kids for a big surprise on Wednesday. Arriving at the circus the next day, the Factoryville students step off a yellow bus and see Amanda lifted to the shoulder of a man in an elephant costume. He and a tiger-suited woman are holding a huge banner that reads, "Amanda Walker-Serrano is Right: Circus Animals Suffer Every Day." Amanda is exultant.

Act I closes with Amanda back at school giving away coloring books that tell the truth about circuses. So far, business is slow. But Amanda is not discouraged, because the play is far from over. She understands that thanks to her and her family, thousands of people now know that something is very wrong with the circus picture.

Gerda Deterer
ERIN GEOGHEGAN

Glancing up and down this quiet suburban street in Dundalk, Maryland, there is little sign of animal life. Surprising, since it would seem that an animal rehabilitation center and sanctuary would stand out like a sore paw. A chorus of bird songs floats gently through the air, its source unknown. Upon further inspection, a blue station wagon labeled "Wild Bird Rescue" sits in front of an average-looking home that is lined on one side with empty Pet Taxis. Hearing the ring of the doorbell, a sturdy woman with a strong voice calls from the window that she'll be right there.

Gerda Deterer leads me to her front room where I am greeted by two friendly German Shepherds, four cockatoos, two parrots, three crates of young squirrels, and countless cardboard boxes full of baby birds poking their beaks through airholes in search of food. The cockatoos call "Hello, Hello," the dogs sniff my unfamiliar clothes, and all at once the phone and doorbell are simultaneously ringing. Gerda smiles, rolls her eyes and politely excuses herself, then returns with three hungry infant birds in hand.

Gerda sighs that spring is her busiest time of year, rotating between squirrel and rabbit litters and the endless flow of orphaned birds. She explains the fledglings need to be fed by hand every fifteen minutes, and so sits down and begins the process that will not end for the rest of our afternoon together.

Through the hectic and noisy atmosphere, through the constant phone calls and feedings, we manage to talk a little about how she came to be the Birdwoman of Baltimore.

Besides the menagerie of living animals in the room, the walls are lined with stuffed ones—hunting trophies of deer, black bears, Canada geese, and ducks. Gerda explains that the "dustcatchers," as she calls the trophies, were donated to her and are used in Wild Bird Rescue's educational programs in place of live animals. The group visits schools around the Baltimore area, in conjunction with the Carrie Murray Outdoor Educational Center, to teach children about the importance of preserving and respecting wildlife and their habitat.

But the primary function of Wild Bird Rescue, Inc., which consists of Gerda and her network of about fifty volunteers, is to rescue, rehabilitate, and release injured birds and other small wildlife species. Gerda receives an average of 120 calls a day from around Maryland with reports of injured or abused animals in need, from orphaned fledglings to victims of poison, pollution, and hunting and auto accidents, plus abandoned "pets" and often those simply considered pests. Her house is the hub where she answers calls and coordinates volunteers who pick up animals and bring them to her so she can repair injuries or arrange for veterinary care. She eventually releases the rescuees back into the wild or places them into good homes. On any given day Gerda could have 100–150 animals in her home, including the permanent residents like her two rescued German shepherds, Nicky and BJ, and a cockatoo named Penelope, who because of a hot temper and special medical needs would be difficult to adopt out.

Luckily, these animals have found themselves a perfect home with this fifty-eight-year-old, German-born bird lover. When asked how she became involved in wildlife rehabilitation, Gerda answers that animals have always been her "undoing," but she only got serious about taking care of them twenty years ago when a child brought her a baby robin, whom she then raised for the next fourteen years. Over the years, she read library books and collected advice from friends with exotic birds, experts at the Baltimore Zoo, and vets who (appropriately) took her under their wing. She saw a need for a group that focuses on these often neglected creatures, and began taking in more birds and small animals.

Wild Bird Rescue, Inc., is funded exclusively by grants and the salary of Gerda's husband, a maintenance supervisor and ex-hunter. She tells how she converted him: by simply handing him a baby squirrel and asking him to feed it. He has not touched a gun in more than twenty years. The group recently received private donations of a motorboat for water rescues and forty-six acres of land in Carroll County, Maryland, where Gerda plans one day to build a full-fledged wildlife hospital and refuge. It's a goal worthy of the considerable time and effort it will take to achieve, but the seemingly ceaseless chirping, squeaking, squawking, and flapping keep her focused on the business at hand; after all, there are hungry beaks to feed, ruffled feathers to smoothe, and wild souls to soothe.

Sally Mackler
Kirsten Rosenberg and Valerie Schneider

❝Who are the animal rights fanatics opposing Measure 34? The following is a profile of Sally Mackler, Southern Oregon Co-Spokesman for the Oregon Bear and Cougar Coalition...❞ read the argument in favor of Measure 34 in the voter information guide for the 1996 Oregon state elections. The pamphlet, sent to all registered voters, went on to say that she lived with many companion animals, eschewed milk products because she felt "dairy cows were exploited," and had even demonstrated against circuses!

Measure 34 aimed to overturn a statewide initiative passed in 1994—with Sally's leadership—that outlawed bear baiting and the hunting of bears and cougars with dogs. But the decision of the measure's backers to make Sally and her "fanatical" beliefs the focus of their campaign (realizing they couldn't defend the barbaric hunting practices they sought to restore) backfired: voters overwhelmingly defeated the initiative. The personal attack proved again the old adage that you can tell a lot about a person by his or her enemies. Wayne Pacelle of the Humane Society of the United States, who worked closely with her on the "No on Measure 34" and other campaigns, concurs. "I have seldom met a more dedicated, credible, and effective activist than Sally," he says.

It all started in the early 1980s after Sally become frustrated with the unchecked breeding of her neighbor's many cats. Living in Southern California at the time, Sally contacted the Pet Assistance foundation, a local spay/neuter group in north San Diego County, and had the cats neutered. She ended up volunteering for the organization, and through her association with its director, Helen Delph, she discovered the world of animal abuse—vivisection, product testing, trapping, etc. The knowledge made her "madder and madder and more and more alarmed, and made me want to get involved," she recalls. Thus, Sally credits her neighbor as a catalyst for her awakening, and says wryly, "I guess I should be grateful, it's what got me into this whole mess."

Her next step down the animal rights path (of no return) was taken when she started a People for the Ethical Treatment of Animals chapter in San Diego in 1983, which later became San Diego Animal Advocates (SDAA), an organization still very much the city's animal rights voice. One of the most memorable notches in Sally's belt came in 1991, when she and former elephant keeper turned activist Lisa Landress made public the San Diego Zoo's involvement in allowing its cast-off animals to be sold to canned hunting ranches. Exposing the renowned San Diego Zoological Society for selling off surplus animals so trophy hunters could shoot them for big money resulted in the practice being halted for a while. The zoo took another blow when Sally, with the encouragement and support of the International Primate Protection League's Shirley McGreal, revealed how some of the primates it disposed of could easily end up in biomedical research facilities. At the University of California at San Diego, where Sally regularly held dramatic demonstrations, she and others succeeded in closing down one of the medical school's dog labs. By ably pulling together sympathetic veterinarians to donate their services and volunteers to help in the process, Sally also launched one of the first feral cat spay/neuter operations in the country, the San Diego Feral Cat Coalition. The organization's success in reducing homeless cat numbers served to help provide a model for the many similar operations that have since sprouted around the country. And the list goes on.

"Sea World, UCSD medical center—they were scared of her when she showed up at meetings because she was so armed with information," recalls Jane Cartmill, director of SDAA. "She was never afraid to take on the big guns."

In 1993, Sally moved to Jacksonville, Oregon, where she continues her special brand of no-holds-barred activism. ("It was a happy day [for the animal users] when she left San Diego," chuckles Jane.) In addition to serving on the board of Predator Defense Institute (PDI) in Eugene, Sally works with Spay/Neuter Your Pet by coordinating the annual Prevent a Kitty Litter low-cost sterilization program. She is also the executive director of Humane Oregon PAC, a political action committee that works to elect pro-animal candidates at both the state and federal level. Following PDI's involvement in successfully persuading Oregon Governor John Kitzhaber to issue an executive decree banning the use of Compound 1080 (a poison used by some sheep ranchers to kill coyotes), Sally is gearing up for the next election cycle. She is working on yet another state ballot initiative [Measure 97], which would codify the Compound 1080 ban and restrict the similar use of sodium cyanide and trapping.

Although her opponents like to paint her as a crazed misanthrope, nothing could be further from reality. Most people are unaware that, for years, Sally and her husband have regularly cared for elderly residents in their communities by driving them to the store or doctors' appointments, or simply providing companionship. Fortunately, Sally is able to focus all her energy on helping others—both human and nonhuman—thanks to "the goodwill of my savings, investments, and my significant other's generous support," she says. When asked what her secret is for staying motivated to engage in one uphill battle after another, without missing a beat she replies, "Anger, just pure rage, plus a healthy sense of revenge."

Editor's note: Measure 97 was defeated in Oregon in November 2000, although a similar measure was approved in Washington state.

Matt and Mary Kelly
KIT PARAVENTI

Just off a winding section of Route 7 on the northwestern tip of Massachusetts lies the Brodie Mountain Ski Resort. In winter, the sprawling 250 acres of hardwood-studded mountain is criss-crossed with blinding fast, heart-thumping ski trails—a favorite pilgrimage for cold-weather recreation-seekers. The names that grace Brodie's rolling slopes ring with an Irish lilt: Killarney Trail, Leprechaun's Loop, Gilhooly's Glade, and Molly's Lane. And thanks to the enduring dedication of Matt and Mary Kelly, their family-owned and run resort has served as a snowy oasis of enlightenment and compassion for the 200,000 visitors who make the trek there annually.

Inside the sprawling, wooden main lodge, the largest standing fieldstone fireplace in the country beckons visitors to warm themselves. Beside it stands a rack covered with literature from animal-, human-, and environmental-interest groups. In the sumptuous dining area, sixteen portraits of vegetarian celebrities are displayed with a friendly printed suggestion that patrons consider cruelty-free menu options. Virtually every indoor sitting and resting nook on the resort is teeming with publications that ignite the quest for social justice.

The list of speakers and lecturers featured at Brodie's events reads like a Who's Who of the animal protection and environment movements, including Howard Lyman, Gene Bauston, Wayne Pacelle, and Karen Davis. "It fills our hearts," says Matt, "to hear so many people say they were personally and positively changed after a Brodie event." For a multitude of visitors, such events triggered a lasting commitment to a vegan lifestyle.

As a child, Matt watched as his father constructed the resort in a stunning expanse of the Berkshire Hills. After putting in more than twenty-seven years at Brodie in various capacities, Matt jokes that, appropriately, the smallest chair lift was named after him "because it's always the first to open and the last to close." Shortly after their marriage in 1984, Matt and Mary returned home from a lecture by John Robbins at the University of Massachusetts with an armload of copies of Diet for a New America and a firm resolve to spread the message of compassion-based living. Already strongly drawn to international social issues, they found Robbins pushed them "over the edge" in terms of an all-encompassing vegan philosophy. As a result, the resort has become a hub of social activism. In addition, the Kellys run a flourishing bird sanctuary whose inhabitants include a host of chickens, ducks, geese, and turkeys rescued from factory farms. In 1999, they were saddened by the passing of one of their most famous residents. Lilly, once nicknamed the "Chinatown Rooster," (see page 152).

On November 11, longtime patrons were stunned by the announcement that Brodie Mountain Ski Resort had been sold to a neighboring lodge. Although initially taken aback by his family's decision, Matt is happy to report that the new owners have agreed to honor all current calendar commitments for 2000, including Farm Sanctuary's "Snowfest for the Animals," the EarthSave Summit, and two of Brodie's famous Veggie Potlucks, slated for the spring and fall. Although the news is good, there is no guarantee that vegetarian events will continue to flourish at Brodie. Matt hopes the success of the scheduled affairs will persuade the new owners to remain compassion-friendly.

"After any door closes, another one opens" muses Matt, who's agreed to stay on at the resort in a marketing capacity until April 2000. Long tuned in to the teachings of Gandhi, Albert Schweitzer, and Martin Luther King, Jr., his faith in the ultimate redemption of all unforeseen circumstances remains unshaken. "Who knows?" he says. "It just may be that we may now be able to go on to fight the good fight in a bigger and better way."

Phyllis Lahti
KIRSTEN ROSENBERG

How natural and good that every cat has a place of love and respect, among them, and especially, the Library Cat.—Inscription on The Library Cat Society membership card

It was the winter of 1987, and a Minnesota blizzard swirled madly outside Phyllis Lahti's home when she heard the pitiful cries of a cat outside her door. Although the distressed tabby was covered with sores and bite marks, Phyllis recognized him as one of the street cats she regularly fed. Because her two resident cat companions made it clear they welcomed the formerly homeless feline about as much as a trip to the vet, the librarian took Regal Reggie (so named because of his "royal bearing," says Phyllis) to live at her place of work, the Bryant Public Library in Sauk. There, he established himself as the library's Cat in Residence, with the reference room being his preferred spot.

Although by no means the first cat to inhabit a library, Reggie served as the inspiration for Phyllis to found The Library Cat Society, whose dozens of member libraries have provided safe havens for many a cat left in library parking lots or dumped in book-return chutes. The group's newsletter, of which Phyllis is editor, espouses its aim: "to advocate the establishment of cats in libraries and recognize the need to respect and to care for library cats." The Society was even featured in a 1997 documentary film, *Puss in Books*, which chronicled the bond between the library mascots and their doting caretakers and the (mostly) admiring public, as well as the sometimes dramatic opposition to the cats' presence by library board members or allergic or cat-phobic patrons.

But Phyllis' concern for animals is not limited solely to *Felis catus librarius*. "The all-too-common attitude towards an abused or neglected dog or cat is 'It's none of my business,' " laments Phyllis, who is not one to butt out when faced with a suffering animal. "I freely express my views to those I know—and those I don't know as well—including animal control officers about the need to have better ordinances that offer real protection for animals, and to enforce the state statutes," she explains in her crisp, cultured voice. Her frustration over a situation in her neighborhood involving the neglect of two dogs by their caretaker, despite her attempts to enlighten the "owner" about proper care, led her to talk with a local councilperson about remedying the problem through strengthening the law protecting animals.

Phyllis emphasizes the importance of remembering the everyday ways that activists can help animals.

She regularly reminds local television stations to give weather alerts for outdoor animals, and frequently expresses her humane views by staying in touch with her elected representatives and writing letters to the editor. "And I have talked to pastors," she adds, "urging them to include the care and love of animals in their sermons." Recently, Phyllis wrote to Minnesota Lt. Gov. Mae Schunk, who is focusing on education issues, about the benefits of incorporating humane education into school curriculum.

Now retired as a librarian, Phyllis contemplates how best to help animals while she works as a book illustrator from home (her water-color paintings of library cats will be included in a forthcoming book on the famed felines). She would like to see the larger, national animal advocacy groups coordinate their efforts more to inform the public better. "The wonderful messages that they espouse are not reaching the guy down the block who neglects his dog," she feels.

These days, Phyllis shares her life and home with rescued cats, Tillie, Thomas, Hansi, Tobie, and Sadie, despite being allergic to them. "I sneeze a lot," she laughs. Considering her history of improving the lives of countless cats, those of us who are "owned" by the creatures might do well to follow (and adapt as needed) the advice she wisely dispenses in the anthology, *Cats, Librarians, and Libraries: Essays for and About The Library Cat Society*:

> The library office can, after all, serve as a refuge for the library cat. It should not lean toward the overly organized, and when possible it should have an inviting open desk or cabinet drawer for catnapping. It need not have a window box, but having one can be therapeutic, both for the cat who is reclining on it and the observer who is watching the cat.

How fortunate for that observer...if they *know* that they are glimpsing the acknowledged master of the art of quiescence. And one may be sure at that moment of mutual encounter, the cat will, in turn, discern to the accurate degree the observer's power of feline insight.

Evelyn Wood
PATRICIA A. WISMER

Nestled along a tree-lined street in a quiet southeast Chico, California, neighborhood, "kitty city" beckoned to a huge gray and exhausted Miss Daisy, a part-Siamese stray. Perhaps, instinctively, she knew the place by reputation: a private no-kill cat shelter where orphaned and abandoned felines are regularly nursed back to health, spayed or neutered, and adopted into loving homes. And they're allowed to stay as long as it takes.

Evelyn Wood, the owner of the modest California home that has housed so many hapless feline victims of human irresponsibility, had just set out a daily buffet for her many rescued charges. Miss Daisy timidly joined the others in the protective yard, seeming to know she had found a safe haven.

Evelyn, a retired widow of nine years and a proud grandmother, promptly phoned several Chico vets and the local humane society to try to locate the family that had once cared for this gentle, spayed female. When no one came forward to claim her, Miss Daisy joined the other fifty or so inhabitants of "kitty city" awaiting new homes. Soon after, another new arrival, a shy gray female, surprised Evelyn by returning one afternoon with her two offspring in tow. Evelyn told friends, "I've never had a kitty bring me her kittens like that before. I just didn't have the heart to tell her we had no room at the inn."

And so it goes on on a daily basis with this quiet heroine who has opened her home to so many strays roaming her neighborhood and the vast expanses of Chico's scenic Bidwell Park, long a dumping ground for unwanted animals. Luckily, Chico doesn't have a restriction on the number of dogs or cats a person can house in a residential neighborhood, although local animal rights activists and city officials have visited the premises and been impressed by its cleanliness—as well as Evelyn's dedication to the cats.

Evelyn and acquaintances Cathi Casamajor and Jim Nakamura fed and rescued groups of felines in Bidwell Park's picnic areas for a decade until the Park Commission suddenly developed a no-feeding policy to help rid it of the unwanted colonies. Jim exercised his right to civil disobedience by continuing to feed the animals and was arrested in 1997; his trial brought national attention to the feral cat issue with assistance from such organizations as United Animal Nations. Joining with her two co-feeders and many concerned citizens who jumped to Jim's defense, Evelyn became a founding member of the Chico Cat Coalition (CCC), a volunteer organization that subsequently removed and fostered more than 300 park cats in the last two years.

Evelyn even managed to add thirty or so of the CCC rescues in the first year alone to her already large feline family of forty. She still visits some of her old haunts in Bidwell Park, sustaining a few remaining ferals whom she hopes to eventually trap and add to the fostered population. There's also room across town in the BG Barn (named for Big Guy, a favorite deceased park kitty) where CCC volunteers care for some thirty felines housed in a large facility modified for their comfort and security by owner Kathy Halloran and volunteer Vance Fowler.

Caring for so many animals is not an easy task for Evelyn, whose health forced her to give up her part-time job as a Costco food demonstrator, but she is committed to it. CCC may soon disband given its successful rescue of the Bidwell Park cats, but Evelyn will continue caring for the city's stray and abandoned felines; for her it is a labor of

love. She is a reminder that lone activists continue where organizations leave off.

Eric Mills

KIRSTEN ROSENBERG

Eric Mills talks so fast it's hard to take in everything he says. Discussing issues from steer
wrestling to turtle rescuing to Southern cooking,
the words fly past. But that's to be expected from
such a man of action.

Eric got his start as an animal activist at the age of three when he
saw a boy in his rural Kentucky neighborhood sitting on a puppy.
Without hesitating, the fearless toddler told the kid to get off the dog
or Eric would knock him off—or so the legend goes according to Eric's
grandma. Spending a lot of time on his grandparents' farm and in the
surrounding woods fostered Eric's budding love of nature. But it
wasn't until he read Cleveland Amory's book *Man Kind? Our Incredible
War on Wildlife* after moving to California in 1966 that his animal
advocacy work really blossomed. He began volunteering at The Fund
for Animals' San Francisco office. In 1983, he launched the Oakland-
based Action for Animals (AFA), the group through which he is now
the bee in so many animal exploiters' bonnets.

One target in particular that has felt the sting of Eric's efforts over
the years is rodeo. "There's too much testosterone in the world," he
says with a smile, "and rodeo is a microcosm of the world." For the
past sixteen years he has been working to improve conditions for
those animals ridden, roped, shocked, and otherwise banged up in
rodeos. In 1984, he convinced the organizers of the annual Hayward,
California, rodeo to implement a policy restricting the use of electric
prods, requiring an on-site veterinarian, padding the arena walls with

gym mats, and banning steer-dressing competitions (where partici-pants forcefully try to put clothes on frightened cattle).

AFA was also an original sponsor of the successful 1994 California bill to outlaw competitions at Mexican-style rodeos in which galloping horses' legs were lassoed ("horse tripping"). In 1996, AFA and other humane groups were victorious in pressing the Professional Rodeo Cowboys Association (PRCA) to require that veterinarians be on site at all the approximately 800 annual PRCA events nationwide instead of merely being on call, so that injured livestock—even those with broken backs or legs—would not languish for hours before being treated or euthanized. He continues to push for a law that would similarly apply to the 200 or so amateur rodeos in California.

Calf roping is another practice that really gets Eric buzzing. He is particularly incensed over ESPN's camera cutaways that shield TV viewers from seeing baby cows jerked off their feet when they hit the end of the rope. "If ESPN showed the event as it really happens, I'm hopeful that public concerns would help bring about changes, or even a ban, in calf roping," Eric states.

Getting the traditionally macho cowboy culture to change its ways is no easy feat for an animal rights activist. Or a gay man.

Eric, who didn't "come out" until he was thirty-eight, never really felt part of the gay community. "When pressed, I always go with the animals when it comes to choosing between gays and animals," he admits. And he's had to make that choice when protesting gay rodeos. "It never crossed my mind gay folks would do to animals what's been done to gay people for eons," he says, marveling at how one class of oppressed individuals could be so insensitive to another.

Yet the full-time activist believes firmly in working with other social causes to build the coalitions he feels are essential for signifi-cantly advancing animal (and human) rights. He also stresses the need to make animal protection a political issue. "[I]f you're not politically involved, you're dead in the water," he wrote in a recent AFA mailing.

In addition to leading AFA's many other activities, Eric now employs his Southern charm as a field representative for The Fund for

Animals. "Eric is the only activist I know who invites his opposition to lunch," says Virginia Handley, California Coordinator for the Fund and Eric's longtime friend and mentor.

For the last six years, Eric (who is still working on becoming totally vegetarian) has also fought to reform live animal food markets—a campaign just as politically incorrect as criticizing gay rodeos because the Chinatown venues primarily serve Asian communities. Thankfully, it now appears that legislation forbidding frogs, turtles, and other animals from being dismembered while still alive—a routine slaughter practice—has a strong chance of passing the California legislature.

But Eric understands what it's like to be attacked for being different from mainstream society. "I never met anyone who thought of himself as unkind and cruel," he says. "I just want to educate and sensitize people about animal issues."

≈

Janet Halliburton
RACHELLE DETWEILER

Years ago, when a young Janet Halliburton dressed up her "pet" roosters at her grandmother's farm north of Guthrie, Oklahoma, she did not imagine that she would eventually get riled up on behalf of other birds much like her childhood companions. Now, as she advocates for a cockfighting ban in her home state (one of three remaining states where it is still legal), she is sparring both for gamecocks and her own protection.

The Oklahoma Coalition Against Cockfighting (OCAC), an Oklahoma City-based political action committee that Janet chairs, began a highly visible campaign more than a year ago to place a ballot initiative before voters that would ban cockfighting and the raising or selling of birds to fight. Since then, Janet has been threatened at home, forced to resign from her job of twenty years, harassed in public, and tailed while driving her car because she and other OCAC members have challenged a barbaric, largely underground tradition. "Cockfighting is cruel," Janet asserts. "It is to the death, and I cannot understand how people can enjoy watching it."

Although a Tulsa Surveys poll showed that sixty-four percent of Oklahomans say they would vote for a cockfighting ban, cockfighters still rely on political clout to protect the "sport." Past legislative attempts to enact bans have flown the coop when amendments created unpalatable bills; one such measure flopped when an added provision made it a felony to leave a saddle on a horse for more than two hours.

To place the cockfighting issue directly before the voters, OCAC completed a massive petition drive last December in which they gathered more than 100,000 signatures in three months. It was then that Janet's harassment escalated. When a picture of her holding a box of knives and gaffs (one- to three-inch-long metal knives that are attached to roosters' legs while they fight) appeared in the *Oklahoma Gazette*, someone claiming to be a cockfighter called her home. He said that he too had knives and that he really enjoyed using them. After the possible death threat, Janet changed her phone number, a precaution not necessary during her involvement in a previously successful campaign that created a felony dog-fighting law in Oklahoma in 1982, or throughout her jobs as a former assistant city attorney in Norman and at the Oklahoma State Bureau of Investigation (OSBI), where people on death row frequently contacted her.

Phone calls also followed her to work at the OSBI, and ban opponents claimed that she used her time and position as chief general council to perpetuate support for the measure. Although no evidence was ever produced to support the allegations, she retired from her position in February 2000 to focus all her energy on the campaign. "She's very tough and doesn't back down from these people," says Wayne Pacelle of The Humane Society of the United States, a major backer of the campaign.

Cockfighters affiliated with the Oklahoma Animal Coalition pursued Janet throughout the petition drive, and the bloodsport enthusiasts frequently passed out flyers vilifying both her and the coalition. At the Oklahoma State Fair, where OCAC was gathering signatures, opponents' disruptions encroached on the fair's activities, causing the management to threaten OCAC with expulsion. Although Janet hired guards for protection during the fair, she was tailgated for miles as she drove back to her house alone.

Legal battles also ensued when the Oklahoma Game Fowl Breeders Association filed several charges against OCAC; one included an allegation currently being debated in court that could thwart the entire effort if the Supreme Court of Oklahoma declares that some petition signatures are not valid. Two gamefowl breeders and two cockfighters also filed lawsuits earlier this year against Janet and OCAC, alleging malicious and reckless defamation by ban proponents who claim that the cockfighting pits were conducive to drug dealing, prostitution, and other crimes. Janet says it was the connection between animal cruelty and other criminal elements that influenced her career path in law enforcement, and drew her into the feud against cockfighting.

One cockfighting supporter tried to debunk OCAC's claims and opened his private pit to the public. Anyone with a voter registration card could watch roosters bob and peck each other at the Collinsville Game Club last season, but the "pitters" cut the fights short. They concealed the bloody puncture wounds, deaths, and mounds of dead birds common among underground fights, and confused some people who could not comprehend the fuss over this use of chickens.

"I would feel differently if it was a dog fight," one spectator told the *Tulsa World* after viewing her first cockfight. "Dogs can become part of the family, but who has a chicken as a pet?"

That newcomer obviously had not heard of Janet Halliburton—yet.

Contributors ∼

Lorri Bauston is president of Farm Sanctuary.

Mark Berman is a program associate for the International Marine Mammal Project of Earth Island Institute, and helped create the Free Willy Keiko Foundation.

Carol Buckley is executive director of The Elephant Sanctuary.

Jill Howard Church is senior editor of *The Animals' Agenda*.

Karen Davis, Ph.D., is president of United Poultry Concerns and author of *Prisoned Chickens, Poisoned Eggs, Instead of Chicken, Instead of Turkey*, and *A Home for Henry*.

Pat Derby is director of the Performing Animal Welfare Society.

Rachelle Detweiler is assistant editor of *The Animals' Agenda*.

Jane Ehrhardt was until recently the editor of *Advocate* and *Shoptalk* for the American Humane Association.

Cathy C. Gaynor is president of Heron Run Refuge Inc.

Erin Geoghegan is a former editorial assistant of *The Animals' Agenda*.

Peter Hnath spearheaded the successful campaign to close New Jersey's Scotch Plains Zoo.

Matt Kelly is a Massachusetts-based vegetarian and animal rights advocate and general manager of Brodie Mountain Ski Resort.

Mia MacDonald is a New York-based independent consultant on environmental issues.

Lynn Manheim writes "Letters for Animals," an animal advocacy column that appears in eight newspapers.

Carol McKenna is a campaign consultant to several U.K.-based animal protection organizations.

Laura A. Moretti is contributing editor of *The Animals' Agenda* and Executive Editor of *The Animals' Voice* web site (www.animals voice.com).

Kit Paraventi is an activist, actor, and communications consultant living in Burbank, California.

Kirsten Rosenberg is managing editor of *The Animals' Agenda*.

Martin Rowe is the founding editor of *Satya: A Magazine of Vegetarianism, Environmentalism, and Animal Advocacy* and is co-founder of Booklight Inc. and its subsidiary Lantern Books, which published *Speaking Out for Animals*.

Valerie Schneider is a student and writer based in Portland, Oregon.

Dawn Willis Solero is a New York-based vegetarian and animal rights advocate.

Kim W. Stallwood is executive director the Animal Rights Network Inc. and editor in chief of *The Animals' Agenda*.

Kim Sturla is director of education for The Fund for Animals, and co-founder of Animal Place.

Rebecca Taksel teaches English and French at Point Park College in Pittsburgh, Pennsylvania.

Pat Valls-Trelles is a supporter of Save a Sato.

Sherryl Volpone spearheaded the successful campaign to close New Jersey's Scotch Plains Zoo.

Patricia A. Wismer is a retired high school teacher and volunteer for the Chico Cat Coalition.

Organizations ≋

Please contact the following organizations for more information.

All-American Animals
328 N. Ocean Blvd., #1108
Pompano Beach, FL 33062
Tel: (954) 786-1831;
www.AllAmericanAnimals.com

Alley Animals, Inc.
P.O. Box 27487
Towson, MD 21285-7487
Tel: (410) 823-0899; http://geocities.
com/Heartland/Hills/8113

Alliance for Animals
122 State St., #406, Madison, WI 53703
Tel: (608) 257-6333;
www.allanimals.org

American Fund for Alternatives to
Animal Research
175 W. 12th St., Ste. 16-G
New York, NY 10011
Tel: (212) 989-8073

American Humane Association
63 Inverness Dr., E.
Englewood, CO 80112
Tel: 800-227-4645;
www.amerhumane.org

Animal Abuse Watch
2882 Pebble Brook Dr.
Buford, GA 30518
Tel: (770) 945-4709

Animal Aid
The Old Chapel, Bradford St.,
Tonbridge, Kent TN9 1AW, UK
Tel: 44-1732-364546;
www.animalaid.org.uk

Animal Care and Welfare/SPCA
P.O. Box 8257
Pittsburgh, PA 15218-0257

Animal Defenders
261 Goldhawk Rd.
London W12 9PE, UK
Tel: 44-20-8846-9777 ;
www.animaldefenders.org.uk

Animal Place
3448 Laguna Creek Trail
Vacaville, CA 95688
Tel: (707) 449-4814;
www.animalplace.org

Animalines/Animal Information Network
The Lodge, Broadhurst Manor, Horsted
Keynes, West Sussex RH17 7BG, UK
Tel: 44-1342-810596;
www.animaline.org.uk

The Animals' Voice
1354 East Ave., #252
Chico, CA 95926
Tel: (530) 343-2498;
www.animalsvoice.com

ArkOnline, Tel: (503) 628-0180;
www.arkonline.com

Australian and New Zealand Federation
of Animal Societies
37 O'Connell St., North Melbourne,
Victoria 3051, Australia
Tel: 613-9329-6333;
www.melbourne.net/animals_australia/

Best Friends Animal Sanctuary
5001 Angel Canyon Dr.
Kanab, UT 84741-5001
Tel: (435) 644-2001;
www.bestfriends.org

The Body Shop
Watersmead, Littlehampton
West Sussex BN17 6LS, UK
Tel: 44-190-373-1500;
www.the-body-shop.com

BRAVE
1 Peterborogh St., #22
Boston, MA 02215
Tel: (617) 262-5761

Brodie Mountain Ski Resort
Route 7, New Ashford, MA 01237
Tel: (413) 443-4752;
www.skibrodie.com

Buffalo Field Campaign
P.O. Box 957
West Yellowstone, MT 59758
Tel: (406) 646-0070;
www.wildrockies.org/buffalo

California Equine Council
P.O. Box 40000
Studio City, CA 91614
Tel: (818) 771-0702

Center for the Ethical
Treatment of Animals
39-3 23 Volzsky Blvd., 109462 Moscow,
Russia

Center for the Expansion
of Fundamental Rights, Inc.
896 Beacon St., Ste. 303
Boston, MA 02215
Tel: (781) 453-0802

Chico Cat Coalition
1620 Muir Ave.
Chico, CA 95973-8611
Tel: (530) 894-1365

Showing Animals Respect
and Kindness
P.O. Box 28, Geneva, IL 60134
Tel: (630) 557-0176;
www.sharkonline.org

Compassion Over Killing
P.O. Box 9773, Washington, DC 20016
Tel: (202) 986-5599;
www.cok-online.org

Earth First! Journal
P.O. Box 1415, Eugene, OR 97440
Tel: (541) 344-8004;
www.earthfirstjournal.org

Earth Island Institute
300 Broadway, Ste. 28
San Francisco, CA 94133
Tel: (415) 788-3666;
www.earthisland.org

The Elephant Sanctuary in Hohenwald
P.O. Box 393, Hohenwald, TN 38462
Tel: (931) 796-6500;
www.elephants.com

Equine Advocates, Inc.
P.O. Box 700, Bedford, NY 10506
Tel: (845) 278-3095;
www.allrealgood.com/equineadvocates

Farm Sanctuary
3100 Aikens Rd., P.O. Box 150,
Watkins Glen, NY 14891
Tel: (607) 583-2225;
www.farmsanctuary.org

Fauna Foundation
P.O. Box 33, Chambly, QC
Canada J3L 4B1
Tel: (450) 658-1844;
www.faunafoundation.org

Fight Against Animal
Cruelty in Europe
29 Shakespeare St., Southport,
Merseyside, PR8 5AB, UK
44-1704-535922; www.faace.co.uk

Friends of Animals
and Their Environment
P.O. Box 27327
Golden Valley, MN 55427-0327
Tel: (612) 822-2720

Free Willy Keiko Foundation/
Ocean Futures Society
325 Chapala St.
Santa Barbara, CA 93101
(805) 899-8899; www.oceanfutures.org

The Fund for Animals
200 W. 57th St., New York, NY 10019
Tel: (212) 246-2096; www.fund.org

Philip Gonzalez / The Ginny Fund
470 East Broadway, Ste. C1
Long Beach, NY 11561
Tel: (516) 889-1831

Heron Run Refuge, Inc.
6565 Belmont Woods Rd.
Elkridge, MD 21227
Tel: (410) 379-0457

Hoofer's Haven
R.R. 6 First Concession Rd.
Thunder Bay, ON P7C 5N5, Canada
Tel: (807) 473-4450;
www.pig.baynet.net

Humane America Animal Foundation
P.O. Box 7, Redondo Beach, CA 90277
Tel: (310) 406-1558;
www.HumaneAmerica.org

The Humane Society
of the United States
2100 L St. N.W.
Washington, DC 20037
Tel: (202) 452-1100; www.hsus.org

In Defense of Animals
131 Camino Alto, Ste. E
Mill Valley, CA 94941
Tel: (415) 388-9641; www.idausa.org

International Marine Mammal Project
300 Broadway, Ste. 28
San Francisco, CA 94133
Tel: (415) 788-3666;
www.earthisland.org/immp

Kennebec Valley Humane Society
Pet Haven Ln., Augusta, ME 04330
Tel: (207) 626-3491

Last Chance for Animals
8033 Sunset Blvd., Ste. 35
Los Angeles, CA 90046
Tel: (310) 271-6096;
www.LCAnimal.org

Library Cat Society
P.O. Box 274
Moorhead, MN 56561-0274
Tel: (218) 236-7205

Metropolitan Guinea Pig Rescue
Tel: (703) 978-6026;
www.houserabbit.org/BaltWashDC/pigs/
rescues.html

National Greyhound Adoption Program
8301 Torresdale Ave.
Philadelphia, PA 19136
Tel: (215) 331-7918; www.ngap.org

Orangutan Foundation International
822 Wellesley Ave.
Los Angeles, CA 90049
Tel: (310) 207-1655;
www.orangutan.org

Peace Abbey
Two North Main St.
Sherborn, MA 01770
Tel: (508) 650-3659;
www.peaceabbey.org

People for Animals
54 Nehru Nagar, Agra 282002, India
Tel: 91-22-361-0218;
www.geocities.com/pfa_agra/index.htm

People for the Ethical
Treatment of Animals
501 Front St., Norfolk, VA 23510
Tel: (757) 622-PETA; www.peta.org

Performing Animal Welfare Society
P.O. Box 849, Galt, CA 95632
Tel: (209) 745-2606; www.pawsweb.org

PIGS, a sanctuary
P.O. Box 629
Charles Town, WV 25414
Tel: (304) 725-PIGS; www.pigs.org

Political Animals
3000 Danville Blvd., Ste. 331
Alamo, CA 94507
Tel: (925) 831-2992

Popcorn Park Zoo/
The Associated Humane Societies
P.O. Box 43, Forked River, NJ 08731
Tel: (609) 693-1900

Poplar Spring Animal Sanctuary
P.O. Box 507, Poolesville, MD 20837
Tel: (301) 428-8128;
www.animalsanctuary.org

Primarily Primates, Inc.
P.O. Box 207, San Antonio, TX 78291
Tel: (830) 755-4616;
www.primarilyprimates.org

Progressive Animal Welfare Society
P.O. Box 1037, Lynnwood, WA 98046
Tel: (425) 787-2500

Royal Society for the Prevention of
Cruelty to Children
Causeway, Horsham
West Sussex RH12 1HG, UK
Tel: 44-870-444-3127;
www.rspca.org.uk

San Diego Animal Advocates
P.O. Box 230946, Encinitas, CA 92023
Tel: (760) 943-0330;
www.animaladvocates.org

Satya
P.O. Box 138, Prince St. Station
New York, NY 10012
Tel: (212) 674-0952;
www.satyamag.com

Save A Sato
Calle C Villas, De Caparra D-2,
Guaynabo, PR 00966
www.saveasato.org

Sherry Schlueter Anti-Abuse
Foundation for Ethical Endeavors
2601 W. Broward Blvd.
Fort Lauderdale, FL 33312
Tel: (954) 321-4830

United Poultry Concerns, Inc.
P.O. Box 150
Machipongo, VA 23405-0150
Tel: (757) 678-7875;
www.upc-online.org

Vegetarian Society
of the United Kingdom
Parkdale, Dunham Rd., Altrincham,
Cheshire WA14 4QG, UK
Tel: 44-161-925-2000; www.vegsoc.org

Ventura County Department
of Animal Regulation
600 Aviation Dr., Camarillo, CA 93010
Tel: (805) 388-4341;
www.ventura.org/animreg/venareg.htm

Wild Bird Rescue, Inc.
P.O. Box 35413, Dundalk, MD 21222
Tel: (410) 288-4546

Wilderness Ranch Sanctuary
for Farm Animals
P.O. Box 1507
Loveland, CO 80539-1507
Tel: (970) 493-7153

Wildlife Rescue & Rehabilitation, Inc.
P.O. Box 1157, Boerne, TX 78006
Tel: (210) 698-1709;
www.wildlife-rescue.org

Zoo Atlanta
800 Cherokee Ave. S.E.
Atlanta, GA 30315
Tel: (404) 624-5600;
www.zooatlanta.citysearch.com

About *The Animals' Agenda*

The Animals' Agenda is a bimonthly news magazine dedicated to informing people about animal rights and cruelty-free living for the purpose of inspiring action for animals. *The Animals' Agenda* is committed to serving—and fostering cooperation among—a combined audience of animal advocates, interested individuals, and the entire animal rights movement. *The Animals' Agenda* is published by the Animal Rights Network Inc., an IRS 501(c)(3) federal tax-exempt, not-for-profit organization founded in 1979.

The mission of the Animal Rights Network Inc. (ARN) is to advance the protection of animals and defend their rights by:

- Working as a news organization that gathers, produces, and disseminates accurate information about acts of cruelty and institutionalized exploitation of animals
- Organizing public education programs to empower people to improve the well-being of all animals
- Leading efforts in the animal advocacy community to encourage dialogue, diversity, understanding, nonviolence, cruelty-free lifestyles, and respect for all members of all species

primary programs are *The Animals' Agenda*, the companion , *Agenda* web site, the library and archive, the Summit for the ials, and international conferences. The long-term goals are to stablish an international network of animal advocacy organizations and individuals, and create an international center for vegetarianism and animal rights.

If you would like more information or a copy of *The Animals' Agenda*, please contact us at:

Animal Rights Network Inc. / *The Animals' Agenda*
3500 Boston Street, Suite 325
P.O. Box 25881
Baltimore, MD 21224, USA
Tel: (410) 675-4566
Fax: (410) 675-0066
E-mail: office@animalsagenda.org
World Wide Web: www.animalsagenda.org